Grammatical categories and cognition uses original, empirical data to examine the Sapir–Whorf linguistic relativity hypothesis: the proposal that the grammar of the particular language we speak affects the way we think about reality. The author compares the grammar of American English with that of Yucatec Maya, an indigenous language spoken in southeastern Mexico, focusing on differences in the number marking patterns of the two languages. He then identifies distinctive patterns of thought relating to these differences by means of a systematic assessment of memory and classification preferences among speakers of both languages.

The study concretely illustrates the new approach to empirical research on the linguistic relativity hypothesis which Lucy develops in a companion volume, *Language diversity and thought*.

Studies in the Social and
Cultural Foundations of Language No. 13

Grammatical categories and cognition

Studies in the Social and Cultural Foundations of Language

The aim of this series is to develop theoretical perspectives on the essential social and cultural character of language by methodological and empirical emphasis on the occurrence of language in its communicative and interactional settings, on the socioculturally grounded "meanings" and "functions" of linguistic forms, and on the social scientific study of language use across cultures. It will thus explicate the essentially ethnographic nature of linguistic data, whether spontaneously occurring or experimentally induced, whether normative or variational, whether synchronic or diachronic. Works appearing in the series will make substantive and theoretical contributions to the debate over the sociocultural-function and structural-formal nature of language, and will represent the concerns of scholars in the sociology and anthropology of language, anthropological linguistics, sociolinguistics, and socioculturally informed psycholinguistics.

Grammatical categories and cognition

A case study of the
linguistic relativity hypothesis

JOHN A. LUCY
University of Pennsylvania

CAMBRIDGE
UNIVERSITY PRESS

Published by the Press Syndicate of the University of Cambridge
The Pitt Building, Trumpington Street, Cambridge CB2 1RP
40 West 20th Street, New York, NY 10011-4211, USA
10 Stamford Road, Oakleigh, Melbourne 3166, Australia

First published 1992
First paperback edition published 1996

A catalogue record for this book is available from the British Library

Library of Congress cataloguing in publication data applied for

ISBN 0 521 38419 2 hardback
ISBN 0 521 56620 7 paperback

Transferred to digital printing 2004

CE

Contents

Figures

Tables

Acknowledgments

The present research received funding from several sources. A Doherty Charitable Foundation Fellowship for Advanced Study in Latin America provided support for my initial ethnographic field research in Yucatan, Mexico. The specific psycholinguistic projects undertaken both in the US and in Mexico were supported by a National Institute of Mental Health Public Health Service Individual National Research Service Award for Dissertation Research (Grant F31 MH07494). These funds were supplemented by a coterminous International Doctoral Research Fellowship Award (Latin America and Caribbean Program) from the Social Science Research Council and the American Council of Learned Societies. Ongoing work, briefly mentioned here, has been supported by the Spencer Foundation (Chicago). I am grateful to all these organizations for their support. Finally, during the writing of this book I had the good fortune to have the intellectual and financial support of the Center for Psychosocial Studies in Chicago. I thank Bernard Weissbourd, Chairman of the Board of Directors of the Center, for making my period of residence possible and Ben Lee, Director of the Center, for giving this project his personal and intellectual support.

Much of the empirical portion of this research was conducted in Mexico; the assistance my wife and I received while doing our research there requires special comment. Norberto González Crespo, then director of Instituto Nacional de Antropología e Historia, Centro Regional del Sureste, gave us a gracious welcome to the local anthropological research community in Yucatan and provided assistance during our first year there. Alfonso Villa Rojas provided useful ethnographic advice on locating an appropriate field site. Juan Ramón Bastarrachea Manzano of the Academia Maya and José Tec Pó'ot (at that time with the Escuela de Antropología de la Universidad de Yucatán) gave assistance in evaluating possible research locations from the point of view of linguistic research. The late Alfredo Barrera Vásquez, doyen of Yucatecan linguists, made various private documentary materials available and was a gracious and encouraging host during our all-too-infrequent visits with him in Merida. Victor Castillo Vales, director of the Escuela del Psicología de la Universidad de Yucatan, was our lone psychological colleague in Yucatan, but he was an ideal one. Over the years, Don Victor has provided intellectual dialogue, research assistance and collaboration, and advice and assistance in innumerable practical matters. Finally Aline and James Callaghan, Americans resident in Merida at the time of our research, provided much practical help and some respite from the always demanding personal task of working in a foreign culture.

In our research location in eastern Yucatan we were assisted by many people. In Valladolid, our supply town, Mario and Lupita Escalante provided us with every imaginable assistance. To them I owe a good part not only of the pleasure but also of the success of my field research. Also in Valladolid, Gabriel Cano Góngora also took a keen interest in my research and provided practical help as well. To all the people of my village field site, I owe my gratitude for their good-natured adoption of me and my family into their midst. In particular, I thank Gonzalo Och Yupit, Maria Eugenia Dzul U'u, and Alfonzo Cupul Pat – my principal informants and closest friends in the village – for patiently guiding me into an understanding of their language and way of life.

This research project was stimulated, guided, and supported by my various teachers at the University of Chicago, including Robert LeVine, Richard Shweder, David McNeill, and Janellen Huttenlocher. Norman McQuown introduced me to the intricacies of the Yucatec Maya language. Michael Silverstein's research on case marking provided the inspiration for the particular grammatical analysis developed in this work. Finally, Susan Goldin-Meadow, through her intellectual enthusiasm and personal support, helped give me the confidence to make the research public despite its imperfections.

I also received much encouragement and help from friends and family. William Hanks and I learned Yucatec together and continue to learn much about Yucatan and ourselves by comparing our field experiences with one another. Alan Fiske and Kathy Mason, friends and fellow students in Human Development, shared with me and my wife the difficulties and rewards – both personal and intellectual – of undertaking anthropological fieldwork. Anna Gaskins cheerfully and competently supervised our US affairs while we were abroad.

Finally, I thank my immediate family – my wife Suzanne Gaskins and my sons Robert and Steven – for their personal support both in the field research and during the writing of this work. Suzanne has also been a partner in the research and there are no words that can adequately express the extent of her contribution to the project. She made it possible.

The editors of the *Australian Journal of Linguistics* generously granted permission to reprint table 15 and other material.

Introduction

The present study forms part of a two volume work that re-examines empirical research on the linguistic relativity hypothesis, that is, the hypothesis that differences among languages in the grammatical structuring of meaning influence habitual thought.

The companion work, *Language diversity and thought: a reformulation of the linguistic relativity hypothesis*, presents an analytic review of the historical development of the linguistic relativity hypothesis and various past attempts to provide empirical evidence directly relevant to it. The review is concerned with methodology in the broad sense, that is, with identifying the general requirements of adequate empirical work on this problem. The review analyzes in detail the flaws and the achievements of existing studies with the aim of formulating an improved approach to such empirical research. The present work provides a concrete case study which utilizes this improved approach.

General goals

The global aim of the project described in the present volume is to demonstrate how the linguistic relativity hypothesis as traditionally conceived can be investigated empirically. Taking Whorf's formulation and subsequent empirical research as the point of departure, four components of adequate empirical research on the linguistic relativity hypothesis were described in the concluding chapter of *Language diversity and thought*. The discussion also indicated which approaches were most likely to lead to significant progress at the present time. These components and the proposed approaches to them can be distilled as follows.

First, such research must be *comparative*, that is, it must present contrastive data on two or more language communities. Without a comparative dimension, nothing can be established about the impact of

1

language differences. Ideally, the languages at issue should contrast widely so that clear, strong differences are at stake. The comparison should also be undertaken with a broad understanding both of the attested world-wide range of language types and of the particular cultural context of the specific language communities being compared.

Second, at present, such comparison should take an external non-linguistic *reality* as the metric or standard for calibrating the content of linguistic and cognitive categories. The development of an adequate, neutral metric represents the crucial analytic problem in any project on the relativity issue. Without such a metric, one cannot say with precision in what respect one language's categories differ from another's or establish that a language category and a cognitive category concern a common domain. Operationally, such a characterization can be formulated by basing it on a wide sample of languages. This assures adequacy since we know that the features of reality captured by such an analysis are those relevant to the actual use of languages, and it assures neutrality since no single language's categories dominate the characterization.

Third, the *languages* of the communities being studied must be contrasted as to how they differently construe a common reality. This will involve a formal analysis of the morphosyntactic categories of the language with special attention to their referential values, that is, their relationship to the contextual surround. Such an analysis should focus on a whole configuration of meaning rather than on an isolated lexical or grammatical category, and it should attempt to state the contrast between the configurations within a unified framework. At present, the focus should be on language patterns as they are habitually used in everyday talk. Eventually, it will be necessary to attend to differences in patterns of use if it turns out that language patterns have some effects on thought.

Fourth, the implications of the language differences for *thought* must be articulated. This involves proposing plausible cognitive entailments of the habitual use of the language patterns at issue. Then there must be some attempt to assess empirically whether the hypothesized cognitive outcomes are present in samples of actual speakers of the languages. Such assessments should be designed so as to present equivalent opportunities to the various language groups, which will involve being sensitive to the cultural context of the assessments. Operationally, this involves asking speakers to engage in tasks with certain materials selected to operationally represent the "reality" at issue. With proper design, such controlled assessment procedures can make alternative explanations of the observed behaviors highly unlikely.

Overview of the study

The specific focus of this study is on whether differences in the grammatical treatment of nominal number (for example, pluralization) in Yucatec Maya and American English correspond with detectable differences in habitual thought as assessed through simple cognitive tasks involving attention, memory, and classification. Because the range of material covered in these chapters crosses a number of traditional disciplinary boundaries, clarity of exposition will be emphasized, in some cases at the expense of full technical detail. In most cases such detail is provided in appendices unless the relevant material is available elsewhere in published form.

The study begins in chapter 1 with a brief ethnographic description of the Yucatecan culture and the nature of the field research. The study compares speakers of English with speakers of Yucatec Maya, an indigenous Indian language of southeastern Mexico. Even though the present study will directly assess individual thought and behavior rather than cultural beliefs and institutions, some basic background in the Yucatec Maya culture is necessary to understand the linguistic analysis and the cognitive assessment. This ethnographic sketch provides this background; it is not intended to be a full-scale cultural analysis.

A detailed explication and analytic contrast of the grammatical patterns of the two languages follows in chapter 2. The goal of linguistic analysis in the present case is to develop a description of a morphosyntactic contrast between English and Yucatec suitable for generating a specific cognitive hypothesis. This involves providing a description of the relevant forms in each language, a meaningful comparison and characterization of the differences, and a way to link the differences to some testable cognitive hypothesis. The category chosen for the present study is that of nominal number. The chapter explains the reasons for selecting this category, provides the relevant descriptive material on the two languages, and contrasts them within a multilanguage framework.

Nominal number as conceptualized here encompasses a variety of ways of marking "number" in the noun phrase and includes both singular–plural distinctions which are obligatory in English and certain modifier forms known as numeral classifiers which are obligatory in Yucatec. Nominal number marking of some sort is frequently used and structurally obligatory in the two languages at issue, thus maximizing the potential for psychological impact from both quantitative and qualitative points of view. Since nominal number frequently has indexical referential value, it is a suitable category in terms of implementing a referential anchor for linguistic comparison. Because it is routinely associated with lexical nouns that themselves can have indexical referential value, it permits the use of pictures and objects as experimental stimuli. Finally, nominal number has been either directly or indirectly involved in nearly all the previous empirical research on the linguistic relativity hypothesis that has dealt with grammar. Thus, by working with nominal number, the present research also addresses the substantive issues raised in the studies by Whorf, Lee, Mathiot, Hoijer, Brown, Casagrande, Maclay, and Bloom which were discussed in *Language diversity and thought*.

The basic formal regularities of nominal number marking are first described for each language. Number marking interacts with the referential content of the lexical noun, with other morphosyntactic categories, with patterns of adjectival modification, etc. The description is focused primarily on the linguistic variables pertinent to the cognitive work to follow but tries to take account of the more significant of these reactances, especially where they suggest a broad, systematic configuration of meaning. In the case of Yucatec, which will not be familiar to most readers, the description of number marking patterns is preceded by a brief description of the global typological characteristics of the language.

These patterns of number marking in English and Yucatec are then contrasted so as to identify similarities and differences. The contrast focuses initially on formal-functional analogues between the two languages. This preliminary contrast is then situated within a broader comparative understanding of number marking patterns, drawing in particular on available linguistic typologies of noun phrase types. The Yucatec–English contrast is then restated in more neutral and precise terms by taking advantage of this broader, comparatively informed perspective. The resulting linguistic description also suggests immediately how other languages can be incorporated into future research.

Finally, the design, execution, and results from the various cognitive assessment tasks are reported in chapter 3. The goal of the cognitive assessment is to identify patterns of habitual thought in the two language groups that could plausibly stem from corresponding differences in the morphosyntactic treatment of nominal number. Habitual thought will be inferred from patterns of attention, memory, and classification exhibited by samples of individuals from both groups engaging in two series of diagnostic task procedures involving identical materials. Even though some naturalistic evidence for habitual thought patterns will also be mentioned, these specially designed, experimentally controlled tasks will provide the crucial evidence for language effects in this study.

The discussion begins by explaining the cognitive implications derived from the linguistic patterns. One set of implications is drawn directly from a straightforward analysis of typical overt referential values. A second set of implications is drawn from considering the underlying (covert) referential values suggested by the configurational logic of each system. A crucial goal is to indicate how these cognitive implications are distinct from the linguistic regularities themselves.

The derivation of implications is followed by a lengthy discussion of the development and logic of the tasks and materials used in the first task series. Included here is a systematic procedure for the comparison of languages on nominal number patterns, a discussion of the rationale for, and development of, the stimulus materials, and an explanation of the various task procedures. The discussion is quite lengthy because the materials and procedures are themselves complex and because they have been explicitly developed for ease of extension to new languages which may exhibit significantly different regularities.

As discussed in *Language diversity and thought*, there are many differences in the behavior of Yucatecan and US samples and many cultural patterns that can potentially account for any given behavioral difference. The various strategies proposed in the final chapter of *Language diversity and thought* such as the use of very specific and highly group-characteristic predictions and the use of multiple means of assessment have been implemented here to help make alternative interpretations of the data implausible. And since, as just mentioned, the assessment procedures have been developed in such a way that they can be readily extended to additional language groups, it will be possible to evaluate any competing hypotheses in future work.

The cognitive section continues with a second task series which focuses on the underlying cognitive implications of the most striking difference between Yucatec and English number marking. The assessment procedure has been designed to maximize information on this difference and so has not yet been generalized for use with other language groups. However, the results of this experiment provide unusually compelling evidence for language effects, clarify the interlocking nature of lexical and syntactic meaning, and suggest a number of interesting lines of future research.

The conclusion in chapter 4 briefly evaluates the success of the empirical project, contrasts the approach with previous approaches, and makes suggestions for future research.

1. Background of the comparative research in Yucatan, Mexico

Effective comparative investigation of the linguistic relativity hypothesis requires direct linguistic, ethnographic, and psychological research in two or more cultures. The present study is based on such research conducted among middle-class Americans and among the Mayan people of Yucatan, Mexico. This chapter provides general background on salient elements of the Yucatecan cultural context since these are likely to be unfamiliar to most readers. Some general comments on the course of the foreign fieldwork and sequence of task administration are also included.

Background on the Yucatec Maya culture

This section provides schematic information about the Yucatecan culture and community where the comparative research was conducted. The account places the rural Yucatecan village culture within the larger array of world cultures and within the Mexican national scene by characterizing its history and social organization in very global terms. Specific details are added where necessary to indicate how the particular village differs from the general Yucatecan pattern, to facilitate interpreting the stimulus materials described in chapter 3, and to highlight salient contrasts with American culture.

History and social geography

The Mayan people of concern in this study are resident in a small rural village in the state of Yucatan in southeastern Mexico. Historically, they are related to the ancient Mayan peoples whose civilization was predominant throughout the region during the pre-Columbian era. This ancient Mayan civilization reached its zenith in a "Classic" period running from approximately AD 300 through AD 900, during which time achievements in the arts and sciences reached a level unexcelled by any other native culture of the New World. This civilization was in decline at the time of the arrival of the first Spanish conquistadors and the subsequent military and religious conquest destroyed most of the remaining "high" culture. However the folk culture, by which is meant the customary beliefs and practices of the great bulk of the people, survived far longer, eventually becoming integrated with elements of colonial Spanish and, later, modern Mexican culture, as a distinctive regional "Yucatecan" culture. It is this regional Yucatecan culture which constitutes the villagers' world both in practical and in conceptual terms, and which forms the background for the present study.[1]

The study was conducted in a village with about 700 people in the Chemax district which lies on the eastern border of the state of Yucatan. (Historical present for this description of the village is 1978.) The village lies in a traditional, corn-farming area which encircles Valladolid (population 50,000), Yucatan's second largest town and the commercial, political, and social center for the eastern region. In many respects the area is one of the last remaining enclaves of extremely traditional culture in the Yucatan peninsula region. To the north is a booming commercial and cattle growing area, around the town of Tizimin. To the west is Yucatan's henequen zone, where henequen (used in making sisal rope products) is grown in a plantation-style agricultural system; Merida, the state capital and source of contact with the outside world, lies in the center of this henequen zone. To the south and west is a region similar in its conservatism to the Valladolid region but which historically has had closer ties to Merida and, therefore, the outside world. The population of this southwestern region has recently become increasingly dependent on a variety of cash crops other than corn. Southeast and east are extensive forests which have been a major source of the chicle used in making chewing gum but which have been logged extensively for timber in recent years. Further to the east on the Caribbean coast is the newly developed resort region of Cancun whose beaches and waters attract thousands of tourists every year.[2]

Historically, contact with the outside world for the villagers required a day's journey by foot or on horseback to Valladolid. Chemax, the local district capital a half day's journey away, was merely a larger version of the village with the addition of a few civil and clerical officials. Merida, the state capital and true locus of peninsular power, exerted its influence through Valladolid and few villagers ever visited it. In the last decade, with the construction of many new roads and with the development of the Cancun resort with its new employment opportunities, village contact with the outside world has increased considerably. For some, Cancun now rivals Valladolid as the most important place outside the village. And for everyone a trip by truck to Valladolid is now a several-times-a-year event, though it is still a notable and exciting event for most. Practical opportunity for outside contact, however, has not always been met by village interest, and, for most residents, the village is still central and the rest of the world either unknown or irrelevant to daily life. Most are happy to live where they do and leave for more than a short trip only when need requires and even then with some reluctance.

Material culture

The journey to the village from Valladolid involves a two hour ride in the back of a three-ton pickup truck which travels the first half of the trip on a modern paved road and the second half on a narrow all-weather gravel road. Truck transport came to the village some years ago (*c.* 1972) and has transformed village life by allowing a flow of goods and people to and from the outside world on a scale not possible before. *En route*, along the road through the scrub jungle, are small individual ranches and farms belonging to private landowners. When the truck eventually arrives at the village, one first sees the new school buildings on the edge of town and then two long lines of huts along the street to the town square. The town square is large and perfectly flat, dominated in the center by a tall colonial church (*c.* 1780) and rimmed on three sides with more thatched huts. The fourth side is bordered by a row of single-story masonry buildings: the original school building and a town hall. It is in front of these buildings that the truck stops, depositing its cargo and passengers, some of whom will continue on by foot or horseback to more remote ranches and villages.

From the top of the church, one can see an expanse of perfectly flat, intensely green jungle stretching off in all directions to the horizon; even houses in the village are not visible beyond the first block or so, being concealed by tall trees. Although the square is roughly rectangular, the town's 150 lots are scattered in a lopsided grid pattern towards the east and north, the directions in which lie most of the men's fields. House lots are typically 50 by 50 meters square and contain one or two oval or rectangular shaped structures made of poles and roofed with thatch (or, in recent years, with thick corrugated tar paper). Some of these structures are houses which are from 3 by 4 meters up to about 4 by 8 meters in size. House floors are made of dirt, sometimes packed over a layer of gravel or small rocks. Additional buildings in the yards provide extra sleeping space, storage, or serve other special functions. Front and back doors are made either of planks with hinges (signifying wealth and/or modernity) or of woven vine (signifying poverty and/or conservatism); houses have no windows. Yards are fenced with rock walls from two to three feet high which mark yard boundaries and supposedly keep animals in or out. (In fact, there are animals everywhere – in streets, yards, and houses.) All water is drawn with rope, pulley, and bucket from wells or natural sink holes which reach the water table. Yard and forest serve as latrine. There is no electricity: wood is burned for heat and cooking, candles and kerosene serve to provide light.

Life is simple in terms of material possessions. Furniture consists of short stools about six to eight inches (15–20 cm.) high made of hewn logs and of short tables about eighteen inches (50 cm.) high used for cooking. Most families also have one large table about thirty inches (75 cm.) high and three feet (1 m.) long which is used to work at standing up and as an altar during special religious events. Often there is a foot treadle sewing machine in the house, in which case modern chairs of standard size are also present since they are needed to sit at the machine. Cooking is done over a fire encircled by three stones which support pots, cooking griddle, etc. Most utensils are made of natural products (e.g., baskets, gourd bowls, etc.) but some are purchased: most families have some ceramic bowls or plates to use on special occasions; pots are enameled steel; ladles are aluminum or steel. Eating utensils are not used; corn tortillas serve in place of fork and spoon. Sleeping is done in hammocks hung from the support beams of the house. And most houses have trunks, suitcases, or cardboard boxes which serve to store each family member's three to six sets of clothing. Clothing is washed in wooden or cement wash tubs in the yard.[3]

Social organization

The village is an *ejido*. This means that the residents and their descendants have petitioned for and been given land collectively and in perpetuity by the national government as an outgrowth of a system of traditional land distribution re-established during the revolution earlier in this century. In rotation, men serve as head (*comisario*) of the *ejido* organization and the men who farm in the village (i.e., all adult men) serve as a committee of the whole in making decisions about matters involving the community. Each man receives from the *ejido* organization a right to cultivate a certain amount of land each year. In return, he is responsible for doing his share in the upkeep of the *ejido*: annual cutting of the *ejido* boundary line, serving guard duty (*guardia*) for the town square, performing communal labor (*fajina/fagina*) (for example, weeding the town square, roofing the schoolhouse), etc. Although not all of these activities are actually mandated by the *ejido* rules of Mexico, there is no real distinction among projects for the villagers: communal projects are decided on by consensus in public meetings (*asambleas*), and everyone is obliged to work upon whatever is agreed upon.[4] A second structure of civil authority comes through the state and district (*municipio*) structure, but it is much less important and involves settling minor disputes such as theft and soliciting funds from state and federal agencies for help with town projects. Beyond these two structures, there are no formal organizations that include all members of the community.

The family is the locus of economic and religious activity. The basic family unit consists of a man, a woman, and their children. Marriage partners may be drawn from within or from outside the village, and both patterns commonly occur. Wedding expenses, which can be considerable, are borne by the man's family. Dissolution of marriage is rare after the first year except by death. Remarriage is common in such a case if the survivor is young.

At marriage, the woman moves to the house of her husband and his parents. Women effectively become part of the man's family for a time. (Women and their families prefer she find a marriage partner from within the village so she can remain close; men and their families prefer he find a marriage partner from outside the village since such a woman will more readily and fully integrate into the new family.) A new wife is trained (or rather, *re*-trained) by her mother-in-law in the proper performance of household chores and in childrearing. The couple continues to live with the husband's parents until their own family grows to the point where it is appropriate to set up their own household unit – usually when they have two or more children. Traditionally, these new household units established by a man's sons were all spatially near if not adjacent to his own. As the village population increases, this is no longer always possible.

Children carry the surnames of both father and mother although the father's name is most often used and is the only one passed on to the next generation. Fertility is high and families are large, although historically childhood disease took its toll and served to limit population growth; six living children is the norm for a mature couple, although ten or more children may actually have been born. With the arrival of modern medicine, child mortality has declined and the population is now growing much more rapidly. The elderly are cared for by their children, especially the youngest son and his spouse.

The widespread Latin pattern of godparenthood (*compadrazgo*) is practiced but is not emphasized as much as elsewhere; baptismal godparents are the most important as they will care for children should the parents (in particular, the mother) die.[5]

Work and leisure

Village life centers on corn farming and associated religious practices. All village men cultivate corn in a swidden (slash-and-burn) system. During fall and winter men fell a section of the jungle. In spring they burn off the now dry timber and, when the rains come, they sow the field. During summer they weed the fields (the most taxing of their chores) and in August they harvest their crop. In the same fields with the corn they grow squashes, tubers, and beans as secondary crops and these four items constitute the bulk of their diet – with corn comprising by far the greatest portion. Most men do not go to their fields every day, taking time each week to build or make needed objects (for example, tables, washtubs, bee hives, raised garden platforms, etc.), maintain the house and yard, travel to town, perform communal labor, etc. All or most of Sunday is taken as a day of rest.

Extra corn beyond that needed for subsistence is grown by nearly all men. This corn is either sold for cash or used to feed animals (turkeys, chickens, pigs) which, in turn, may themselves be eaten or sold for cash. Many men also keep colonies of honeybees which provide another source of cash. Most families also have gardens in their yards in which they have fruit trees and some vegetables; these are usually consumed domestically, but are also sold for cash by some. When the corn crop is insufficient or when expenses are unusually high (due to illness, planned marriage, etc.), men seek wage labor either by working in their neighbors' fields or by going away, usually to Cancun where they work carrying water for masons building the tourist hotels.

While the man is in the field, the woman is also performing a taxing round of daily chores. Twice each day she must prepare corn for grinding and two or three times she must prepare meals. When not engaged in food preparation, she usually is washing clothes, drawing the water used in bathing, cooking, and irrigating the garden, or gathering firewood (this last is a job also done by children and men). She also spends a lot of time watching children and supervising the work and caretaking responsibilities of the older children. Women's work is continuous and long. Just preparing corn to eat involves many hours and many steps: husking the ears, shucking the dried kernels, drawing water, boiling the corn with lime, rinsing the boiled corn three or more times, taking the corn to the motor-driven grinding mill (hand grinding was supplanted many years ago), and finally making by hand and cooking over a wood fire the dozens of tortillas to be consumed at each meal. As with the men, corn is the center of daily life for women.

Of the 156 men in the community, very few (the elderly aside) do not farm corn for themselves. Four of those who do not are brothers: one is a butcher; one is the driver of the truck that goes to Valladolid once each day; one runs a store, operates a corn grinding mill, and owns a cattle ranch; and the fourth does very little if anything. Two other men cannot work in the fields for medical reasons and hence make money through stores and butchering. There are a few other men in the village who supplement their farming by performing other services. Three men own corn grinding machines; several have a small stock of "store" goods which they sell to their neighbors at a markup; one man does carpentry of a simple sort (for example, making chairs, doors, and coffins); one man is a tailor; one man is learning to be a mason; and one man serves as a "doctor" in his capacity as a trained representative of the federal rural health-care program dispensing drugs and shots. Five men say prayers at special events in exchange for food, but this is more a ritual responsibility undertaken from a sense of duty or a desire for prestige rather than as a money making activity. Women specialists include a woman who represents the rural health-care program in matters of pregnancy and child health care, two traditional mid-wives, a few women who sew or embroider especially well make clothing for their neighbors, and three women who serve as cooks at large social gatherings which is a ritual responsibility carrying considerable prestige but negligible economic benefit. All of these occupations are sidelines to the main business of farming and domestic maintenance. In recent years, government programs to expand agricultural opportunities have led to the organization of groups for more extensive vegetable farming, bee raising, and hardwood production, but these have yet to establish themselves as long-term and productive income sources, and no one really relies on them yet.[6]

Leisure activities such as dancing, bull fighting, visiting, drinking and eating special food are primarily associated with the religious activities that are discussed in the next section. Villagers also engage in a variety of secular recreational activities such as hunting, playing baseball (which may involve a trip to a neighboring town), and watching movies. Finally they engage in many small diversions such as simply watching activities in the village, gossiping and joking, card playing (mostly young men), visiting neighbors and relatives, and listening to the radio.

Religion

Religion dominates all aspects of village life. The religious practices represent a creative fusion of colonial Catholic and pre-Columbian native belief. Central to nearly all the religious activities is the theme of inviting the gods to come and share a meal with the participants; hence, food offerings predominate in any religious setting. There are religious beliefs and practices associated with each stage in the agricultural cycle; with various points or periods in the life-cycle; with various days of the year associated with patron saints or with anniversaries of recent deaths and the like; and with illnesses, emergencies, or times of need. On any given day there is almost sure to be some religious activity somewhere in the community. Some of the observances are private, family affairs, some encompass small groups of families, and still others involve nearly all villagers and even persons from neighboring villages.

Work, social status, recreation, courtship, and general worldview are all implicated in the religious system. Most surplus wealth eventually ends up being spent on religious observances in one way or another and to some extent status is linked to the amount spent sponsoring religious events. Events associated with religious observances – food preparation and meals, small gatherings of worshipers, dances, bullfights, etc. – constitute the bulk of organized recreational social life in the village and, from the native point of view, constitute the highlights of a given day, week, or year. It is these events which are looked forward to and which provide relief from the monotony of the daily round.

For most of this religious activity the village is self sufficient. The Catholic clergy is needed and thought of only for baptisms, marriages, and an occasional mass (which occurs about four times each year). Even in these ceremonies, the follow-up activities in the households once the priest has gone constitute the more significant elements in the minds of the villagers. Here public nervousness and a certain blind formality give way to religious care and deep belief.[7]

Language, education, and intellectual life

Maya is the language of the village. Only a handful of men are truly bilingual in Spanish, although most men know enough Spanish to interact with government officials, Valladolid shopkeepers, and Cancun employers – and it is usually in these contexts that Spanish is spoken. Men between the ages of 20 and 30 (i.e., who have reached adulthood since the coming of the road and the development of the tourist resort), speak more and better Spanish on the whole, as a result of having worked outside the village. Very few women know much Spanish; most can be characterized as monolingual with supplemental Spanish phrases and vocabulary. In fact, many Spanish lexical items have essentially become part of Maya, accepting Maya verbal and nominal inflectional patterns, and are not distinguished by native speakers from indigenous Maya. Many shopkeepers and doctors in Valladolid (traditionally the major point of extra-village contact) require their employees to know Maya, and hence people who know only Maya can live in a more or less monolingual environment.

Education in the village is of two kinds: formal and informal. Formal education in the school system is provided by a federal agency especially concerned with indigenous peoples which sends in teachers each week to the village. The first two or three grades are taught in Maya with Maya materials; thereafter, the attempted transition to Spanish is instituted, but even in the upper grades, Maya is used heavily. There are six grades available in the village; further education entails leaving the village for a boarding school run by the same federal agency. Most children probably go to school once in a while, but less than half attend seriously and only a small minority attend beyond the third grade. Prior to the coming of the road, teachers came irregularly, infrequently, or both, hence many older people have no education at all; many men cannot sign their own name or read simple printed signs. Those adult men who can read derive some prestige from that fact and are more likely to serve in the higher public offices and to run stores. They may also take up official prayer reading, which involves reading the prayers appropriate for a given occasion or day for other members of the community. In recent years the school has become an important source of new information in the village, but this has more to do with the efforts of a few dedicated and enlightened directors and teachers than with any general influence of school as an institution.

An informal education is provided by parents and by general exposure to life in the village. There are few pre-made toys and little parental attention to children's play activities; but with sticks, leaves, tin cans, etc. the children do play and explore their world. All children from the age of four onward are liable to be given a younger sibling to take care of; this duty lasts off and on until the older child becomes more valuable in other chores. By age six or seven the young boy begins to help his father in the field in small ways and slowly he makes the transition by late teens to a self-sufficient farmer. Young girls begin helping their mothers at about the same age with water drawing and other simple chores and later move on to learn cooking and other skills by their late teens.

The intellectual demands of village life are not high. Few of the tasks in the culture are conceptually difficult and complex, but there is plenty of time to master these and all young adults are competent in the basics by age twenty. There is no stigma to slow learning, and people are ready to laugh at themselves and others when they can't learn easily; but there is great stigma to not knowing what one should do or in not doing well something all men and women are expected to do perfectly. Such overlearning of basic skills brings its own sort of social pressure: failure can correctly be ascribed to lack of effort, not ability. Because of this overlearned aspect of intellectual tasks, it is often difficult to pick out individual differences at first. But with time one finds that some are more efficient in their activities and that some are adding new skills beyond the basics even as adults. Differences show up, too, in ability to calculate or estimate sums in one's head, to make and understand jokes, and to deal with novel situations. The most striking difference from the perspective of the familiar modern situation in the West is the general absence of certain sophisticated individually held intellectual skills (for example, ability to do mental multiplication). The society in many ways is structured to minimize dependence on such individual intellectual skills. For example, people need not do extensive mathematical computations when shopping in the stores since items are purchased one at a time: you ask for what you want, ask its price, pay the price, get your change, and then go on to buy the next item after checking with the shopkeeper that your funds are sufficient. Only the storekeeper needs to be routinely capable of making change correctly at the simplest level. (Consequently, in the trade town of Valladolid, villagers depend very much on a shopkeeper's honesty, and successive generations of people go to the same stores in part because of trust in these shopkeepers and their families.) As this example shows, social routines effectively substitute for complex, individual intellectual procedures of mental calculation.

However, some responsibility for specific *knowledge* does rest with the individual and people retain elaborate quantities of information. A particularly notable example is the nearly universal ability to recall exactly the price paid for many personal or household items – even years after the date of purchase. This information is widely discussed and the information serves as some protection against overcharge when the individual travels alone to town to make a purchase from shops where prices are never posted.[8]

Information on fieldwork and task administration

Site selection

The decision to work with the Yucatec Mayan people (as opposed to some other group) was guided in the first place by several practical methodological requirements. Principal considerations were proximity to the United States given the expectation that multiple field visits would be needed, widespread use of a non-Indo-European language, a relatively stable cultural situation, and a wider context of political stability. Subsequent to these considerations, the availability of prior ethnographic and linguistic research on the area was decisive given the specific topical focus of the research. Before undertaking the field portion of the project, a considerable amount of background research was conducted on the language and culture so that more field time would be available to take up particular research topics.

Similar methodological (or logistical) factors influenced the selection of a site within Yucatan. Ample size of village was important in providing a large enough sample of individuals, especially when some control over age or sex might be necessary. Size was also a consideration in terms of finding housing. An upper limit on acceptable size however was presented by the fact that only smaller villages were as culturally and linguistically conservative as was desired. Maya language dominance (rather than Spanish) was a crucial factor. Cultural conservatism was deemed important to minimize the complicating factors associated with modernization. The village met all of these requirements.

Timing and focus of field research

The fieldwork itself was conducted over a three-year period from December 1977 through December 1980 during which time three separate trips to the field site were made. Intervals between field stays were used for analysis of data and preparation of materials for the next stage of the research.

During the first and longest stay (twenty months in Mexico, seventeen in the village) basic ethnographic and linguistic research was conducted. The ethnographic goal was a basic understanding of community life, that is the people, objects, activities, and ideas which were part of the round of daily life. The existence of particularly good descriptive material on the culture (for example, Redfield and Villa Rojas, 1934) greatly facilitated understanding during this early period despite an initial language barrier. Residence in the village and participation in its activities provided the personal background necessary for an operative (as opposed to abstract) understanding of the details of village life.

It soon became apparent that each individual acted with great independence in most spheres of Mayan social life. It was not possible therefore to gain the confidence of one person (or some few persons) of importance and thereby obtain the cooperation of the many individuals necessary for a systematic project. It was necessary, in short, to befriend each person individually and an enormous amount of time was spent therefore developing personal ties with as many villagers as possible. Although such friendship was a prerequisite of future cooperation as an informant, it was in no way a guarantee.

In addition to the usual ethnographic topics, considerable attention was paid to details which might prove of eventual value in the psychological portions of the work. These included, for example, degree of education, literacy, familiarity with photos and pictures of other sorts, and games. Degree of literacy was important not merely because of its obvious intellectual implications, but also because it was an index of comfortableness in working with written (including pictorial) materials.

The linguistic goals during this first trip included both gathering enough systematic data so as to be able to draw a contrastive linguistic comparison with English and becoming fluent enough in the language to use it comfortably for interviewing and for administering the various experimental procedures. Initial entry into the language was facilitated by the existence of good training and background materials (especially Blair and Vermont Salas, 1965). Daily contact with the language over many months provided the practice necessary to be able to speak the language easily.

Although a variety of grammatical topics were investigated in some detail, only a few seemed to be straightforwardly amenable to psychological assessment of the sort contemplated in this project. Greatest concentration, therefore, was directed toward these aspects of the grammar. A break after the first field stay provided the time necessary to refine the preliminary notions developed in the field setting and to make a contrastive analysis of English and Yucatec.

A second field trip in July and August 1980 was made to conduct more systematic assessment of certain details of the linguistic hypotheses which had been settled upon and to pretest various possible stimuli and task procedures for the nonlinguistic assessment. Following this trip, final experimental tasks and stimuli were prepared. During a third field visit in November and December 1980, the tasks reported here were administered to a group of Mayan men. Finally, during the first half of 1981, the same tasks were administered to a group of English-speaking American men. Additional work with these tasks and modified versions of them was undertaken in 1988 in the context of pilot work for a further study. These results are described here only when they help clarify problematic issues in the original study.

Administration of the experimental tasks

Two series of experimental tasks were administered to each group. The overall sequence of administration for each series is presented in table 1. The experiments in series 1, which concerned the referential range of certain body-part terms, will not be discussed here. However, this series

Table 1. *Sequence of experimental tasks*

<hr>

Tasks in series 1
1. Picture depiction
2. Picture recall
3. Picture recognition (A)
4. Picture recognition (B)
5. Picture description

Tasks in series 2
1. Picture description (immediate)
2. Picture description (recall)
3. Picture similarity judgment
4. Picture recognition (short term)
5. Picture recognition (long term)
6. Object forced-choice triads (direct)
7. Object forced-choice triads (indirect)

<hr>

did serve (by design) to introduce speakers to the general format of experiments and to most of the specific task procedures as well. Thus, by the time they got to series 2, the tasks relevant to the current project, the men were familiar in a general way with most of the task requirements.[9] Undoubtedly there remain substantial differences between the English and Yucatec samples in general familiarity with the experimental procedures typically used in cognitive studies, but it was hoped that the preliminary exposure to series 1 would help to minimize the significance of such differences on series 2 which followed.

The experiments were designed to provide a variety of types of information as shown schematically in table 2. Experiments 1, 3, 6, and 7 concerned immediate classification of stimuli (which, in the present case, included attention, categorization, and similarity judgment) whereas experiments 2, 4, and 5 concerned memory, that is, response to stimuli after a time delay. Experiments 1 and 2 provided systematic information on verbal responses both to verify linguistic patterns observed through less systematic techniques and to provide specific information on the verbal patterns associated with the stimulus materials to be used in the nonverbal experiments 3, 4, 5, 6, and 7. Experiments 3, 4, and 5 provide information on performance using pictures as stimuli, in contrast to 6 and 7 which involve actual objects.

Table 2. *Variables involved in series 2 experiments*

		COGNITIVE DIMENSION				
		Classification	Memory			
M R						T S
O E						Y T
D S	Verbal	Exp. 1	Exp. 2			P I
E P					Picture	E M
O		Exp. 3	Exp. 4, 5			U
N	Nonverbal					L
O S		Exp. 6, 7	----		Object	O U
F E						F S

Mayan sample

Adult Mayan men from the village were asked to perform the tasks. These men ranged in age from 18 to 45+ years of age with fairly even representation across this span. Educational experience ranged from zero to three years. (Ages and years of education for older men are estimates.) The primary motivations for participation were personal friendship and curiosity. Although financial compensation equal to a half day's wage was given, and was a decisive factor in a few cases, in no case was it alone sufficient.

The experiments were conducted in my house usually during daylight hours and the work was done at a small table at which we both sat. A portable procedure would have offered certain advantages (for example, I could have shown up at a man's house at an agreed upon time and by my presence help assure fulfillment of the commitment to participate), but the privacy available in my house outweighed these considerations. In general the men found the tasks interesting and easy – although some grew tired or bored by the last few experiments. Men coming in the morning tended to be more energetic and cheerful. However, those coming in the afternoon included more reliable and responsible men who would come only when the day's agricultural work was completed. Details of stimuli and task procedures are outlined below where the particular experiments are described.

The experiments (both series 1 and 2 together) took from 2 to 3 hours depending on the individual. This was an extraordinary amount of time for these men to be engaged in concentrated intellectual work, and it undoubtedly influenced their performance somewhat adversely. However, previous experience indicated that using a single session was the best approach for a variety of reasons. Like many cultural groups, the Maya do not put the same emphasis that we do on either temporal punctuality or verbal obligation. Thus, men would say that they would come at a certain time and then not come, or they would eventually show up hours later; alternatively, they would come as planned only to announce that they had other commitments. Secondly, by design the experiments were sequenced as to difficulty and order of exposure of certain stimuli so that a single administration was desirable. Finally, the desire to get equivalent data on all men argued for a uniform approach. By repeated advance visits on the day before or even a few hours before to reaffirm the commitment to come, by withholding the compensation until the entire series was completed, and by utilizing some verbal persuasion, it was possible to administer the tasks to about five men a week.

Questions can be raised about the willingness of Mayan men to participate, as this is a common difficulty in cross-cultural work of this sort. It should be emphasized that I had no special power over these men and that, by the time these experiments were administered, this was clear to everyone. The basic egalitarian norm of male interaction in the village, namely, that no man can or should coerce any other man, was operative for me and, I believe, made men comfortable in refusing to participate if they wished. Several did refuse. Men who were explicit about not wanting to participate were not asked again. There are a number of extremely subtle, indirect cues as to genuine interest which are too complicated to elaborate on here (for example, suggesting we do the task tomorrow signifies "I'm not interested," suggesting tomorrow at some specific time such as four o'clock signifies "I'm seriously interested"). Implicit refusals were also honored to the extent they were recognized. The most difficult situation, as indicated above, arose when a man failed to appear as agreed because this might indicate reluctance to participate, but could not, in and of itself, be taken as a reliable index of such reluctance. Some men genuinely forgot to come, others encountered more pressing demands on their time, and so forth. These are common occurrences in village life where neither the clock nor informal arrangements of the sort involved here count for much. In the end, some of the men who agreed to participate clearly showed some ambivalence about doing so. I believe their hesitancy was usually due either to uncertainty about what was required and/or insecurity about their skills in "bookwork." No one remained uncomfortable once the tasks were begun and they saw what was involved. Many wanted to come "work" again another time and have done so on subsequent field visits.

American sample

College-aged men from the University of Chicago were also asked to perform the tasks. All were native speakers of English. These men were all known to me from previous contact in the University housing system and the primary motivations for participation were personal friendship and curiosity. The tasks were administered in my apartment in an informal atmosphere using the same procedures as with the Maya. The men experienced no special difficulties with the tasks and usually completed them in about two hours. One or two men showed excessive concern with their performance – what might be called "test anxiety" – but their patterns of performance were not noticeably different from those of the other men on the substantive measures reported below.

2. Comparison of grammatical categories: nominal number in English and Yucatec

Introduction

An examination of the relationship of linguistic diversity to thought requires the identification and analysis of a specific case of such diversity. Ideally, following Whorf, the contrast would be of large-scale "fashions of speaking." This ideal guides the approach taken here in two respects. First, the focus is on a structurally and semantically significant aspect of the grammar rather than on a little used or structurally marginal pattern. Second, some preliminary indications are given as to how these patterns fit together into larger semantic structures in each language.

It would also be desirable to investigate a substantial sample of languages. This is approximated here in that the linguistic characterizations and comparisons explicitly take account of typological data on an array of languages. Further, the analysis has been constructed, both methodologically and substantively, to facilitate extension to additional languages. However, detailed linguistic discussion will be provided only for American English and Yucatec Maya – the two languages for which cognitive assessments will be undertaken.

The phenomenon of concern in this chapter can be loosely labeled in traditional terms as *nominal number marking*. Notionally, it involves various indications of the multiplicity, number, quantity, or amount of some object of noun phrase reference relative to a predication. Formally, it includes such things as plural inflection, plural concord, and indication of singular or plural by modification of the lexical head of a noun phrase with a numeral or other adjective indicating quantity or specificity of amount. Nominal number has been chosen for several reasons. First, it is one of the most commonly encountered and most central noun phrase categories; as such it is ideal for comparative purposes. Secondly, in many cases the formal patterns have clear referential value, an important consideration from the point of view of developing controlled language comparisons and nonlinguistic cognitive assessment procedures. Finally, it is the locus of some of the more striking differences between the structure of English and that of Yucatec.

The primary goal of this chapter is to describe and interpret the basic contrasts in number marking between English and Yucatec from which a meaningful cognitive analysis can be developed. The approach taken is to sketch first the number marking patterns of the two languages in broad terms, showing the place of the specific patterns of interest within the larger pattern of number marking and the general grammatical organization. In the case of Yucatec, a brief general introductory sketch of the language in terms of some standard typological categories is also included. These descriptions are then followed by an explicit comparison of the two languages on the major points of difference – bringing in additional comparative information and perspectives to clarify the interpretation. The chapter concludes with a brief summary statement of the major patterns of differences.

Any given linguistic utterance represents the intersection of a number of complex functional levels into a single formal representation. Inversely, each individual form within an utterance may simultaneously play a role at several of these functional levels or even several roles within a single level. This multifunctionality of speech forms lies at the heart of the difficulties of linguistic analysis. The present analysis by being focused as it is on only one subsection of the grammar – number marking – must necessarily simplify (hence, distort) some aspects of the actual patterning of the two languages. Yet if all the meanings of a formal pattern, all the formal manifestations a given meaning may take, or all the interactions the form–meaning combinations undergo were explored, one would inevitably be led away from the original focus of research to a description of the structure of the entire grammar. Such a comprehensive grammatical description is not the goal of this chapter. Further, it will also become evident during the discussion that there are substantial difficulties with the traditional characterization of number marking itself. Although some indications are given as to the direction a reconceptualization might take, a full theoretical reworking will not be undertaken here.

Description of English

Overview of English noun phrases

The focus of the present analysis will be on number marking as part of the constitution of a *noun phrase*. A noun phrase forms part of a *proposition* (clause or sentence) which is, in turn, usually part of a longer utterance in a *sequence of discourse* consisting of many linked propositions. The category of number functions significantly at these higher structural levels, aiding in the establishment and maintenance of coherent discourse. So these levels, although they are not the focus, must also play a role in the analysis.

The emphasis here will be on lexical noun phrases. A *lexical noun phrase* consists of a phrase with a *lexical noun* as its endocentric *head* and may include various *modifiers*. The head noun itself may be intrinsically a noun (i.e., a noun root), may be derived from a non-noun root (for example, verb root), or may be formally neutral (for example, becoming a noun or verb with equal facility). The *derivational processes* which essentially convert non-nominal material into nouns may be signaled by morphological marks or may consist merely of placement in a noun phrase framework. The head noun may be modified in various ways either by *inflectional processes* (usually affixation) with various grammatical categories (for example, number), by *lexical modification* (for example, determiners, quantifiers, and descriptive adjectives), or by various *phrasal and clausal modifiers*. Various *pronominal* forms which necessarily index some element of the immediate speech situation (for example, personal pronouns, demonstratives, etc.) can function as full noun phrases from a formal point of view without involving a lexical noun. However, some of the grammatical categories (especially inflectional categories) applied to or characteristic of lexical noun phrases also receive explicit marking in these pronominal forms (for example, pronouns may differentiate number and gender).

Overt indications of grammatical number

Lexical content versus grammatical number

Some lexical nouns indicate a multiplicity of referents as part of their inherent referential meaning. So for example *herd* refers to an aggregation of animals and *people* refers to more than one person. Although such lexical indications interact with grammatical number, they are not equivalent to it. Thus *herd* may take both singular and plural number marking to indicate the number of herds (for example, *one herd, three herds*, etc.); the existence of a multiplicity of animals within the aggregation is grammatically irrelevant in this construction. *People* likewise can function in this way (for example, taking a plural as in *the peoples of the earth are threatened*), but in other situations the inherent multiplicity of the lexical meaning will be reflected in grammatical number marking patterning (for example, plural verb agreement with nonplural lexical noun: *the people of the earth are threatened, a people are united by their traditions, people are angry*, etc.).

The interaction of grammatical number with inherent lexical content is a central concern of this chapter. For this reason, the initial account of the number marking patterns in English will be made without reference to the lexical content of the noun head. Care has not always been taken on this point in traditional grammatical accounts. It is quite common to use a given pattern of number marking to sort or define lexical nouns into classes (for example, nouns that can take plural inflection are "count" nouns, those that cannot are "mass" nouns). Then the lexical division is used to explain the application of number marking (for example, this noun can be pluralized because it is a "count" noun). The circularity here is quite clear. This purely formal approach provides no explanatory value in the absence of some notional grounding outside the circle. One alternative is to characterize the lexical content of the nouns independently of number marking and number marking independently of specific lexical content and, only then, to analyze the interactions.

Marking noun phrase number by inflection

Plural is a basic inflectional category of English lexical noun phrases. Individual lexical nouns typically take a *plural* suffix *-s* (∼ *-es*) to refer to a multiplicity of referents – hence the traditional notional interpretation of the category as having to do with *number*. The nature of the multiplicity depends on the meaning of the lexical noun; two meanings predominate: multiplicity of a recurrent unit (for example, *pens*) and multiplicity of various kinds (for example, *wines*). Lexical nouns without such a mark (i.e., no suffix or "zero" suffix [-∅]) are frequently interpreted as being "singular," that is, as necessarily having reference to a single unit or kind, but in fact they need not be. Many nouns cannot be inflected for plural nor take plural meaning (for example, *zinc, heat*); it is misleading then to call these lexical forms singular to the extent that doing so suggests a specific sense of "singularity" in formal opposition with plural. All other things being equal, that is, in the absence of some other indication of number, the lexical forms without *-s* are best interpreted as being *nonplural* from the point of view of number.

Singular, then, is not an inflectional category in English. If there is an overt indication of singularity it lies elsewhere in the noun phrase or clause. However, for most nouns the nonplural form of a lexical noun will be the one used to form noun phrases with *Singular* meaning and thus, in many cases, "singular" is a plausible residual interpretation of the number of these lexical nouns. It will be important in what follows to distinguish clearly between nonplural form of the lexical noun and the

Singular number marking of the noun phrase as a whole. To indicate this difference orthographically, the capitalized terms Plural, Singular, and Neutral will be used to designate the overall number value of the noun phrase; uncapitalized forms such as plural and nonplural will be used to refer to the value of specific markings within the utterance.

Many lexical nouns in English depart from this basic inflectional pattern. They show irregularities in the formation of the plural form often because of the preservation of an older plural marking form (for example, *ox* versus *oxen*) or because of the foreign origin of the lexeme (for example, *criterion* versus *criteria*). The characterization of these forms as plurals depends on both an understanding of their usual referential meaning and on the fact that the forms themselves pattern in certain ways like ordinary plurals. Even so, the very fact of their irregularity is a clue that there may be something unusual about the typical meaning of these nouns. Sometimes both the ordinary and an irregular plural coexist leading to three-way oppositions with special semantic senses for the irregular forms: *brother, brothers, brethren*.

Marking noun phrase number by modification[1]

Lexical nouns may be modified in English by a variety of adjectival forms which precede the noun in the following general sequence: *determiners* (including articles, quantitative determiners, demonstratives, possessives), *quantifiers* (including ordinal numbers, cardinal numbers, and certain phrasal forms indicating groupings, partitives, and measures), and *qualifiers* or descriptive adjectives (including everything else). Determiners consist of a relatively small set of frequently used forms some of which can show agreement with, or mark the number of, the lexical noun head and, from a syntactic point of view, act much like the head of a noun phrase (Lyons, 1977, secs. 11.4, 15.2). Quantitative adjectives comprise a moderately large set of lexical forms which interact with, and directly indicate the number of, the lexical noun. Qualitative adjectives comprise a large set of lexical forms which interact with number indirectly by the information they provide about the inherent lexical meaning of nouns. This discussion will concentrate for the most part on determiners and quantitative adjectives.

Determiners

Indefinite article and similar forms. The indefinite article *a* (~*an*) occupies an interstitial status between determiner and quantitative adjective. Along with certain other forms it is sometimes referred to as a quantitative determiner. It is in structural alternation with other determiners, but means 'one' or 'singularity'. Historically, *a* apparently derives from *an*, Anglo Saxon numeral 'one' and the full form *one* emerges in deictic and anaphoric uses: *give me one*. This indefinite article form thus signals *singular* and, when occurring with a nonplural lexical noun head, is one of the most important indications of Singular meaning within the noun phrase as a whole. For example, the nonplural lexical noun *cake* when preceded by article *a* produces Singular noun phrase: *I ate a cake*. This can be readily distinguished from a *Neutral* noun phrase where number is not positively specified and therefore is neither Singular or Plural (for example, *I ate [some] cake*) and, of course, from a Plural noun phrase (for example, *I ate [two] cakes*). Several other forms also mark Singular noun phrases in the same fashion as the indefinite article: *every, each, either, neither*.

Other indefinite forms.   The absence of the indefinite article or similar form, that is, when the determiner is *0* (phonological zero), a *nonsingular* lexical noun is indicated. It can occur with a plural lexical noun to form a Plural noun phrase (for example, *He brought cookies*) or with a nonplural lexical noun to form a Neutral noun phrase (for example, *He brought wine*). Table 3 shows how the plural/nonplural alternation in inflectional patterning interacts with the singular/nonsingular patterning of the quantitative determiners to yield a three-way patterning of number at the noun phrase level. Several other forms also mark nonsingular noun phrases in the same fashion as *0* (phonological zero): *some* (unstressed), *any* (unstressed), and *enough*. These forms can stand alone in anaphoric or deictic uses.

Definite article and similar forms.   Number is not signalled by the definite article *the*: *I ate the cake*, *I ate the cakes*. Other determiner or determiner-like forms that are neutral with respect to number are the possessives *his, her, its*, etc., *some* (stressed), *any* (stressed), *no*, and various *wh*-forms (*whose, which, whichever*, etc.). These forms can stand alone in deictic or anaphoric uses.

Demonstratives.   Demonstratives agree with the number of the lexical noun head: *this cake, that cake, these cakes, those cakes*. So demonstratives do not modify the number of the lexical noun, that is, they apparently do not contribute to creating number at the level of the noun phrase. However, they can be diagnostic of number in ambiguous cases for noun phrases headed by irregular lexical nouns. Like other determiners, these forms can stand alone in deictic or anaphoric uses.

Table 3. *Interaction of noun inflection and determiner modification in English to produce number marking at the noun phrase level*

Formal marking	Number of the noun phrase		
	Singular	Neutral	Plural
Noun inflection	nonplural		plural
Determiner modification	singular	nonsingular	

Quantitative modifiers

Quantitative modifiers generally involve explicit or implicit mention of number and usually can follow a determiner such as *the*. In general the quantifier modifiers indicate either singular or plural number. A couple of forms can be used either way.

Ordinal indicators.   Ordinal modifiers include the true ordinals *first, second, third,* etc. and certain forms which resemble them semantically and grammatically such as *next, last, another, additional, other, main, precise*. The true ordinals other than *first* require a nonplural lexical noun and indicate singular as part of their meaning. *First* allows a broader range of meanings and does not reliably distinguish number. The remaining ordinals other than *last* and *another* are also compatible with either plural or nonplural lexical nouns, but with the nonplural nouns they all indicate singular as part of their meaning. *Last* like *first* allows a broader range of meanings especially when referring to temporal ordering and therefore does not reliably distinguish number. *Another* usually co-occurs with a nonplural noun and signals singular. We may generalize that ordinals tend to exclude a meaning of Neutral at the level of the noun phrase.

Cardinal indicators.   Cardinal indicators include the true cardinals *one, two, three,* etc. and certain forms which resemble them semantically and grammatically such as *many, few, several, only. One* occurs with nonplural lexical nouns and inherently indicates singular by its meaning. With one exception, the remainder of the true cardinals and cardinal-like forms occur with plural lexical nouns and indicate Plural noun phrase. The exception is *only* which does not distinguish number. Like the

Table 4. *Number marking implications of English quantitative modifiers*

Formal marking	Number of the noun phrase		
	Singular	Neutral	Plural
Ordinal Modifiers			
First	singular		plural
True ordinals	singular		
Ordinal-like[a]	singular		plural
Cardinal modifiers			
One	singular		
True cardinals			plural
Cardinal-like[b]			plural

[a] Except *last, another.*   [b] Except *only.*

ordinals, the cardinal indicators tend to exclude a Neutral interpretation at the noun phrase level.

Table 4 summarizes these patterns. Since the plural meaning of these modifiers is redundant with the inflectional pattern on the lexical noun in the ordinary case, the main relevance of the ordinals and cardinals from the point of view of grammatical number is to distinguish the Singular noun phrases from Neutral ones. For irregular lexical noun forms, however, the marking of plural may not be redundant at the noun phrase level and then provides crucial information about grammatical number (for example, *two deer ran by*).

Other quantifier modifiers.   The adjective *much* indicates quantity or amount but without actual reference to number in the sense of singularity or multiplicity. The form is also syntactically unusual in that, unlike other quantitative modifiers, it virtually never co-occurs with the determiner *the*. Since *much* occurs with nonplural lexical noun forms yet does not have reference to singular meaning, it is often taken as a positive specification of Neutral noun phrase number. Another adjectival modifier *little* may also be mentioned here since it contrasts in use with *much*. When used to indicate quantity, *little* refers to size with some nouns (for example, *the little box I bring*) and amount with other nouns – where it can be regarded as being elliptical – (for example, *the little [bit of] money I earn*). Correct interpretation depends on knowing certain aspects of the meaning value of the lexical noun head.

Marking noun phrase number by concord

Verbs

In addition to indications of number within the noun phrase itself or its equivalents, there are sometimes other positive indications of number at the larger clause level. Neutral and Singular noun phrases in English nominative case take special verbal concord (usually suffix *-s*) in the present indicative in contrast to Plural noun phrases. So *a/some cake sits on the table* contrasts with *two cakes sit on the table*. Absence of this special concord indicates that the noun phrase is Plural. But no such rules of agreement with verb phrases separate Singular from Neutral noun phrases – so the pattern of number marking in the present indicative verb matches exactly the patterning for the inflectional forms of the lexical nouns.

Pronouns

Number distinctions are also represented in the patterning of third person pronouns which are functionally equivalent to complete noun phrases. By looking at the cross-referencing relations with lexical noun phrases with known number (as well as by many other indications) it can be established that the third person pronouns *they/them* are Plural, *he/him* and *she/her* are Singular, and *it* can be either Singular or Neutral. Parallel patterns operate for cross-referencing with possessives: *their*, *his*, *hers*, *its*. In cases where these pronouns (excepting *it*) substitute for and/or cross-reference full noun phrases of uncertain number status, the pattern of agreement can signal the number of the corresponding noun phrase. Notice that number marking on the pronouns, like that on the present indicative verb, generally follows the patterning for the inflection of lexical nouns (i.e., segments out Plural from everything else). But for nouns with masculine or feminine gender value, a true Singular is signaled.

Covert indications of grammatical number

Syntactic potential of lexical nouns

Any given lexical noun can be characterized as to the set of syntactic constructions that it is compatible with. Often there will be constructions into which a given lexeme will not fit. Such interaction effects were called reactances by Whorf and identifying such reactances is an important part of modern grammatical analysis. We can take the criterial frames so far described for number categories and ask whether various individual lexical nouns can fit into them. Plural is distinguished from both Singular and Neutral by inflectional -s and absence of special verbal concord when serving as the subject of a present indicative verb form. Singular is distinguished from Neutral by modifiers of various sorts, especially the application of the indefinite article *a* (~ *an*) in certain contexts. Neutral is thus the residual number category at the noun phrase level, but as a positive criterion we can look for simultaneous compatibility of *0* (phonological zero) indefinite article (or, alternatively, *some* [unstressed]) with nonplural lexical noun and nonplural present indicative verb.

Some nouns such as *zinc* only fit this Neutral frame: *0 zinc is hard*. Such nouns are typically called "mass" nouns in grammatical descriptions of English. Some lexemes such as *truck* never fit this Neutral frame but do fit both Singular and Plural frames: *a truck is coming* / *(some) trucks are coming*. These are the nouns typically called "count" nouns in grammatical descriptions of English. Other nouns fit all three frames – Singular, Plural and Neutral. The noun *cake* mentioned earlier is such a noun. Many nouns change their meaning considerably depending on the frame, a consideration taken up further below.

Some forms do not readily fit into these criterial patterns. For example, a form may meet one criterion of Plural but not another: *the news is on* shows plural suffix without plural concord, *the cattle are coming* shows plural concord without plural suffix. Disambiguating these cases requires examining the overall patterning and giving priority to some criteria over others. And general knowledge of the language may be essential here, for example, in recognizing the significance of the implicit alternation of *cattle* with *cow* and *cows*. Other nouns may appear to be plural but lack

Table 5. *Distribution of some lexical nouns into various English number marking frames*

	Grammatical frames					
	1	2	3	4	5	6
Formal marks:						
1 definite article: *a*	+	+	−	−		
2 plural inflection: *-(e)s*	−	−	+	+	−	−
3 plural verb concord: *are*	+	−	−	+	+	−
Examples of noun types						
beef						x
cattle					x	
dreg				x		
linguistic			x			
scissor		x?		x		
truck		x		x		
cow		x		x		
measle		x	x	x		
sand				x		x
stone		x		x		x
duck		x		x	x	x
family		x		x	x	x
people	x?	x		x	x?	x

Each grammatical frame is characterized by a specific pattern of presence (+) or absence (−) of the three formal marks. If a lexical noun can fit into one of the frames, an *x* is entered into the column under the number of the frame.

any corresponding nonplural form: *He gave me only the dregs* shows what appears to be a plural form in *dregs* but there is no corresponding nonplural form **dreg*.[2] Some forms of this type will slowly undergo reanalysis to conform to the dominant pattern as in the creation of nonplural lexical noun *scissor*. (It also appears that the reverse process can occur as in, for example, the virtual disappearance of the nonplural form of *galoshes* in some dialects.)

If we add in these additional patterns of the grammar (for example, nonplural noun inflection with plural verb concord; cf. *cattle* earlier) we can define more distinctive frames and get more varieties of lexical nouns. So for example *duck* fits at least four frames: Singular *a duck is flying overhead*; Plural (*some/three*) *ducks are swimming in the pond* (also *ducks are good to eat*); Neutral *duck is fatty*; "Aggregate" [?] *duck are in season. Family* also fits many frames: Singular *a family is waiting*; Plural *two families are waiting* (also *families are important*); Neutral *family is important*; "Collective" [?] (in some dialects) *the family are agreed*. Sorting out the semantic and pragmatic subtleties of some of these formal variations is a considerable task. Table 5 represents schematically some of the English lexical nouns mentioned above as well as some others with indications of how they distribute relative to the three formal attributes which have been emphasized here: inflection, modification, and concord.

Implicit (or deducible) number

In many syntactic constructions, some of the distinctions among kinds of grammatical number are formally neutralized. Nonetheless, number may be semantically implicated in these cases if we include as part of the meaning of each lexical noun the potential range of grammatical relations. For example, although there is no overt difference in number between *the hammer is hard* and *the zinc is hard*, the first sentence implicates Singular number and the second does not because of the selectional restrictions on the two nouns. *Hammer* can take the criterial Singular and Plural frames (*a hammer is, two hammers are*) and can never take the criterial Neutral pattern (**0 hammer is hard*). Therefore, in a case like this where there is formal neutralization of the number distinction, that is, when Singular and Neutral cannot be distinguished by any overt mark, we can deduce nonetheless that the noun *hammer* must be singular because it can never take the overt, diagnostic Neutral pattern and hence that meaning. We may say that the noun phrase contains *a covert indication of Singular* by virtue of the broader distributional potential of the lexical noun. *Zinc*, by contrast, can take the overt Neutral pattern (*0 zinc is hard*) but can never take overt Singular or Plural patterns (**a zinc* or **two zincs*). So noun phrases containing *zinc* are always Neutral and the lexical noun itself may also be so construed. This sort of reasoning underlies the standard division of nouns in English into "count" and "mass" which essentially amounts to a description of the distributional pattern characteristic of each noun. It also underlies the reasoning which disambiguates number for constructions containing irregular lexical nouns.

The situation for nouns which fit all three criterial frames is obviously more complicated and in some cases we would want to say that a given noun has no fixed or preferred selectional pattern. For these nouns, when number is formally neutralized it is also semantically neutralized as well. The number of these nouns must be specifically marked in the utterance if it is important. So, for example, the utterance *the cake was hard* in and of itself makes no commitment as to number, quantity, amount, multiplicity, etc., outside of a context such as prior speech or actual physical copresence where it might be deduced, because neither the covert limitations of the lexical noun *cake* nor the overt syntactic marking provides the information necessary to deduce number.

These rules of deducibility depend completely on there being a reliable difference in *meaningful* structural potential among the nouns of a language. If the structural difference had no semantic consequences there would be nothing to deduce. For example, if *a hammer is hard* and **0 hammer is hard* were equally valid expressions for referring to the properties of a single hammer then there would be no basis for establishing a category of singular in the first place. If such a semantic difference is signaled and the noun routinely takes both forms, then there is no basis for deciding in the neutralized case. So if both of the expressions just cited were syntactically possible and semantically different (as is, in fact, the case with nouns such as *cake*) there would be no reliable way of differentiating on structural grounds which meaning must be present in the case of formal neutralization (i.e., in cases where *the hammer* is used). Finally, if all nouns had this same structural potential, and hence the same semantic ambiguity, then there would be nothing to add to the semantic specification of any given noun. Only when (1) a syntactic construction is meaningful, (2) its application is somewhat obligatory, and (3) there are restrictions on which nouns can enter that construction, can we then say that structural potential of this sort is a part of the meaning of noun phrases containing the noun. The most reliable difference is an absolutely obligatory syntactic distinction, although systematic statistical differences can sometimes serve.

Meaning: interaction of lexical content with grammatical number

Some lexical nouns when they take the plural inflection refer to a multiplicity of individuals or tokens of a given object. So *three boys* usually refers to three individual boys. Other nouns when they take the plural inflection imply a multiplicity of kinds or types of a given object. So *three wines* usually refers to three kinds of wine. From the point of view of number marking, the two situations are the same since in both cases multiplicity is being indicated. Whatever difference in meaning obtains for these two noun types must be a function of the meaning of the lexical noun itself. Similar arguments can be made for the application of marks for singular.

It has been common, as noted above, to regard nouns of the first type as "count" nouns. They are usually defined from a formal point of view as entering only Singular and Plural noun phrase construction types. In fact they can enter into Neutral noun phrase construction types precisely when the referent is being construed as a kind; this is usually made explicit: *what kind of boy would do that?*[3] Nouns of the second type are regarded as "mass" nouns. They are usually defined from a formal point of view as entering only Neutral noun phrase construction types. But many such nouns can enter into Singular and Plural noun phrase construction types with a rather straightforward interpretation in terms of a singularity or multiplicity of kinds: *we had a good wine last night, we had some good wines last night.* To refer using these mass nouns with the sense of 'individuals' usually requires some overt signal that the referent is being construed as an individual: *a bottle of wine.*[4]

If a distinction is to be drawn between the referential potential of various nouns with respect to number, it should not be developed solely in terms of formal distributional categories where terms such as count and mass refer to nothing more than the compatibility of the noun with Singular/Plural or Neutral construction types. On the one hand, this approach produces a kind of tautology: nouns which can take a plural can take a plural and those which cannot, cannot. Such tautologies account for nothing. On the other hand, this approach ignores the large number of cases which violate the regularity and yet produce completely inter-pretable constructions. Rather, what is needed is a semi-independent description of the referential value of various types of lexical nouns which can be used to account for their meaningful interaction with number categories at the noun phrase level.

One clue to such an analysis in the present case lies in the meanings of the forms just cited. Whereas *boys* means multiplicity of individuals, *wines* means multiplicity of kinds. This suggests that one lexical noun type refers to individuals or units and the other to kinds or types. This is confirmed by the consequences of trying to reverse these emphases which produces the phrasal forms *kind of boy* and *unit of wine.* (It will be important in this regard to have some information about the operation of some of these phrasal forms in English; this is provided in the next section.) There seems to be some sort of inherent contrast among lexical noun types, then, as to whether they essentially refer to units or to kinds. (Alternative characterizations of this difference can be made in terms of an opposition in reference to forms or substances, to intrinsically bounded or unbounded entities, etc.) The important point is not to define this dimension of difference solely in terms of selectional restric-tions with respect to grammatical number but in terms of inherent lexical content as manifest in a variety of ways. The nature of this particular unit/kind opposition will not be explored further at this point but will be taken up later in the comparison with Yucatec.

Phrasal modifiers of quantity

A variety of phrasal constructions in English of the form "Noun Phrase 1 *of* Noun Phrase 2" can also be used to indicate quantity or amount (for example, *a piece of meat*). These forms provide a unit for those lexical nouns which essentially refer to kinds and indicate the specific nature of the unit for those lexical nouns which essentially refer to units. Understanding their operation will be important in the comparison with Yucatec. The relevant phrasal constructions can be grouped into partitives – including general partitives (for example, *piece of cake*), specific (or typical) partitives (for example, *slice of cake*), and measure partitives or measure phrases (for example, *pound of cake*) – and into quantitative estimators such as *lots of* as in *lots of cake*. Some of the so-called pre-determiners (for example, *all [of]/both [of]/half [of] the cakes*) also pattern like the quantitative estimators.[5]

For the partitives the lexical head of Noun Phrase 1 is usually the syntactic head of the larger phrasal construction and this fact is reflected in the patterning of grammatical number. Thus, in the clause *two quarts of lemonade are already chilled*, the adjective *two*, the plural suffix *-s*, and the verbal agreement *are* all center on *quart* and not *lemonade*, the head of Noun Phrase 2. Even though it might appear that the referent of Noun Phrase 2 in such constructions is the real focus of interest and that its lexical head (*lemonade* here, *cake* in the examples in the previous paragraph) should therefore be the head of the larger noun phrase, this is not the case for the partitives, nor is it the case in general in English for constructions of this type. Compare here two syntactic reductions which preserve this focus on Noun Phrase 1: *two quarts are already chilled* and *sóme lemonade is already chilled*; by contrast the following example shifts the focus: *some lémonade is already chilled* where the lexical noun *lemonade* is usually given contrastive stress.

In short, the partitive term (i.e., lexical head of Noun Phrase 1) functions syntactically as the head of the larger noun phrase even though it seems to be modifying Noun Phrase 2 by indicating its quantity. The syntactic focus, and ultimately the semantic focus, in these noun phrases is on the *unit* of grouping, containment, measurement, or segmentation and not on what the unit is a unit of. In line with this focus on units, Noun Phrase 1 tends to be Singular or Plural rather than Neutral.

Not all partitives can occur with all lexical nouns, and the pattern of selectional restrictions is quite complex. Nonetheless, relatively large

Table 6. *Number marking in English partitive and estimator constructions*

English forms	Noun phrase number						
	Noun phrase 1			*of*	Noun phrase 2		
	S	N	P		S	N	P
Partitives[a]							
General (e.g., *piece of, bit of*)	+	−	+		+	+	+
Typical (e.g., *slice of, roast of*)	+	−	+		+	+	+
Measure (e.g., *pint of, pound of*)	+	−	+		+	+	+
Estimators[b]							
Quantitative (examples)							
lot of	+	−	+		−	+	+
large/small quantity of	+	−	+		−	+	+
large/small amount of	+	−	+		−	+	+
large/small/great/ good number of	+	−	+		−	−	+
great/good deal of	+	−	−		−	+	−
plenty of	−	+	−		−	+	+
Pre-determiners (examples)							
half (of)	+	+	+		+	+	+
all (of)	−	−	+		−	+	+
both (of)	−	−	+		−	+	+

Letters heading columns indicate number for either Noun Phrase 1 or 2 as follows: S = Singular, N = Neutral, P = Plural. A plus (+) in a column indicates that the given number marking option is available for the particular type of partitive or estimator; a negative (−) indicates that the option is not available. Only general patterns are shown.
[a] Verb agrees with Noun Phrase 1. [b] Verb agrees with Noun Phrase 2.

groupings of nouns can be developed by working with the very general partitives. For example, if the lexical nouns compatible with the partitive phrasal *(a) part of (a)* are separated out, the nouns traditionally regarded as count nouns will be included. Finer groupings can be gotten with some of the more specific partitives. For example, *(a) slice of (a)* when applied to concrete referents will sort out solids of firm shape (for example, *a slice of baloney*) from liquids (for example, **a slice of water*). Such sortings may represent one way in which characterizations of inherent lexical content relevant to number patterning could be developed.

The quantitative estimators differ considerably from the partitives. Number agreement is with the lexical head of Noun Phrase 2:

> *lots of zinc ends up being wasted*   [*zinc* ⇒ nonplural verb]
> *a lot of zinc ends up being wasted*   [*zinc* ⇒ nonplural verb]
> *lots of pens end up in the trash can*   [*pens* ⇒ plural verb]
> *a lot of pens end up in the trash can*   [*pens* ⇒ plural verb].

In these cases Noun Phrase 2 has to be regarded as the head of the noun phrase in terms of its verbal concord. Further, this pattern can be used to infer the status of the lexical head of Noun Phrase 2 even when it is not formally expressed:

> *lots ends up being wasted*   [nonplural verb ⇒ nonplural noun]
> *a lot ends up being wasted*   [nonplural verb ⇒ nonplural noun]
> *lots end up in the trash can*   [plural verb ⇒ plural noun]
> *a lot end up in the trash can*   [plural verb ⇒ plural noun].

This is deviant from the general pattern for partitives in English but does accord with the intuition that Noun Phrase 1 in some sense modifies Noun Phrase 2 (i.e., tells us "how much" of the referent of Noun Phrase 1 there is). These syntactic facts suggest that Noun Phrase 1 is acting here like a lexical modifier – a sort of frozen form equivalent to lexical modifiers such as *many* and *much*.

The number of Noun Phrase 2 is never Singular so that we can say that the estimators apply essentially to Plural or Neutral noun phrases. (In the examples just given, the implicit nonplural noun can actually be characterized more precisely as part of a Neutral noun phrase construction.) There is, however, some variability in their ability to take Plural or Neutral noun phrases and the pattern must be worked out for each individual estimator form. Some examples of these patterns and those of the relevant pre-determiner estimators are shown in table 6 along with the pattern for the partitives.

Summary

The basic English pattern overtly distinguishes Plural from both Singular and Neutral in the noun phrase. This is the pattern evidenced in lexical noun inflection and in concord with verbs, most pronouns, and demonstratives. For certain irregular nouns, the concord patterns may be the essential criteria for assigning number. At the level of the noun phrase,

Singular may be overtly signaled by the use of the indefinite article *a* (~*an*) and by the use of certain quantitative modifiers such as *one*, *second*, etc. Neutral noun phrases are either residually indicated by the use of certain determiner forms or by the absence of an article in indefinite noun phrases showing nonplural inflection and concord.

In many cases, especially for definite reference, overt number marking adequate to distinguish Singular from Neutral is not present. In such cases number can often be imputed on the basis of knowing the general distributional potential of the lexical noun head. Many traditional analyses use these distributional potentials to generate noun classes such as count and mass nouns. These analyses typically ignore a good part of the actual range of usage of the lexical forms and, from the point of view of giving an account of number marking, are fundamentally tautological. A more adequate approach would involve characterizing lexical noun types independently of grammatical number marking and then exploring the attested distributional potential in terms of an interaction of inherent lexical meaning and grammatical or structural meaning. A careful analysis of phrasal modifiers relevant to number and quantity might provide one source of classification of nouns into types. In the comparison with Yucatec developed below, certain others will be identified.

Description of Yucatec

Since most readers will have little familiarity with the Yucatec language, a brief sketch of some of the main typological characteristics of the language precedes the more detailed discussion of number marking.

Overview of Yucatec Maya

This sketch of Yucatec is intentionally brief and selective. The language is located socially and typologically. Emphasis is on the noun phrase since this may be useful in reading and (re)interpreting the main text or the materials in the appendices.

Geography and history

Modern Yucatec Maya is spoken throughout the northern Yucatan peninsula area in southeastern Mexico. Along with the related languages Lacandon (Chiapas, Mexico), Itza (Peten, Guatemala), and Mopan (southern Belize and Peten, Guatemala), it is part of the Peninsular

Table 7. *Phonemic inventory of modern Yucatec Maya consonants*

Manner of articulation	Place of Articulation					
	L	LD	DA	AP	V	G
Stop						
Plain	**p**		**t**		**k**	
Glottalized	**p'**		**t'**		**k'**	**'**
Voiced	**b'**		*d*		*g*	
Affricate						
Plain			**¢**	**ch**		
Glottalized			**¢'**	**ch'**		
Fricative		*f*	**s**	**š**		**h**
Resonant						
Nasal	**m**		**n**	**ñ**		
Lateral			**l**			
Median	**w**		*r*	**y**		

L = labial, LD = labio-dental, DA = dental/alveolar, AP = alveopalatal, V = velar, G = glottal. Boldface font indicates indigenous Yucatec consonant; italicized font indicates consonant introduced from Spanish. (*r* is apparently indigenous in some dialects.)

Maya subgroup (often termed Maya Proper or Yucatecan) within the Mayan family of languages (McQuown, 1956). There are some 350,000 speakers in all, but probably fewer than 50,000 monolinguals (Kaufman, 1974; Dirección General, 1973). Modern Yucatec is little changed from Classical Yucatec Maya, the language of the post-Classic era in northern Yucatan at the time of first Spanish contact (McQuown, 1967, p. 202; but cf. Bricker, 1979, pp. 113–15; 1981b). Many believe some variant of Yucatec was the language of the Classic period of Maya civilization and hence the basis of the written inscriptions of that era as well, but definitive evidence is still lacking; the principal alternative is the Cholan subgroup of Mayan languages (Kaufman, 1974; Morley, Brainerd, and Sharer, 1983, p. 504; cf. McQuown, 1967).

Phonology

Modern Yucatec has the consonantal phonemes shown in table 7 (Blair, 1965 [1964]; Straight, 1972). There are five vowels that each occur in four phonemic length–tone combinations: short–neutral: **i, e, a, o, u**;

long–low: ìi, èe, àa, òo, ùu; long–high: íi, ée, áa, óo, úu; and long–[high] broken (or glottalized): i'i, é'e, á'a, ó'o, ú'u (Blair, 1965 [1964]; Straight, 1972). Vowel alternation has both morphological and syntactic significance. Paralinguistic patterns affect the overt expression of vowels (McQuown, 1970). In rapid speech a considerable number of consonants and vowels may be omitted, but in relatively predictable ways.

Roots

Roots tend to be of monosyllabic Consonant–Vowel–Consonant form and there are estimated to be 2,000 such roots in the language (McClaran Stefflre, 1972, p. 262; McQuown, 1967, p. 208). Many, if not most, roots readily enter into both nominal or verbal constructions, that is, form nominal or verbal stems, with minimal derivational apparatus (McClaran Stefflre, 1972, p. 83), hence the categories of noun and verb appear to be modulus rather than selective (Whorf, 1956, pp. 93–99). These stems in turn anchor complex morphological affixing (predominantly postfixing) and infixing (especially in verbal constructions) to form lexical nouns and lexical verbs. These "lexical" items are equivalent in many cases to full phrases and, especially in the case of verbs, to complete clauses or sentences.

Noun phrases

Case

Noun phrases as such do not have overt morphological marks for the primary syntactic case relations of intransitive subject and transitive agent and patient;[6] lexical meaning, word order, and cross-referencing verb- or preposition-bound pronominal markers carry this information. A generic preposition *ti'* ~ *t-* serves to express locative, directional, and other relationships: *ti' mèesa* 'to/at the table'. If an additional noun is related to the predicate, it is preceded by this generic preposition thereby overtly marking the additional case relation. Possession is marked by a pronominal prefix on the possessed noun cross-referencing to the possessor which follows immediately (if it is expressed): *'u-kib' Juan* 'his-candle John [i.e., John's candle]'. Many specialized locative expressions combine this pattern of possession with the generic preposition; the first noun indicates relative placement and the second indicates with respect to what object: *t-u-ȼel nah* 'to-its-side house [i.e., to the side of the house]'.

Number and gender

Noun phrases are not obligatorily marked for number and gender and are apparently neutral on these dimensions. However, some lexical nouns, primarily animates, are often marked optionally for number (Singular or Plural) and gender (Masculine or Feminine). Neither of these requires agreement with other material within the noun phrase. Most often, number is marked by pronouns forming part of the verb complex; agreement is not obligatory.

Modification

Demonstratives frame or bracket the noun phrase with a prefix/postfix combination: for example, *le-* . . . *-o'* 'that' frames *máak* 'man' to yield *le-máak-o'* 'that man'. Enumeration with Yucatec numerals requires the insertion of a numeral classifier between numeral and lexical noun (if there is one) which provides information about the unit being counted: *ká'a-túul máak* 'two-animate man [i.e., two men]'. The noun need not be pluralized and usually is not. Enumeration with Spanish numerals does not require a classifier. Constructions with a Yucatec numeral and classifier serve a variety of syntactic functions that in other languages might be handled by articles or gender marking. Thus, the unstressed numeral 'one' along with the appropriate classifier can be used to indicate indefinite reference: *'un-túul máak* 'one-animate man [i.e., a man]'. In general, adjective modifiers precede the lexical noun and derivational affixes (which often have adjectival value) follow the stem. Relative clauses follow the modified lexical noun.

Verb phrases

A copula or equational verbal relation is not expressed morphologically (i.e., it is a phonological zero). Other verb forms fall into three classes depending on the suffixation necessary to form a transitive from a verb stem; further subclasses can be defined by other inflectional patterning (Blair, 1965 [1964]). There is as yet no adequate analysis of the full semantic implications of these classes and subclasses although some preliminary work has been done (McClaran Stefflre, 1972; Owen, 1969 [1968]). Perfective (or completive), imperfective (or incompletive) and optative (or subjunctive) aspects are marked in the verb complex. Perfective is not further differentiated by other essentially aspectual distinctions; imperfective and optative are differentiated into a variety of

Table 8. *Yucatec Maya bound pronoun forms*

Meanings		Forms	
		A Series	B Series
Person	Number		
1st	singular	(')in-(w)-	-en
1st	plural₁	(')in-(w)- ... -ó'on	-ó'on
1st	plural₂	k-	
2nd	singular	(')a-(w)-	-ech
2nd	plural	(')a-(w)- ... -é'eš	-é'eš
3rd	neutral	(')u-(y)-	-ø ~ -ih ~ -eh
3rd	plural	(')u-(y)- ... -ó'ob'	-ó'ob'

different forms referring to temporal contour distinctions (Blair, 1965 [1964]; Bricker, 1981a). Many of these forms involve some tense-like meanings, but in general tense is subordinate to aspect in terms of formal elaboration and semantic significance.

Pronouns and case marking

Two bound pronoun sets (shown in table 8) occur within both minimal and verbal constructions. There is a prefixing set, traditionally called the A series, which marks agent with transitive verbs and possession with nouns, and a postfixing set, traditionally called the B series, which marks patient with transitive verbs and forms equational constructions with nouns. For intransitive verbs, subject pronouns vary as a function of aspect: perfective and optative intransitives take the B series (i.e., case-marking in these aspectual paradigms, taken alone, looks ergative–absolutive), and the imperfective group of intransitives take the A series (i.e., case-marking in the imperfective paradigm, taken alone, looks nominative–accusative). Reflexives are indicated by a special form that follows the predicate and inflects with the A set.

   The A and B sets overlap in the plural where the postfixing B series plural forms are used with the prefixing (A series) nonplural forms to produce A series plural verb complexes. In most parts of Yucatan, the first person plural form of the A series (marked 1st plural₂ in table 8) is irregular from a formal point of view. In the village, a regular form (marked 1st plural₁ in table 8) is also used. (Speakers of other Yucatec dialects apparently do not use this form.) These two plurals are not in any readily definable paradigmatic alternation.

Word order and syntax

Basic word order has been regarded as VOS or SVO depending on the criteria used. (See the discussions of these alternative basic word orders in Durbin and Ojeda, 1978, and in Bricker, 1979.) All six basic word orders are acceptable each with specific pragmatic and semantic effects. As yet, higher level syntactic structures (i.e., above the level of morpho-tactics) have been little studied in Yucatec.

Discourse structures

Discourse structures in the sense of general devices for linking clause and sentence level structures to one another to form a coherent utterance in Yucatec have as yet received little research attention. Larger discourse patterns defining genres of speech have also received little attention. Preliminary work has been conducted on some of the more readily definable forms of speech, for example, poetic structuring of prayers, letters, stories (historical and fictional), and short proverbs and riddles (Bricker, 1974; Burns, 1983; Hanks, 1986; Lucy, 1992). Nearly every-thing still remains to be done with respect to characterizing the general structure of everyday speech patterns.

Uses of language

The Maya use language primarily for social communication. Speech varies markedly as to topic and manner depending on the participants in the interchange. Four global spheres can be defined by reference to the typical addressees or audience: private speech to near kin, public speech to fellow villagers, diplomatic speech to outside officials (for example, of government or church), and ritual speech to deities. In moving along the gradient from private to ritual speech, the content of speech becomes less important and the form relatively more important. Each of these is cross cut in significant ways in terms of the sex, age, social status, and social role of speaker and addressee. The net result is a complicated cultural system, but one which is essentially socially anchored.

There is no general pattern of sustained use or specialized involvement with language by lone individuals, for example in meditation, philosophizing, entertainment, problem solving, etc. Even ritual specialists tend to conform to this pattern, although Bible reading has become a solitary religious activity for one or two men in the village. There are no elaborate debates about the true meanings of words or about the relation of words to reality. The occasional conversations as to the correct way a speech or ceremony should be given stress the traditional form rather than the referential content of what is said. What individual psychological uses may be made of language categories remain tacit and undeveloped. Reading, writing, and education in general are recognized as valuable accomplishments but they are closely tied to Spanish and have little to do with Yucatec.

Overt indications of grammatical number

To the extent possible, Yucatec will be described in terms of the same formal framework as the English discussion so as to highlight the similarities and differences. Whenever possible, illustrations from English are provided which suggest the meaning value of the Yucatec forms.

Marking noun phrase number by inflection

Yucatec lexical nouns can be marked for plural by suffixing *-ó'ob'* to the lexical noun head, so *pèek'* 'dog,' plus *-ó'ob'* '[plural marker]' yields *pèek'-ó'ob'* 'dogs'. This suffix is identical to the one suffixed to verbs to indicate the presence of third person plural complement. The suffix is usually used to indicate explicitly that the noun phrase refers to a multiplicity of referents; sometimes it apparently suggests that all of a given group of referents are being referred to.

The suffix is optional or *facultative* in that it need not be used for correct reference when a multiplicity of referents does in fact exist, but it can be used to clarify or emphasize such multiplicity. For example, *yàan pèek' té'elo'* 'there-is-dog over-there' is ambiguous syntactically as to whether it refers to a multiplicity of referents or not. Specifically, it can refer to more than one dog: 'there are dogs over there'. This is quite similar to the ambiguity of some definite noun phrases in English: in the sentence *I saw the deer this morning* it is not clear on morphosyntactic grounds (either overt or covert) whether the person saw one deer or many deer or whether the intent is to contrast having seen deer with having seen some other kind of animal. In the absence of the plural suffix, then, Yucatec noun phrase heads have truly *neutral* form with respect to number. The term *neutral* makes clear the semantically indeterminant status of the uninflected form: the lexical nouns themselves can be used just as well with a multiplicity of referents as with one referent. The lexical head cannot be called nonplural (as in English) since it is not in obligatory alternation with an available plural form. And the facultative nature of the plural is consistent with this neutral status of the lexical noun. (Notice that this use of the term "neutral" is slightly different from, although consistent with, that developed in the discussion of English. In English, Neutral was applied to a noun phrase not formally marked Plural or Singular and where number could not be deduced on lexical [selectional] grounds. The form of the lexical noun itself in such a Neutral construction was nonplural. Here we are saying the lexical noun itself is neutral.) The application of the *-ó'ob'* suffix is also syntactically optional in that it is not required even when there are other indications of a multiplicity of referents in the noun phrase or associated verb phrase. So one can speak of *ȼ'éeȼ'ek pèek'* 'few dog' without any need to attach the plural suffix to *pèek'* 'dog'.

One complication in the interpretation of Yucatec noun phrases arises from the pattern for indicating possession. In general, under traditional interpretations, possession is indicated by attaching an A series pronoun. For the third person possessive, the forms are neutral *'u-* 'its [~ his, hers[7]]/their' and plural *'u- . . . -ó'ob'* 'their'. For example, *'u-pèek'* 'his/their dog' and *'u-pèek'-ó'ob'* 'their dog'. Of course, this last form is further ambiguous since it could also represent the neutral form of the possessive (*'u-* 'his/their') attached to the plural noun (*pèek'-ó'ob'* 'dogs') to yield 'his/their dogs'. The difficulty lies in the fact that the *-ó'ob'* could arise from two different sources: plural noun inflection or plural possessor. In fact, some analysts have argued that the same form can even cover both senses, one of the two instantiations being deleted in the noun phrase, and so 'their dogs' is also a viable interpretation. Hence the form *'u-pèek'-ó'ob'* is usually interpreted as triply ambiguous. The fact which is overlooked in these analyses is that the form *'u-pèek'* (i.e., neutral possessive with neutral noun) can also take each of these three meanings (i.e., 'his dogs,' 'their dog,' 'their dogs') as well as the additional meaning 'his dog'. The semantic ambiguity is present in the noun phrase quite independently of any plural marks because of the neutrality of Yucatec nouns and third person pronouns with respect to number; no arguments in terms of referential value will help in assigning a status to *-ó'ob'* in such cases. All we know for sure is that something is definitely plural in (or about) the noun phrase. However, in terms of simple frequency, *-ó'ob'* in such constructions usually emphasizes the multiplicity of the head noun rather than the possessor. When the nature of the possession is inherently unique, however, plurality of the possessor seems to be the appropriate interpretation. For example, in the expression *'u-nàah-il-ó'ob'* 'their houses/homes' each individual can be understood to have only one house – as suggested by the *-il* '[inherency]' suffix on the root – and so the primary multiplicity must be of possessors although this guarantees a multiplicity of houses as well.

There are few unusual cases in the formation of Yucatec plurals. The only significant irregularity involves the suffix *-al* which applies to a few forms in the language. So for example *pal* 'child' can become *pal-al* 'children'. The form may be a collective (similar to *family* in English): 'children of one person'. Note for example the latter can itself take *-ó'ob'*, hence *pal-al-ó'ob'* 'children [for example, the children in the village]'. Another striking though perfectly predictable pattern arises with Spanish loan words. In some cases the plural inflectional form of the Spanish lexical noun has been taken into Yucatec as a neutral form which can then be pluralized in the usual fashion: Spanish *vaquero-s* 'cowboy' plus Yucatec *-ó'ob'* '[plural]' yields Yucatec *vaquero-s-ó'ob'* 'cowboys [i.e., a group of young men who assist a bullfighter]'. As Spanish becomes better known, the original value of *vaqueros* as plural reasserts itself for some speakers – at least in formal settings. However, for words with more phonological alteration from the original Spanish, this does not happen: Spanish *vacas* 'cows' becomes Yucatec *wàakaš* 'cow, bull' which is always pluralized *wàakaš-ó'ob'* 'cows, bulls'.

Marking of noun phrase number by modification

The principal modifiers relevant to indicating number are the quantitative adjectives. Neither descriptive adjectives nor most determiners routinely indicate grammatical number, although interactions with specific lexical content can occasionally produce such effects. The only determiner forms which signal grammatical number are the forms used to establish indefinite reference. But these forms are actually unstressed quantitative adjectives containing the numeral prefix 'one'. For this reason, these "indefinite articles" will be treated here with the quantifier adjectives.

Quantitative modifiers involving numerals

Singularity or multiplicity of referents can be signaled in Yucatec as in English by a modifier containing a numeral. Noun phrases of this type obligatorily involve a special type of morpheme known as a *numeral classifier* which is bound to the numeral. Understanding the structure and

Table 9. *Examples of Yucatec numerical classifiers used with nouns*

Wholes:
-ç'íit	'one dimensional shape'
-wáal	'two dimensional shape'
-p'éel	'three dimensional shape' (i.e., formally and semantically unmarked)
-túul	'self-segmenting shape'
-kúul	'agricultural or other socially significant plant'

Aggregates of wholes:
-ç'áam	'pair'
-çàap	'stack' (usually of two-dimensional items)

Parts of wholes:
-táan	'side, face'
-tú'uk	'corner, edge'

Portions of wholes:
-tìich'	'strand'
-šóot'	'slice'

Measures:
-lùuch	'jicara-full' (a half gourd holding 250–500 milliliters)
-méek'	'armful'
-kúuch	'load's worth'
-ç'áak	'mecate's worth' (one mecate = 20 meters by 20 meters)

Irregulars (only with *'un-* 'one'):
-p'íit	'(little) bit's worth'
-páay	'kind-of-thing' (irregular when used to emphasize contrast) (cf. English "on the one hand ... on the other hand")

functioning of these classifiers is crucial to understanding number marking in Yucatec.

Explanation of the term "numeral classifier." A large number of languages in Asia and the New World exhibit a syntactic pattern known as numeral classification. When counting or enumerating in these languages, an extra morpheme must also be used in addition to those expressing the number and the referent. This additional morpheme expresses or makes explicit further information about the nature of the referent. For example, whereas in English one can say *two turkeys* (i.e., number + plural lexical noun), in Yucatec Maya one must say *ká'a-túul 'úulum* (i.e., number + extra morpheme + neutral lexical noun). Usually a language which makes use of such a construction contains a number of these morphemes. Because each of the nouns in a language

C

tends to co-occur primarily with one such morpheme, the nouns are effectively grouped into classes – hence, the traditional label numeral classifiers.

Commonly used classifiers in Yucatec.   It is difficult to state exactly how many classifiers there are in Yucatec since the system is partially productive, that is, new forms can be created if necessary. Also, there appear to be differences in both regional and individual usage. If we restrict ourselves to commonly used items, Classical Yucatec had well over 200 and Modern Yucatec has somewhat fewer than 100 (cf. Miram, 1983). For present purposes it will suffice to indicate the principal types of numeral classifiers used with lexical nouns and some examples of frequently used items of each type. These are given in table 9.[8]

Syntax of noun phrases containing numerals.   Numeral classifier morphemes can form part of a full noun phrase or, along with the accompanying numeral, stand for such a noun phrase. The order of the morphemes is as follows: Numeral (or equivalent) + Classifier + Lexical Noun (or equivalent).

The preposed numerals.   Four Yucatec numerals are still in common use, each with a number of phonologically conditioned variants:

'un-	(~ *'um-* ~ *hun-* ~ *hum-*)	'one',
ká'a-	(~ *ká'-* ~ *ká'ab'-*)	'two',
'óoš-	(~ *yóoš-*)	'three', and
kan-	(~ *kam-*)	'four'.

Any of these four numerals may occur with each classifier with the exception of a few forms (examples are listed as irregularities in table 9) which are restricted to *'un-* and its variants. *háay-* 'how many' can also occur in place of a numeral:

   háay-túul máak   'how many men [in a question]'.

   Numerals require the presence of a classifier with two exceptions. First, numerals may be prefixed to verbal stems as adverbials to indicate multiple iterations of the predicate:

   yàan a-ká'a-b'in   'you must go a second time [i.e., again]'.

Second, they may appear with a set of related suffixes *-eh*, *-he-ak*, and, perhaps, also *-ak*, which are used for counts of days:

ká'ab'-eh	'two days from today'
'óoš-eh	'three days from today'
ká'a-fi-ak (< *ká'a(b')-he-ak*)	'two days ago'
'óoš-fi-ak- (< *'óoš-he-ak*)	'three days ago'.

It is possible to give all these forms an adverbial interpretation and generalize that *numerals in conjunction with nouns* (or their equivalents) *always take classifiers.*

Numerals may be reduplicated to indicate special senses:

hu-hum-p'íit-il	'little-by-little',
ká'a-ká'a-túul-il	'two-by-two',
ká'a-ká'a-teh	'(until) later'.

Spanish numerals may also be used with classifiers. They are usually used to indicate counts larger than four and they take a slightly different syntactic construction:

diez 'u-túul-ul máak	'ten men',
diez 'u-túul-ul	'ten [men]'.

The syntactic significance and interpretation of these mixed constructions is quite complicated and will not be taken up here.

The postposed lexical noun (or equivalent).[9]   Most classifiers can be followed by a lexical noun. Usually, these are common nouns, but proper nouns also occur:

'óoš-túul máak	'three men',
'óoš-p'éeh Juan	'three Johns'.

Inversely, every lexical noun in Yucatec can follow some such classifier. In fact Blair (1965 [1964], p. 46) uses this as one of his criteria for identifying nouns in Yucatec. So the ability to take a numeral modifier with a classifier does not in and of itself separate out subsets of nouns in Yucatec. (Note: *p'éeh* is an alternate form of the classifier *p'éel*.)

The lexical noun may be replaced by a pronominal form (in particular a suffix from the B series) producing an equational sentence:

'óoš-túul-ó'on	'the three of us/we are three'.

First and second persons pronominal suffixes tend to occur only in the plural and mostly with *-túul*, but there are exceptions. Third person forms also tend to occur mostly with *-túul* but can be used more widely. All these pronoun forms presuppose the nominalization of the Numeral + Classifier combination and then use it as a base to form an equational sentence. Further, since in many cases the third person neutral pronoun form can emerge as a phonological zero, *-∅*, classifiers with no following nominal material can often be interpreted as taking this pronoun form. This is, for example, the underlying structure in cases in which the classifier is followed by a clause:

'óoš-p'éel-∅ 'u-b'in	'three [more] to go'.

Use of classifiers as ordinal indicators.   Numeral classifier constructions can be augmented by the use of an "inherency" marker *-il* (often realized as *-ih*) to derive ordinal indicators:

(*le-*) *yá'aš um-p'éel-ih*	'the first [one]',
(*le-*) *'óoš–p'éel-ih*	'the third [one]',
(*t-u-*) *ká'a-p'éel-ih*	'both'.

Use of classifiers to establish reference.   Numeral classifier constructions, as has already been mentioned, frequently serve to establish initial reference in cases where an indefinite article would be used in English. The most frequently used forms in this context are the three most general classifiers in conjunction with the numeral prefix signaling 'one':

'un-túul máak	'a man',
'um-p'éeh nàah	'a house',
'um-p'íit ha'	'a little bit of water'.

Modification of the lexical noun by the numeral 'one' in conjunction with the classifier is the basic way of indicating Singular in Yucatec. But, since all nouns require a classifier construction, the Singular frame does not in itself distinguish out any subgroups of nouns. However, the various lexical nouns can be sorted into categories on the basis of their semantic compatibility with specific classifiers.

The Numeral + Classifier construction can also be used alone without a following noun phrase as a deictic or anaphoric form much like English *one*:

ȼíit ten 'um-p'éeh	'give me one'.

Thus the close connection in English between indefinite article *a*, numeral *one*, and anaphoric *one* is also found in Yucatec, but with the important difference that the classifier morpheme is obligatorily involved in all such constructions. Therefore, in the process of introducing a referent or signaling Singular, considerable additional semantic information will be signaled. *It is as if Yucatec has a large array of indefinite articles, numerals, and pro-forms each with a somewhat different meaning.*

Quantitative modifiers without numerals

There are several important quantitative modifiers in Yucatec which do not involve numerals. Of these, only *ȼ'éeȼ'ek* 'few' seems to imply as part of its lexical meaning that the noun phrase has Plural meaning. Three others imply as part of their lexical meaning that the noun phrase has Singular meaning: *'u-láak* 'another [emphasizing otherness]', *'u-heh* 'another [emphasizing sameness]', and *máakal máak* 'which'. The four remaining forms hold no reliable implications for grammatical number even though they indicate quantity: *lah* 'all', *t-u-láak-al* 'all, every one', *yá'ab'* 'many, much', and *miš* 'no, not'. For the purposes of comparison, table 10 shows the Yucatec forms used to convey the English senses discussed in the previous section.

Marking noun phrase number by concord

Pronominals bound to the verb

Number is optionally marked on the verb complex by cross-referencing bound pronominal affixes. For example, the third person intransitive forms (A series) are as follows:

> *'u-VERB*   'it/he/she/they VERB [i.e., neutral form]',
> *'u-VERB-ó'ob'*   'they VERB'.

Notice that the agreement in these cases is asymmetric in an important respect: plural pronoun implies that the cross-referenced noun phrase is Plural whether or not it is inflected for plural; however neutral pronoun does not imply anything specific about number in the cross-referenced noun phrase. In fact, a neutral pronoun form can cross-reference a noun phrase explicitly marked by inflection for Plural. Nonetheless, to repeat, in those cases where the verb complex contains a plural pronoun, it indicates that the cross-referenced noun phrase can be construed as Plural. For transitive and other verbs with multiple noun phrase complements, there can be semantic ambiguity about which cross-referencing noun phrase the plural mark applies to: *t-u-bis-ah-ó'ob'* can mean 'he took them', 'they took it', or 'they took them'.

Pronominals not bound to the verb

The pattern for free pronouns is the same. So both *pèek'* 'dog [neutral]' and *pèek'-ó'ob'* 'dogs [plural]' can be cross-referenced by free pronoun forms *leti'* 'it/he/she/them [neutral]' or by *leti'-ó'ob'* 'they [plural]'; but *leti'-ó'ob'* directly implies that the overtly neutral *pèek'* is part of a noun phrase Plural whereas *leti'* implies nothing about noun phrase number.

A similar asymmetrical agreement pattern applies for several other bound pronominal forms:

Table 10. *Comparative list of Yucatec quantitative modifier forms and their English senses*

Cardinal indicators

'um-p'éel	'one'
ká'a-p'éel	'two'
hay p'éel	'how many'
yá'ab'	'many, much, a lot of, lots of'
b'uká'ah	'how much, how many'
ma'-yá'ab'-i'	'not many, not much, not a lot'
miš-yá'ab'- . . . (-i')	'no – not many at all'
yá'ab' kach	'quite a lot of'
ȼ'éeȼ' ek	'few'
algunos [Spanish]	'some, several'
chen	'only'
lah	'all (of it, of them)'
chúum-uk	'half (of it, of them)'
túul-is	'all (complete)'
le-ká'a-p'éel-ih	'both (of)'

Ordinal indicators

yáaš ('um-p'éel)	'first'
le-ká'a-p'éel-ih	'second'
'u-láak ('um-p'éel-ih)	'another, next'
'u-heh	'another'
'u-šúul	'last'
mas	'more, other' [Spanish]
'u-láak ('um-p'éel-ih)	'additional'

Quantitative determiners (includes relatives)

'um-p'éel [unstressed]	'a (an)'
t-u-láak-al	'all (every one)'
cada 'um-p'éel [Spanish *cada*]	'each, every'
máakal máak	'which one, whichever'
. . . wa . . .	'(either) . . . or . . .'
miš . . . miš	'neither . . . nor . . .'
?	'some, any' [both unstressed]
suficiente [Spanish]	'enough'
'um-p'íit	'some, any' [both stressed]
miš	'no(t)'
b'á'aš	'what'
wa-b'á'aš	'something'
he-b'á'aš	'whatever'
má'aš	'who'
wa-má'aš	'someone'
he-má'aš	'whoever'

ti'	'to it/him/her/them',
ti'-ó'ob'	'to them',
kih	'like so from it/him/her/them' [used primarily to quote],
ki(h)-ó'ob'	'like so from them'.

Covert indications of grammatical number

Given the pattern of facultative number marking in Yucatec, lexical nouns cannot be categorized on the basis of taking obligatory marking. Yucatec lexical nouns can only be separated into groups on the basis of frequency of plural inflection or concord, that is, nouns which frequently take suffix *-ó'ob'* either as a direct inflection or as part of the cross-referencing bound pronoun on the verb. There is an overwhelming tendency in everyday speech to limit plural inflection and concord to animate entities or to objects in one-to-one relation to an animate possessor (for example, heads, houses, etc.).

Lexical nouns can be distinguished by their compatibility with various quantitative modifiers – including the numeral classifiers. However, membership in such a semantic class does not reliably correspond with any pattern of obligatory number marking and therefore cannot serve as a diagnostic for syntactic potential with respect to number. Nonetheless, as will become clear below, such modifier classes can be revealing from a comparative point of view.

Given the facultative nature of plural marking in Yucatec it is impossible to develop the argument that some set of lexical nouns has distinctive inherent lexical content such as "countability" which would allow us to assign grammatical number in ambiguous cases on the basis of overall configurational pattern. Notice that two of the criteria for deducibility mentioned in the discussion of English have been met: there is a *meaningful* category (signaling multiplicity) with a *regular* pattern of distribution (tending to apply to animates). But the distinction is not *obligatory*. Therefore, there can be no criterial frameworks (distinctive reactances) which reliably distinguish among lexical nouns which must have a specific grammatical number. In general, then, grammatical number is not syntactically deducible in Yucatec by reference to underlying lexical content.

Summary

The basic Yucatec pattern is to disregard number, and most lexical noun phrases are Neutral in number. Plural may be distinguished facultatively (for example, for emphasis) either by lexical noun inflection or by concord with cross-referencing pronouns in the verb complex. Singular and Plural may also be signaled facultatively by a variety of specific quantitative modifiers. (None of these modifier forms either with or without numerals require any other formal plural or singular marks in the noun phrase or the clause.) In the absence of any pattern of obligatory number marking these facultative signals can not be used to ground or provide any reliable information concerning inherent lexical number. Number distinctions as such simply do not have the general significance within Yucatec grammar that they do in English, and grammatical number is expressed very indifferently in comparison with English.

Comparison of Yucatec and English

Both English and Yucatec represent number in the noun phrase and do so in somewhat similar ways: they both mark Plural by inflection and concord, they both mark Singular by adjectival modification (determiners and/or quantitative adjectives), and they both provide a variety of specialized modifiers to indicate other number distinctions. However, the overt expression of Plural is more important in English, where it is obligatory for a large range of noun phrases, than it is in Yucatec, where it is optional for a relatively small range of noun phrases. And the structure of quantitative modification involved in the overt expression of Singular differs considerably – most notably the obligatory use of numeral classifiers for all numeral modification in Yucatec. This section characterizes these two differences more precisely and places them within a broader comparative framework.

Contrast in plural marking (inflection and concord)[10]

The pluralization patterns of the two languages differ in several ways. The goal of this section is to characterize these differences more precisely and in a form which will be suitable for generating hypotheses about cognitive consequences. The analysis will proceed from a general, interpretive characterization to a more specific, formal characterization. Then some indications will be given as to how the analysis can be extended to additional languages and patterns of pluralization. For the purposes of this section, no distinction will be made between Plural marking by inflection and Plural marking by concord.

Clarifying the contrast between English and Yucatec

English obligatorily marks Plural for a wide range of lexical noun phrases whereas Yucatec optionally marks Plural for a relatively small range of lexical noun phrases. Thus there are two dimensions of difference: scope of application and obligatoriness of application. At the outset I will conflate these two dimensions by speaking of *typical* patterns of pluralization. By focusing on typical patterns of pluralization we incorporate both semantic requirements and pragmatic regularities into a unified formulation. Alternatively, one could represent only obligatory pluralization (in which case one focuses on semantic requirements and the differences between the languages become larger) or one could represent only the existence of the option of pluralization (in which case one focuses on pragmatic possibilities and the differences between languages become smaller). Later, when we examine other languages where information about pluralization may be incomplete or when we try to account for underlying semantic structure, it will be fruitful to attend to patterns of obligatory marking.

The distributional pattern

The differences in typical patterns of pluralization in English and Yucatec can be characterized more precisely in terms of groups of lexical noun phrases. A sample of more or less equivalent minimal lexical noun phrases with concrete reference can be selected from each of the two languages so as to include some noun phrases which both languages typically pluralize (Group 1), some noun phrases which neither language typically pluralizes (Group 3), and some noun phrases for which the two languages differ in their typical pattern (Group 2). These three noun phrase groups have been defined, then, purely on formal, distributional grounds. These distributional facts can then be represented as shown in table 11.[11]

Providing a notional characterization

Since the three noun phrase groups in table 11 are defined purely distributionally, that is, they are defined solely in terms of whether or not they take plural marking in the two languages, they cannot be used to characterize or account for those distributional patterns. However, each of these groupings of lexical noun phrases corresponds to a grouping of

Table 11. *Scope of typical pluralization in English and Yucatec lexical noun phrases in terms of preliminary formal groupings*

	Lexical noun phrase group		
Language, marking	1	2	3
Yucatec, plural	yes	no	no
English, plural	yes	yes	no

referents. These groups of referents, it turns out, are not mere aggregations, but can each be characterized in terms of certain typical attributes. Group 1 noun phrases tend to refer to *animate beings and similar self-segmenting*[12] *entities* (for example, dogs, automobiles), Group 2 noun phrases tend to refer to *discrete objects and similar stably segmented entities* (for example, shovels), and Group 3 noun phrases tend to refer to *tangible materials (or substances) with malleable form and similar segmentable entities* (for example, mud). These regularities raise the possibility that the noun phrase groups and their referential meaning values can be established on *independent* grounds and then used to characterize the scope of plural marking in the two languages.

The groupings involved here do not directly correspond to, and are not reducible to, those that might be made on nonlinguistic grounds. For example, from a strictly biological vantage the group of typically pluralized referents singled out by Group 1 (i.e., the lexical nouns typically pluralized in both languages) does not include all biologically animate beings (for example, insects) and does include some entities that are not biologically animate (for example, trucks). Thus, the grouping reflects something about the organization of experience *for the purposes of speech* rather than solely some independent regularity in the world. This can be stated more generally: languages (both individually and collectively) construe entities *from the point of view of language as a referential and predicational device* and not solely or consistently in terms of extra-linguistic (or natural) characterizations.[13] Thus, to continue the example, when Group 1 is described as typically referring to animates, it indicates that most noun phrases in that group refer to biologically animate referents but that some also refer to referents which share the typical volitional, agentive, or motive properties of such animates as these are relevant to predication.

The development of noun phrase groups, then, cannot proceed either by simply characterizing the formal distributional regularities of a given language (language as pure form) or by simply characterizing the objects of reference (the world) in nonlinguistic terms and treating language categories as a reflex of them (language as transparent content). Rather, we want to characterize distributional regularities insofar as they represent or refer to the world in a characteristically linguistic fashion, that is, in terms of characteristic language–world (form–content) relationships.[14] Specifically, we want to characterize *noun phrase types* in terms of cross-linguistically grounded *(proto)typical features of referential meaning*. In essence, we need a metalanguage for the description of noun phrase types (typical linguistic meanings) that will be independent of the formal categories of any particular language yet dependent for its terms on the way languages in general construe reality.[15]

Such a feature-based description of the noun phrase types relevant to any given grammatical category can be developed by cross-linguistic comparison of an array of morphosyntactic structures within the framework of markedness theory (Silverstein, 1976, 1981, 1986, 1987). Development and justification of such a referential feature description for noun phrase types specifically relevant to pluralization is a complicated task beyond the scope of the present work. Nonetheless, a beginning can be made by employing referential features already identified by others to characterize the particular noun phrase types in question. Then some indications will be given as to how the approach can be extended to new languages and further referential features. Finally, the general procedure for developing a feature-based characterization of noun phrase types will be discussed.

Comparison in terms of referential features

Two referential features are sufficient to generate the three noun phrase types suitable for the comparison of Yucatec and English plural marking.[16] The first feature is [±animate]. Noun phrases marked [+animate] specifically signal reference to an animate entity in the special sense clarified above.[17] By contrast, those marked [−animate] are not specified one way or the other as to animacy from a linguistic point of view – they may, in fact, refer to both animate or inanimate entities. However, under appropriate conditions, by residual interpretation, noun phrases marked [−animate] can be considered to have a negative value, that is, to refer to "inanimates."

The second feature is [±discrete].[18] This feature stands in a regular markedness relationship with the first, that is, the two features do not freely cross-cut each other and [±discrete] is only specified if the noun phrase is [−animate]. In other words, in the context of a noun phrase marked [+animate], the distinction [±discrete] is generally not operative, that is, the applicability of the broader, less specific feature [±discrete] is contingent on the narrower, more specific feature not being specified (i.e., having negative value [− animate]):

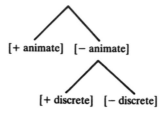

Thus, noun phrases overtly specified [+ animate, + discrete] should not ordinarily occur. To avoid possible confusion on this score, the values of a more general feature such as [± discrete] will be indicated (written out) only when the more specific feature actually has negative (neutral) specification such as [− animate]. This should not obscure the fact that the positive value of the general feature will usually be guaranteed when the more specific feature is positive (for example, any animate is perforce discrete, etc.).[19]

Noun phrases marked [+ discrete] specifically signal reference to distinct, stably bounded objects.[20] By contrast, those marked [− discrete] are not specified one way or the other as to distinctness from a linguistic point of view though they may refer to a perceptually distinct entity. Again, under appropriate conditions by residual interpretation, noun phrases marked [− discrete] can be considered to have a negative value, that is, to refer to "materials" or "substances."

Using these two features we can characterize three types of lexical noun phrases: Type A[21] is specified [+ animate], Type B is specified [− animate, + discrete], and Type C is specified [− animate, − discrete]. We can now express the scope of pluralization in the two languages in terms of these three noun phrase types as shown in table 12. Unlike table 11 which made no reference to the meaning value of the noun phrase groups shown, table 12 indicates clearly that the application of plural marking is contingent on (a function of) the meaning value of noun phrases as these are embodied in referential features.

Secondary advantages of a feature representation

In addition to incorporating referential meaning into the representation of the contrast of scope of plural marking, the characterization of such differences in terms of referential features presents several secondary advantages. First, it allows regularities in the application of grammatical

Table 12. *Scope of typical pluralization in English and Yucatec lexical noun phrases in terms of features of reference*

		Lexical noun phrase type		
		A	B	C
	Features:	[+ animate]	[− animate] [+ discrete]	[− animate] [− discrete]
Language, marking				
Yucatec, plural		yes	no	no
English, plural		yes	yes	no

Features are defined more fully in the text.

number to be related to other grammatical categories within the language that are contingent on the same or related referential features. This provides the foundation for an analysis of a larger "fashion of speaking" involving multiple, cross-cutting categories. Second, it allows the expression of the cross-linguistic comparison in terms of general types of noun phrases. This allows the comparison to accommodate and utilize a larger array of lexical items since cross-language comparison does not depend on comparing a specific fixed set of equivalent lexical items across languages. Third, to the extent the features are ordered with respect to one another by marking relationships, they can provide a common framework for ordering or relating the various patterns of pluralization among languages. Such a framework will be discussed in the next section.

Generalizing the analysis for further comparisons

A central goal of the present work is to indicate how this analysis could be extended to encompass other languages and other grammatical categories. This section indicates the procedure for extending the analysis begun in the previous section to additional languages and features by providing some further examples.

Generalizing to additional languages

We can take the comparison just developed and apply it to additional languages. For each language, lexical noun phrases with various feature

Table 13. *Multilanguage comparison of obligatory pluralization of lexical noun phrases*

Language, marking	Lexical noun phrase type		
	A	B	C
Features:	[+ animate]	[− animate] [+ discrete]	[− animate] [− discrete]
Chinese, plural	no	no	no
Yucatec, plural	no[a]	no	no
Tarascan, plural	yes	no	no
English, plural	yes	yes	no
Hopi, plural	yes	yes	yes

The English and Yucatec data have been given earlier in this chapter. The Hopi pattern is reported in Whorf (1946; 1956, pp. 139–42); further details appear in Voegelin and Voegelin (1957) and Kalectaca (1978). The Chinese (Mandarin) pattern is reported in Chao (1968, ch. 7, section 2) and Li and Thompson (1981, pp. 11–12, 40–41); see also Smith-Stark (1974, p. 663). The Tarascan pattern is reported in Friedrich (1970); see also Smith-Stark (1974, p. 663).
[a] Facultative marking of plural is common with Type A noun phrases.

specifications can be identified and evaluated as to whether they typically take plural marking. In many cases, such comparisons will have to operate with incomplete information. For example, many grammatical descriptions do not report on the scope of plural marking or, if they do, they tend to report on the scope of obligatory marking and provide little or no information on optional or facultative marking. Therefore, comparisons made on the basis of existing descriptive materials will generally have to be done in terms of obligatory or highly regular patterns. Further, although comparison would best be done at the level of the whole noun phrase in relation to the verb phrase so that the multiple formal means of marking (for example, inflection, modification, concord, etc.) employed by different languages could be represented, adequate information may not be available on all the relevant means of marking. As a rule, morphological patterns such as inflectional marks for plural are most adequately described in grammars.

Despite these difficulties, however, useful comparisons can still be made. In table 13 a few additional languages are added to English and Yucatec to show how these two stand in relation to some other patterns of plural marking. Table 13 shows the presence or absence of *obligatory* morphological marking of plural on lexical noun phrases of the three types defined earlier. (Notice, now, that because we are dealing with obligatory patterns, the coding of Yucatec for Type A noun phrases shifts to "no.") It should be clear that both languages fit easily into an orderly array of language types.

Generalizing to additional features

The format of table 13 clearly represents the differences among languages at issue in the present discussion. However, other referential features than the two discussed so far govern the scope application of plural marking in many languages. Smith-Stark (1974) has proposed a preliminary list of such features developed by examining published grammars of a sample of 25 languages.[22] To the extent relevant data were available, he divided the nouns (including pronominals) of each language into groups on the basis of whether or not they took certain forms of plural marking including verb–argument concord, noun–modifier concord, and direct morphological marking on the noun and whether or not these patterns were optional or obligatory. In most cases, each number marking pattern split at a certain point, that is, with respect to a certain referential feature, such that each mode of pluralization applied to some noun types and not to others. The features identified by Smith-Stark were as follows: [± speaker], [± speech event participant],[23] [± kin], [± rational], [± human living], [± human], [± animate], [± neuter]. The ordering of the features is significant: Smith-Stark pointed out that these features are ordered such that if plural marking of a given type applies to nouns characterized by one feature, then it will apply to nouns characterizable by the higher, more specific features. Where there are multiple modes of marking the plural, multiple number marking patterns sometimes emerge each with its own characteristic division or split of the nouns of the language. Still further subdivisions of pattern are possible if one sorts on the basis of the specific morphological forms actually used for marking.

Smith-Stark's preliminary work is flawed in a number of respects. Most importantly, he did not develop an argument and evidence to indicate that these features could be identified and ordered independently of considerations of plurality (cf. Smith-Stark, 1974, pp. 662–67). As will be discussed below, this argument is important so that the approach does not become tautological. There are minor problems as well: in many

Table 14. *Scope of obligatory pluralization of lexical noun phrases in various languages using an expanded array of referential features*

		Lexical noun phrase type						
		A	B	C	D	E	F	... etc.
Features:								
a.	kin	+	−	−	−	−	−	
b.	human		+	−	−	−	−	
c.	animate			+	−	−	−	
d.	discrete				+	−	−	
e.	(etc.)					+	−	

Language, marking

Chinese, plural	| ←———————————————————— no |
Yucatec, plural	| ←———————————————————— no |
Coos, plural	| yes ——→ | ←———————————— no |
Kwakiutl, plural	| yes ——————→ | ←——————— no |
Tarascan, plural	| yes ——————————→ | ←——————— no |
English, plural	| yes ——————————————→ | ←——— no |
Hopi, plural	| yes ———————————————————→ |
(etc.)	

Coos and Kwakiutl patterns are reported in Smith-Stark (1973, pp. 660–63). Sources for the remaining languages are provided in table 13.

cases his analysis is based on scanty data; some of his features are not of the same order as others (for example, [± neuter] would not usually be considered a referential feature). Despite these various problems, Smith-Stark's work seems sufficient to indicate that with additional research a richer set of well-grounded features can be developed to characterize differences among languages in scope of pluralization and that additional languages can be compared in the way Yucatec and English have been compared above.

The format of table 13 can be expanded to accommodate such additional features. Table 14 shows such an expanded format incorporating for illustration a couple of additional features proposed by Smith-Stark. Because it becomes increasingly cumbersome to list the features at the head of each column, the features themselves have been listed to the left and only the positive and negative specifications entered at the column heads. The scope of application of pluralization for several languages is then indicated below by indicating the range of lexical noun phrase types which are obligatorily pluralized ("yes") and which not ("no"). More details could be incorporated into such a display if we wanted to indicate the full range of relevant detail such as the possibility of facultative plurals, the formal nature of the plural mark (for example, inflection or concord), or the different types of plural (for example, duals or paucals) within a language.

It should be clear at this point that many additional languages can be incorporated into the analysis proposed here for English and Yucatec. This insures that cognitive implications developed in chapter 3 on the basis of the differences between these two languages can be developed for many other languages as well. We are dealing in the present instance, then, with differences between languages, but not isolated, idiosyncratic differences. In fact, although it is not on the agenda here, it is only against such a typological backdrop that isolated, idiosyncratic differences can eventually be analyzed as such and welded to a more culturally specific set of implications.

Developing appropriate referential features

In the previous discussion, referential features, related to one another in terms of markedness relations, were used to characterize the various noun phrase types. These referential features were to be developed independently of the facts of plural marking so that they could be used not merely to provide an alternative description of those patterns but also, in a limited sense, to account for them as well. But no argument was given as to how to find and order such features in a principled manner independently of the facts of number marking. Indeed, a full explanation of the procedures involved in defining such features would take us well beyond the scope of the present study and is certainly not necessary for understanding the basic contrast between Yucatec and English. But, in order to indicate how referential features suitable for characterizing noun phrase types can in fact be developed, the present section briefly sketches the procedure and provides an illustration of such a set of features developed for case marking.

General procedure for developing referential features and characterizing noun phrase types

A strategy for developing a general cross-linguistic characterization of noun phrase types in terms of features of referential meaning has been developed by Silverstein (1976, 1981, 1986, 1987). Only key elements of his approach relevant to identifying and ordering referential features will be schematized here.

We first need to recognize what sorts of features we want. Every noun phrase can be characterized by a large number of referential features, but not all those features are *grammatically relevant*. So, for example, [+ wheeled] might be considered to be a feature of meaning inherent in the noun phrase *the wagon*, but it is not a good candidate for our feature space since it has no syntactic significance, that is, no grammatical category is ever contingent on its value. When we seek features of noun phrase reference which might govern plural marking, then, we want features which are inherent to noun phrase meaning *and* which have attested value as grammatically relevant. The process of developing such features typically begins, then, by identifying common referential values inhering to noun phrase groups created by patterns of formal morpho-syntactic distribution within various individual languages.

Second, the analysis of these morphosyntactic distributions is under-taken within the framework of *marking theory*. This involves attending to such factors as the regularity and ubiquity of formal expression of categories and the behavior of one category with respect to others under neutralization (suspension) where the emergent patterns "constitute diagnostic considerations leading to an hypothesis about markedness structure" (Silverstein, 1987, p. 18). (The general strategy of analysis involved in establishing marking relations cannot be elaborated here. See the discussions in Greenberg, 1966; Lyons, 1968, pp. 79–80, also pp. 120–27; Silverstein, 1976, pp. 116–22; 1986, 1987.) The features emergent from such an analysis, as we have seen above, are asymmetric in an important respect: a noun phrase marked [+ f] specifically indicates that the given feature of referential meaning is present whereas a noun phrase not so marked, that is, [− f], is neutral as to whether the feature is present or not (i.e., the given meaning is not specified at all – either positively or negatively). (Under appropriate conditions of usage this failure to specify may be taken by speakers as a positive indication of negative specification.) Further, the relationship among features (or the morphosyntactic categories they govern) is also typically asymmetric: one of the two morphosyntactically significant features (categories) is relevant only when the other is not. Typically, a more general feature of meaning (category) is signaled only when a more specific feature is not signaled.

The patterns of marking (or neutralization) among feature categories within a language allow them to be ordered with respect to one another. Some features do not stand in a marking relationship to one another – usually within well-defined limits – and give the appearance of being freely cross-cutting binary features. Such features actually define distinct subspaces (orthogonal dimensions) of referential meaning, and these subspaces can also be ordered with respect to one another by reference to their expression (or neutralization).

Third, since we want these features to serve for comparisons across a variety of languages, it becomes crucial to compare similar morphosyntactic groupings and to extract, when possible, a common recurring referential feature value. This extraction of a *cross-linguistic notional core* (or *salient contrast*[24]) to characterize the commonality among groups is no simple task and an appropriate characterization may not be obvious. In general these core values will not be definable with reference to the distributional facts of any one language. Nor will they necessarily correspond precisely to some set, extralinguistic property of the referents themselves (for example, psychophysically defined "color"). Rather, these core values will characterize objects of reference as their properties are relevant to the morphosyntactic patterns of a range of languages. (Notice, however, that a given cross-linguistically valid feature may not be functional in every language, that is, no morphosyntactic distribution may be contingent on such a feature in a particular language.) By calibrating the language-specific feature orderings with reference to these notional similarities, a composite cross-linguistic ordering of features and subspaces can be produced.

Fourth, in principle, we would like the features to be developed and ordered independently of the specific grammatical pattern at issue – number marking in the present case. Only if the referential feature is independently defined can it be used to account for the pattern of distribution. So, for example, a feature [+ count] cannot account for pluralization patterns in English because it can only be defined in the first place relative to the specific distributional patterns of pluralization in English. This independence can be secured by defining the features relative to a variety of other grammatical categories in a broad sample of languages. Since sets of referential features can be built one by one for each of the various morphosyntactic categories relevant to the noun phrase, however, the process ultimately becomes circular in one sense: features relevant to the description of each category are derived from all the others and vice versa. The features are nonetheless ultimately defined relative to the overall constellation of grammatical categories in many languages and remain, from this point of view, *independent of any particular category and any particular language*. In fact, since only one category is being excluded ("controlled for") each time, considerable overlap among the features is virtually guaranteed, and it may be possible to develop a core set of features ordering the space as a whole.

Finally, combinations of features define possible noun phrase types of cross-linguistic significance. That is, by analogy with phonological processes where each phoneme consists of a "bundle" of distinctive feature values of sound, we may characterize each noun phrase type (A, B, C . . . in table 14) as a bundle of distinctive feature values of reference (a, b, c . . . in table 14). The overall ordering of features and subspaces allows these noun phrase types themselves to be ordered. Various patterns of morphosyntactic marking such as case marking and number marking can be characterized in terms of their scope of application with respect to such an ordering of noun phrase types.

An illustration: Silverstein's feature space for case marking

As discussed in *Language diversity and thought*, chapter 4, Silverstein (1973, 1976, 1981, 1986, 1987) has built such a feature representation to account for some of the patterns of case marking of noun phrases evidenced in languages. In his approach the features are defined and ordered independently of the facts of case marking itself, so they constitute an independent variable from the point of view of case marking.[25] Various generalizations about case marking – in particular the regular *splits* of case marking between nominative–accusative and ergative–absolutive paradigms – are then shown to be readily characterizable in terms of the resultant ordering of noun phrase types derivative from the hierarchical ordering of referential features. Silverstein (1986) has suggested that similar spaces can be constructed for other grammatical categories.

Table 15 reproduces Silverstein's (1981; see also 1986, 1987) feature space. To the left is the hierarchically ordered list of features. To the right are various columns each corresponding to a combination or intersection of relevant feature specifications which serve to characterize a given type of noun phrase A, B, C, etc.[26] By consistently placing the positive feature specifications toward the top of the vertical feature axis, an ordering of noun phrase types is produced. (The apparent violation of this convention in the diagram with features b through d – creating the appearance of cross-cutting features – is due to the two dimensional layout of the space. With additional dimensions, the positive feature values would be contiguous – bunched around the axis.) A provisional label for each noun phrase type (A, B, C, etc.) is given in the table. For the purposes of comparison, the subset of features and noun phrase types developed for grammatical number in table 14 has been marked within the space in order to clarify the way these features might be situated within a larger scheme.

Silverstein's feature space for case marking cannot simply be borrowed directly for use with number marking for several reasons. First, the

Table 15. *Silverstein's two-dimensional "Hierarchical array of noun phrase types in referential feature-space (approximation)"*

segmentable 'natural kind' things
social beings
social indexicals (potential)
social indexicals (specific)
indexicals of speech event
indexicals of speech
participants
speaker
spkr & adrsee

feature	A 1 du incl	B 1 pl incl	C 1 singular	D 1 du excl	E 1 pl excl	F 2 singular	G 2 dual	H 2 plural	I 3 du anaphor	J 3 pl anaphor	K 3 sg anaphor	L 3 du demonst	M 3 pl demonst	N 3 sg demonst	O proper name	P kin-term	Q status term	R being	S perceived obj	T container	U spatial	V sensual entity	W essence	X
a. ego	+	+	+	+	+	−	−	−	−	−	−	−	−	−	−	−	−	−	−	−	−	−	−	−
b. tu	+	+	−	−	−	+	+	+	−	−	−	−	−	−	−	−	−	−	−	−	−	−	−	−
c. unique			+	−	−	+	−	−																
d. plural									+	+	−	+	+	−										
e. enumerable	+	−							+	−		+	−											
f. coreferential									+	+	+	−	−	−	−	−	−	−	−	−	−	−	−	−
g. deictic												+	+	+										
h. proper															+	−	−	−	−	−	−	−	−	−
i. kin																+	−	−	−	−	−	−	−	−
j. human																	+	−	−	−	−	−	−	−
k. animate																		+	−	−	−	−	−	−
l. discrete																			+	−	−	−	−	−
m. containing																				+	−	−	−	−
n. locative																					+	−	−	−
o. concrete																						+	−	−
p. quality																							+	−
⋮																								
x. defined	+	+	+	+	+	+	+	+	+	+	+	+	+	+	+	+	+	+	+	+	+	+	+	−

Silverstein (1981, p. 240, table 1).
Features discussed in the current study are enclosed in the L-shaped box.

feature spaces for different categories need not be identical; features relevant to case marking need not be relevant to number marking although, as indicated above, one can expect considerable overlap. Second, and more specifically, Silverstein's array actually includes features such as [± unique], [± plural], [± enumerable] that directly refer to the number status of indexical noun phrases and that cannot, therefore, be taken as independent variables in characterizing number marking.[27] Third, number marking has been taken into account in the ordering of the features and so the array cannot be construed as independent of number even if the obvious features such as [± plural] were eliminated. A new set of features needs to be articulated for number marking (and each other grammatical category of interest) such that the target category's patterning is kept out of the feature defining and ordering process.

An aside: Silverstein's interpretation of the ordering of noun phrase types

An important issue is whether the noun phrase ordering articulated in table 15 is interpretable, that is, whether one or more notional principles can be articulated which correspond to the ordered array of noun phrase types A, B, C, etc. As Silverstein indicates in the bracketed labels above the ordered noun phrase types in table 15, various nested subgroups of the noun phrase types can be given coherent interpretation. Each subsequent layer of the nesting includes all the groupings at lower levels and adds further noun phrase types by loosening the criterion of inclusion. The question of what orders the noun phrase types then becomes one of what principle governs the criteria of inclusion.

The noun phrase types to the left in the table are forms which depend on the immediate context of speech for their interpretation: pronouns and various anaphoric and deictic forms. This suggests that the ordering is linked in some way to speech events themselves, in contrast, for example, to context-independent properties of the objects of reference. As we move to the right (O, P, Q, etc.), the link to the immediate speech event becomes weaker. It is this ordering which provides the key to Silverstein's interpretation.[28] He introduced the notion that the self-referential quality of speech, that is, the ability of the forms to refer to their own relationship to the speech situation, is reflected in the ordering. Silverstein's (1981) initial[29] proposal was that the ordering of noun phrase types reflects the degree to which a given type of noun phrase both indexes something about the speech event in which it occurs and simultaneously refers to the nature of that indexical relationship itself. He expressed this in more technical terms as follows:

> It would appear that, insofar as the markedness of noun phrase categorizations is concerned, languages follow an ordering principle based on what we can term THE UNAVOIDABILITY AND TRANSPARENCY OF METAPRAGMATIC REFERENCE. This can be explained as follows.
>
> That language signs are used in contexts of situated social encounters is, of course, a truism; let us restrict the usage of the term 'pragmatic' to the study of such relationships, indexical relationships, between signs and their contexts of occurrence ... Then any linguistic forms that essentially describe (refer-to and/or predicate-of) the very terms of such indexical relationships are inherently 'metapragmatic' (employing the ordinary formation with prefix 'meta-'). In particular, any referring form in language, whose instantiation in speech at once indexes and describes its counterpart term in an indexical relationship [for example, the pronoun *I*], is unavoidably and transparently metapragmatic. Note that for such a form to occur felicitously, its use must presuppose the existence of the contextual entity it indexes (lest it be a pragmatic misfire), and at the same time its use achieves consummated reference to the contextual entity.
>
> (1981, p. 241)

Thus, in Silverstein's account noun phrases bear indexical relationships to socially situated speech events. The degree to which noun phrases guarantee or express this relationship as part of their referential meaning when they are used gives rise to their position in the noun phrase ordering.

Another way of expressing this regularity is to say that socially situated speech itself is the ground against which noun phrase types are ordered:

> To be interpretive for a moment, it is as if language use itself in the instant of referring, an activity with an 'agent'–'recipient'–'instrument/vehicle' structure in the speaker–addressee–signal roles, were the creative structuring model against which unavoidable transparency of metapragmatic referentiality is measured by the markedness system of noun phrase categories.   (Silverstein, 1981, p. 242)

This is an important claim for it indicates directly what is distinctive about linguistic categories: they take speech (or speaking) as their ground. "The reference space . . . is not a model of entities in the world that happen to become potential denotata of language" nor "a model of some pre-linguistic 'reality,'" but rather a model of "the way language structures its presentation of denotata through coding categories of Noun Phrase form" (1987, p. 30). A deeper analysis of number marking will have to proceed in this direction by searching for a characterization of the morphosyntactic value of pluralization not solely in terms of decontextualized semantic values but in terms of its role in the pragmatic and metapragmatic dimensions of discourse.

In recent work, Silverstein (1987) has provided a more detailed semiotic–functional interpretation of the noun phrase ordering, in terms of the different weightings of certain basic conditions on correspondence (bases for reference) across different groups of noun phrase types. This approach is especially promising in that it both indicates the dominant factor apparently governing the placement of a noun phrase in the ordering, and also accounts for the possibility of meaningful variation in, and manipulation of, specific noun phrase reference. For example, this approach promises to give a more direct account of the shift in fundamental referential value of lexical nouns from units to kinds across the ordering, and also of the possibility of both kinds of reference occurring at both ends of the continuum.

Summary of the contrastive analysis

Yucatec and English use similar morphosyntactic devices to mark pluralization, but they are implemented quite differently. The Yucatec marking is optionally applied to a small range of noun phrases whereas the English marking is obligatorily applied to a larger range of noun phrases. A characterization in terms of typical application of the plural marking can capture these distributional facts in a single representation. Examination of this representation suggests that a notional characterization can be given to the scope of pluralization in terms of differences in the inherent meaning values of various noun phrase types. The discussion proposed two referential features that adequately characterize the three noun phrase types relevant to the Yucatec and English comparison and then illustrated how such an analysis can be extended to encompass additional languages and additional features. The concluding section discussed important elements of Silverstein's general procedure for developing such features. Brief mention was also made of his attempts to interpret the emerging ordered array of noun phrase types.

Contrast in singular marking (numeral modification and unitization)

Whereas English establishes Singular indefinite reference with the indefinite article *a* (~ *an*) (including here various indexical uses of the form *one*) or with one of various quantitative modifiers, Yucatec usually establishes Singular indefinite reference by a single modifier type consisting of the numeral prefix *'un-* 'one' in conjunction with a numeral classifier. So the key difference between the two languages lies in the existence and obligatory use of numeral classifier constructions in Yucatec – in particular in those cases where English requires only the indefinite article. This discussion will center on explaining the functioning of the classifier forms in Yucatec and their implications for Yucatec lexical and grammatical structure.

Clarifying the contrast between English and Yucatec

Why does Yucatec require numeral classifiers whereas English and other related languages of Europe do not? What function do the classifiers serve in the grammar? The concern here is not with the use of any given classifier, but with the reasons for the existence of the whole set of forms. Although an exhaustive account will not be developed here, it will be possible to indicate in a general way the semiotic function of the system and the logic of its operation. The approach of the present analysis will be comparative, that is, Yucatec Maya will be compared with other non-classifier languages such as English for functionally analogous structures, and with other classifier languages such as Chinese for formally analogous structures. A crucial cross-linguistic regularity will then be articulated which allows the two types of languages to be encompassed in a unified way in regard to both their similarities and their differences.

Comparison with non-classifier languages

Semantic value in the proposition. The first and most obvious characteristic of the classifiers is that they are necessary for enumeration. This suggests that lexical nouns could not be modified by a numeral (or their referents enumerated) without them. If we look to English for parallels, we find a similar phenomenon in those lexical nouns such as *zinc* and *cotton* which are not usually modified by a numeral, for example, **two zincs*, **two cottons*. These lexical nouns have traditionally been called "mass" nouns (i.e., when they are noun phrase heads, the noun phrase is always neutral). Such mass nouns are generally conceptualized as lacking any intrinsic specification of unit as part of their referential meaning. Since such a unit would be necessary for enumeration of the referent of the noun, a unit must be explicitly specified by some additional morphological forms – typically of phrasal form: *two blocks of zinc, two balls of cotton.* (See Lyons, 1977, p. 462.) The morphosyntactic process which converts the lexical noun phrase into one which explicitly signals the unit of the referent can be called *unitization*, and the specific forms used (phrasal modifiers in this case) can be called *unitizers* or *unitizer constructions.* Each mass noun in English is typically compatible with an array of different unitizers.[30]

This interpretation of English mass nouns can illuminate the pattern of numeral modification for Yucatec lexical nouns. It suggests, by analogy, that all the lexical nouns of Yucatec are unspecified as to unit since they all require supplementary marking (i.e., numeral classifiers) in the context of numeral modification.[31] Under this analysis, the numeral classifiers serve to specify the unit or boundedness of the referent of the lexical noun, that is, they are unitizers which supplement the meaning of the lexical noun head so that it will accept numeral modification. We can say, then, that the difference between the two languages is really one of scope (or range) of lexical nouns requiring unitization in order to be suitable for numeral modification: English requires unitization for a limited range of lexical nouns whereas Yucatec requires unitization for all lexical nouns.

This interpretation, that Yucatec lexical nouns are unspecified as to unit and somewhat like English mass nouns, is consistent with the fact that lexical noun phrases in Yucatec do not require pluralization in the context of reference to a multiplicity of entities. If the lexical noun does not inherently signal a specific unit, then the multiplicity of these units is not *semantically* relevant – at least on these grounds. If the expression of multiplicity is pragmatically important, of course, it can be signaled optionally. But if this interpretation is correct, then the plural itself in Yucatec must have a somewhat different meaning than the plural in English in that it need not apply to, or signal, *multiple units* as such, but rather some looser notion of quantity – somewhat equivalent to our expression *lots of*. Significantly, the general adjective modifier for quantity, *yá'ab'* 'much, many', also conforms to this pattern of indifference to presence of a unit.

Also consistent with this interpretation is the fact that Yucatec lexical forms often include a range of meanings which would be subdivided into separate, and semantically quite different, lexical items in English. For example, the word *che'* 'wood' is used not only to refer to the material itself, but also to refer to a variety of objects that are composed of wood and have distinctive shapes such as 'tree, stick, board'. English, by contrast, as the preceding translation equivalents indicate, can focus on the distinctive shapes by using a different lexical item for each (i.e., they conflate unit and material into a single lexical form). Yucatec lexical nouns can be used in conjunction with a classifier to approximate the referential values of the various English lexical items:

'un-č'íit che'   'one stick [lit. 1-dimensional unit] of wood'.

Most Yucatec nouns can combine with a variety of different classifiers just as the English mass nouns can enter a variety of phrasal forms. For example, consider the following set of forms:

'un-č'íit	há'as	'one/a 1-dimens. banana (i.e., the fruit)',
'un-wáal	há'as	'one/a 2-dimens. banana (i.e., the leaf)',
'un-p'éel	há'as	'one/a 3-dimens. banana (e.g., the fruit)',
'un-kúul	há'as	'one/a planted banana (i.e., the tree)',
'un-kúuch	há'as	'one/a load banana (i.e., the bunch)',
'um-p'íit	há'as	'a-little-bit-of/some banana'.

Again, as in the example with *che'* ('wood'), it is as if these Yucatec lexical forms have reference to a common material or substance that may take a variety of manifest shapes or forms.[32] From an interpretive point of view the classifiers resemble the inflectional category of aspect in the verb phrase which gives the logical or temporal perspective being applied to or presupposed of the predicate. Numeral classifiers clarify the logical or spatial perspective being applied to, or presupposed of, the noun phrase complement. In this way Yucatec speakers achieve by means of a single grammatical formation what English speakers achieve by a combination of lexical alternation, determiners, and quantitative modifiers.

With this specific dimension of noun phrase meaning isolated in a separate morpheme, the opportunity is created for manipulation of this dimension to signal subtle referential distinctions. For example, in the following pair of expressions the classifier *-túul* usually associated with animate entities is in opposition with the most neutral classifier *-p'éel*:

> *'un-túul noh-och máak*   'one old man (known to me)',
> *'um-p'éeh noh-och máak*   'one old man (not known to me)'.

Many such alternations are pragmatically conditioned, that is, depend on the immediate context of use for their effect, and a given opposition may represent a different meaning in a different conversational context.

Pragmatic value in discourse.   Yucatec numeral classifiers also serve pragmatic, or discourse-based functions. The numeral one ('*un*- or one of its variants) along with a classifier is used to indicate that a new item is being introduced into discourse. These forms thus bridge the propositional and discourse levels. By indicating additional semantic information at the propositional level, they effectively signal at the discourse level that the item is not already present and/or presupposable (definite) in the speech context. In many ways these constructions are quite similar in their usage to the indefinite articles in English (*a ~ an*). This suggests, then, that the classifiers play a crucial role in establishing reference.

Numeral plus classifier constructions (i.e., standing alone without an associated lexical noun) can also serve in deictic and anaphoric uses. This means that they refer by virtue of indexing something in the immediate context (whether non-speech or previous speech) hence their referential value can only be computed by reference to that context. In this they follow closely the usage of *one* in English. For example, *tàas ten 'un-ȼ'íit chamal* 'bring me a (1-dimensional) cigarette' would, in appropriate contexts, routinely be reduced to *tàas ten 'un-ȼ'íit* 'bring me one (1-dimensional)'.

However, as should be clear, these forms carry a greater semantic load than similar English forms precisely because each one represents a selection from a much larger array of possibilities. It is as if Yucatec has a whole array of indefinite article forms where English has only a two way alternation of *a* (*~ an ~ one*) versus *some* (*~ 0*). In these cases the additional semantic information signaled by the numeral classifier construction is exploited to help establish and maintain reference. Attempts to analyze the use of classifiers purely in terms of their contribution to propositional value will be inadequate, just as similar attempts to characterize English determiners in such terms have been.

Comparison with other classifier languages

Other languages which have numeral classifiers show patterns parallel to those characteristic of Yucatec numeral classifiers. In particular, individual lexical items in these languages have a type of reference that is consistent with their being neutral as to intrinsic unit. Classifiers typically provide such a unit for numeral modification and many nouns can occur with more than one classifier, each of which produces a different semantic effect. At the discourse level, in almost every language with genuine numeral classifiers, these forms with their associated numerals can be used as deictic or anaphoric forms. Thus, both the semantic and the discourse level functioning of the Yucatec forms are not isolated and idiosyncratic phenomena, but rather perfectly regular characteristics of many languages.

Another common claim about numeral classifiers deserves mention. Most analysts divide numeral classifiers into two broad groups: *sortal* and *mensural* (Lyons, 1977, pp. 463–64). Sortal classifiers apply to "whole" entities and sort them into "classes." Mensural classifiers indicate the "measure" or "quantity" of some amorphous substance.[33] One characteristic of the sortal classifiers is that there is usually a very general classifier, somewhat neutral in its sense, which can be applied in place of any of the sortals with the possible exception of the classifier(s) for animate entities (Greenberg, 1972). This pattern is most closely paralleled in Yucatec by *-p'éel* which can be used for reference to almost any object where a "sortal" classifier would be expected, although it is not usually used to substitute for cases where *-túul* would be appropriate, that is, for reference to most animate objects. In Yucatec, then, a class much like the sortals can be detected by identifying those lexical nouns that are compatible with one of the two general classifiers *-túul* 'animate' and *-p'éel* 'three dimensional [formally and notionally unmarked]' supplemented by the pattern of interaction with the quantitative adjective *ȼ'éeȼ'ek* 'few'. There is a second very general classifier *-p'íit* 'a little bit of, a few' which can be used in almost every case where mensural classifiers could be used. Many nouns (especially edible plants and animals) fit both categories because *-p'íit* itself is neutral with respect to unit and can cover the two English senses 'a little bit of' and 'a few'.

Outside of certain restrictions on compatibility with other classifiers, little in the grammar of Yucatec appears to hinge on, or correlate with, this "sortal" (*-túul/-p'éel*) versus "mensural" (*-p'íit*) distinction, and it is difficult to know what status it should be given. But it *is* interesting that groups of lexical nouns compatible with the three general classifiers correspond roughly to those serving as heads of the three lexical noun phrase types ("animates," "objects," and "materials") developed in the analysis of pluralization patterns. This suggests that something like a three way split of lexical noun types operates within the sphere of unitization as well.

Table 16. *Complementary distribution of obligatory unitization and obligatory pluralization in English and Yucatec by lexical noun phrase type*

		Lexical noun phrase type		
		A	B	C
	Features:	[+ animate]	[− animate] [+ discrete]	[− animate] [− discrete]
Language, marking				
Yucatec		unit	unit	unit
English		plural	plural	unit

Interrelationship between pluralization and unitization

A striking fact which emerges when we examine numeral classifier languages is that there is a general absence of obligatory pluralization. Sanches ([with Slobin], 1973; see also Greenberg, 1972, 1978; Gil, 1987) has shown that, in those languages which have numeral classifiers for all or nearly all nouns, obligatory pluralization is usually either absent or infrequent.[34] Since we have seen that the scope of typical pluralization varies as a function of noun phrase type, and that there is interesting variation within classifier systems by lexical noun type, it is reasonable to ask whether a more precise specification of this complementary relationship between these two grammatical phenomena can be achieved by working at the noun phrase level.

We can explore such a possibility with Yucatec and English by using the three noun phrase types developed earlier. To accomplish the comparison, we need to shift our focus to obligatory pluralization and we need to treat English quantitative phrasal constructions as unitizer constructions that are functionally equivalent to Yucatec numeral classifiers. We can then characterize the *scope of obligatory unitization* by noun phrase type in the two languages and ask about its relationship to the *scope of obligatory pluralization* by noun phrase type.[35] Table 16 portrays the relationship that obtains between these grammatical patterns in English and Yucatec using the referential features and noun phrase types developed earlier. The complementary relationship between these two patterns emerges clearly: not only is there a global difference in that Yucatec tends to obligatorily unitize across the whole spectrum of lexical noun phrase types which are not obligatorily plural-

Table 17. *Multilanguage comparison showing complementary distribution of obligatory pluralization and obligatory unitization of lexical noun phrases*

Language, marking	Features:	Lexical noun phrase type		
		A	B	C
		[+ animate]	[− animate] [+ discrete]	[− animate] [− discrete]
Chinese		unit	unit	unit
Yucatec		unit	unit	unit
Tarascan		plural	unit	unit
English		plural	plural	unit
Hopi		plural	plural	plural

Sources of data for individual languages indicated in table 13. Additional data for Chinese drawn from Li and Thompson (1981, pp. 104–13) and Killingley (1981).

ized, but also a pattern exists in English of unitizing precisely for those lexical nouns that do not take obligatory pluralization. This pattern indicates the close relationship between unitization and pluralization and the appropriateness of treating numeral modification as part of the number marking system of a language. It also indicates the close relationship between grammatical number marking patterns and lexical noun phrase structure – and vice versa. The semantic structure of lexical noun heads is ultimately at issue.

Generalizing the analysis for further comparisons

Sanches's work suggests that the complementary relationship between numeral classifiers and pluralization is a general phenomenon. The discussion in the previous section suggests that the analysis can be made more precise by examining the relationship in terms of noun phrase types and can be broadened to incorporate nonclassifier forms of unitization. However, in the absence of previous work examining this problem in terms of noun phrase types, only a few general suggestions can be made at present as to how the analysis can be extended to other languages and features.

Generalizing to additional languages

The complementary distribution of unitization and pluralization at the noun phrase level apparently holds for at least some additional languages. Table 17 shows the complementary distribution of obligatory pluralization and obligatory unitization for the set of languages used earlier in terms of the same three noun phrase types. For languages such as Tarascan that have both obligatory pluralization and true numeral classifiers, a statement of the complementary distribution of these two marking patterns by noun phrase type has the advantage of more adequately characterizing such languages. By contrast, in Sanches's comparison at the level of whole languages, such languages appear to be anomalous.

Although much more work would be required to fully document and qualify the generality of such a complementary distribution, these data should be sufficient to indicate that the differences between Yucatec and English are not mere local, accidental phenomena, but rather form part of a much larger, cross-linguistic regularity. This regularity seems to center on an interaction between patterns of number marking and fundamental structure of lexical nouns.

Building a more general feature analysis

In the immediately preceding discussion, the features characterizing the scope of unitization and its complementary relationship with pluralization were borrowed from the analysis of plural marking because they were appropriate. It is likely, however, that a larger set of features will be required to characterize a larger sample of languages and, in fact, to treat some of the languages in table 17 more adequately. It also may be possible that the features relevant to bounding the scope of unitization may not in fact generally correspond to those bounding the scope of pluralization, so it is desirable to distinguish the two sets of features until this is established. I know of no previous attempts to characterize the scope of application of unitization in general or of numeral classifiers in particular, and no further attempt to develop such an analysis will be made here since it is not necessary for the present contrast between Yucatec and English. The previous discussion of the procedures for extending the analysis of pluralization can, however, serve to indicate the general course such an analysis would have to take.

There have been a number of works attempting to generalize about the sorts of referential meanings involved within numeral classifier systems (for example, Allan, 1977; Denny, 1976, 1979). These deserve some comment both because they differ somewhat from the approach favored here and because they hold important implications for the interpretation of the semantic structure of lexical nouns. These accounts all suffer from a set of common weaknesses.

First, they all tend to assume that classifiers reflect something about the lexical noun rather than contributing new information to the meaning of the noun phrase. Attention is confined to some purported common value of the lexical items associated with the classifier (or, worse yet, to a simple list of such lexical items) rather than being extended to the actual change in referential value entailed by the application of the classifier. Co-occurence relations with lexical nouns can provide clues to the meaning of the classifier by suggesting contexts in which their meaning values are relevant, but the meaning of the classifier cannot be reduced to the common value of the lexical items. In short, the fundamental role of the classifier in the grammar typically goes unrecognized.

Second, and relatedly, they do not recognize a linkage between the need for classifiers in numeral modification and the overall structure of the grammar as expressed in the inherent semantic structure of lexical items and other number marking patterns, such as pluralization. Thus, classifier systems are analyzed on their own terms without reference to the rest of the grammar and the contribution of the classifiers to the coherent system of reference is often not recognized.

Third, within the analyses, they seek a set of decontextualized semantic features and do not incorporate features sensitive to the immediate and/or cultural context of speech. Use of a classifier to augment the inherent meaning of the lexical noun provides the opportunity not only for semantic modification, but also for pragmatic modification – for example to signal the introduction of a new referent in discourse or to suggest speaker attitude towards the referent. In short, the pragmatic potential of classifiers to tailor the reference of the modified lexical noun head and the utterance as a whole to the context (including the view or perspective of the speaker) is simply ignored.

One extended example from Yucatec can serve to illustrate these points. One of the most commonly recognized aspects of classifier systems is the presence in most such languages of a separate classifier co-occurring with lexical nouns referring to animate entities. The classifier *-túul* in Yucatec is such a form:

> *'un-túul k'éek'-en*   'one/a live pig'.[36]

The usual claim about such forms is that *k'éek'-en* 'pig' is an animate noun and therefore it "takes" the animate classifier. In this sort of analysis, the classifier contributes nothing to the meaning of the utterance. Classifiers are essentially construed as if they were empty formal categories that merely agree with the lexical noun head. If, however, the classifiers as a group signaled such a purely formal category, then we might expect a given noun to take only one classifier. This by no means occurs: many lexical nouns can take a variety of classifiers which produce clear and reliable shifts in meaning. For example, *k'éek'-en* can take the following meanings with some other classifiers:

'um-p'éel k'éek'-en	'one/a whole pig (dead or alive)',
'um-p'íit k'éek'-en	'a-little-bit-of/some pork',
'un-šéet' k'éek'-en	'one/a piece/shred of pork'.

One way to account for this variability is to suggest that classifiers have typical uses which are extended analogically. For example when an animate classifier form is applied to non-animate lexical nouns it suggests that they are "like animates" by virtue of their typical use.[37] For example, *-túul* sometimes occurs with inanimates:

'un-túul camión	'a/one truck [Spanish loan]',
'un-túul botón	'a/one button [Spanish loan]'.

The claim would be that, in the specific circumstances of use, the truck and button in question were regarded as being like animates in some way: the truck passed by under its own power, the button popped from the fingers of the person attempting to sew it on. This approach explains the extension of the syntactic distribution of the classifier, but still leaves the classifier without significant referential value. This is a less than satisfying explanation for the existence and functioning of a highly regular and obligatory pattern of syntactic marking: the exceptional applications of the classifier are meaningful, but the routine uses are not.

The obvious alternative is to attribute to the classifier itself some referential value. For example, one could attribute the meaning "animate" to the classifier itself so that it makes any noun phrase containing it animate as well. This leaves the relevant lexical nouns without a semantic value of [+ animate] (i.e., they are [− animate], or neutral, if some nouns are so marked or, if none are, then the feature is simply not relevant at all) unless it is provided by one of the classifiers. This may strike us, as speakers of English, as odd, but it is not at all implausible given the operation of the classifier constructions in these languages. For example, the lexical item *k'éek'en* used in the above example can refer without any special marking to 'dead pigs' and 'pork' which suggests that animacy is not a necessary element of its meaning: *tàal-en in-màan k'éek'en* 'I have come to buy a/some pig/pork'.[38] If the lexical noun *k'éek'en* is neutral with respect to animacy and the classifier *-túul* provides this dimension of meaning, then *'un-túul k'éek'en* refers to a living, animate pig by virtue of *-túul*, not by virtue of the meaning of *k'éek'en*. And some alternative such as *'um-p'éel k'éek'en* 'a/one whole pig' or *'un-šéet' k'éek'en* 'one piece/shred of pork' can be used to refer to a dead pig.[39]

One problem with this analysis is that it puts us in the position of saying that every item occurring with *-túul* is being specified [+ animate]; so, for example, the truck and the button referred to in the examples given above would be marked [+ animate]. This is fine if we understand [+ animate] in the technical sense indicated above as a label for the volitional, agentive, or motive properties of a referent.

An alternative to this latter proposal is to argue that the classifier does contribute something to the meaning of the lexical noun phrase but that it is not [+ animate]. For example, one might claim that *-túul* signals a feature such as [+ mobile] or [+ self-segmenting] where these are to be understood as defined relative to a specific event of speaking and not as a permanent attribute of an object. This use of a not-inherent-to-the-referent feature accords well with the perspective-signaling character of numeral classifiers.[40] Thus one could regard particular referents such as trucks which pass by on their own power or buttons which slip from one's hand as [+ mobile] or [+ self-segmenting] in a particular speech context without having to regard the lexical nouns used for denoting trucks or buttons as being inherently [+ mobile] or [+ self-segmenting]. This approach also squares with the availability of a variety of classifiers for each lexical noun since the relevant *unit* appropriate for enumeration may vary by the referential context. Of course, most of the time such a description would be applicable to animate referents and therefore occur with the lexical nouns referring to them. This would account for the strong association of *-túul* with such lexical nouns in Yucatec. But notice, now, under this interpretation, that it is not the classifier alone nor the lexical noun alone that indicates (or suggests) animateness, but rather such a meaning is deducible from their joint operation.

Either of these last two solutions seems preferable to leaving the classifier semantically empty (at least in the usual case). These approaches also incorporate a crucial shift of emphasis towards considering the classifier as a creative referential device signaling meaningful information in the noun phrase, and support the view that the appropriate level of analysis for cross-linguistic analysis of number marking is the noun phrase and not the lexical noun.

Summary of the contrastive analysis

Singular marking in Yucatec is basically accomplished by means of modifiers consisting of a numeral plus classifier combination. By contrast

English uses the indefinite article and/or quantitative modifiers. The pattern in Yucatec is functionally similar to that used for mass nouns in English, and this relationship is used to suggest that Yucatec lexical nouns are all inherently unspecified for unit. The Yucatec pattern of lacking obligatory pluralization is also consistent with other classifier languages. Combined comparison of the two languages shows a complementary relationship across noun phrase types in the requirement of obligatory unitization and the requirement of obligatory pluralization. This analysis in terms of the two features developed for pluralization can be extended to some other languages, although there is as yet no generally worked out set of features governing the scope of unitization. The discussion closes by recognizing the need to assign referential feature values to classifiers and some of the difficulties in doing so.

General summary

The number marking systems of the two languages show a number of striking convergences. Plural and Singular are marked using similar morphosyntactic devices. Yet when we look more closely, we find that the languages differ in which elements of structure require obligatory, overt specification and which do not. The two analyses together suggest some fundamental asymmetries of structure at the level of lexical nouns. Interpretively, in Yucatec all nouns are like our mass nouns in that they are neutral with respect to logical unit or shape. Although individual classifiers may appear and disappear within Yucatec, it would require a major restructuring of the grammar to eliminate classifiers altogether. This lexical structure is consistent with the obligatory unitization to indicate Singular (and specific quantitative multiples) and with the optionality of Plural marking. English divides its lexical nouns into two groups, those with a presupposable unit as part of lexical structure and which may take Plurals and Singular marking with indefinite article, and those lexical nouns which function like the Yucatec lexical nouns in requiring unitizers and lacking the plural.

Much more could be said to make these generalizations more specific and to explore their further ramifications in morphosyntactic structure. But the analysis presented thus far should be sufficient to meet the criteria established for the current project. We have identified a difference in morphosyntactic structuring that corresponds with a significant difference in the referential meaning value of fundamental forms in the two languages. The difference penetrates a variety of formal and substantive structural domains in the two languages and reveals an intimate relationship between lexical and syntactic patterning. The comparison has been developed in terms of a "neutral" cross-linguistic descriptive framework which characterizes both commonalities and differences among languages within a unified treatment. And indications have been given as to how the analysis can be extended to other languages.

3. Cognitive assessment

The objective of this chapter is to illustrate an approach capable of addressing whether or not different linguistic configurations of meaning produce cognitive consequences. This will be accomplished by seeking evidence that the linguistic patterns described in chapter 2 have correlates in cognition. If cognitive performance corresponds with linguistic structure in a distinctive way, the proposal that the specific structure of a language is related to thought gains support. As discussed in *Language diversity and thought*, chapter 7, it is not possible with correlational techniques to establish unequivocally that language is the shaping factor in such a relationship; the language patterns may in fact derive from culturally specific thought patterns, or both patterns may derive from some third cultural factor. But correlational evidence can be extremely suggestive of a causal role for language if the relationships are strong and distinctive and if no other explanation for the contrasting cognitive patterns seems plausible. It will be difficult to achieve conclusive results in a single study – especially when it is exploratory, as the present one is – and further work using additional assessment procedures and other linguistic and cultural groups will be needed to establish the reliability and generality of the present findings and to rule out plausible alternative explanations. Nonetheless, the results reported here are suggestive of some interesting and reliable relationships between linguistic patterns and habitual thought.

General approach

To find connections between language and thought, specific hypotheses concerning potential linkages must be formulated. The move from the linguistic forms of English and Yucatec to an assessment of possible psychological connections requires three analytic steps. First, *implications of patterns of linguistic meaning for the interpretation of experi-*

ence must be clarified. Second, the *locus of cognitive effects*, that is, specific cognitive activities likely to be affected by such interpretations of experience, must be identified. Third, *practical techniques of assessment* for revealing or diagnosing the presence of cognitive effects must be developed so as to test whether or not the predicted associations actually exist.

Implications of patterns of linguistic meaning for the interpretation of experience

The goal here is to provide examples of the kinds of questions which can be posed given the differences in number marking between English and Yucatec. However, the two predictions developed here by no means exhaust the possible cognitive consequences of these differences.

Types of linguistic patterns which are of interest

It is worth recalling at the outset that we have followed a specific agenda in producing the linguistic comparison developed in chapter 2. We have focused on *basic morphosyntactic categories* with *denotational referential* value that seem to coordinate into a structured *configuration of meaning*, the description of which can be given *cross-linguistic characterization and justification*. We are concerned now with how these different morphosyntactic structurings of reference might have broader implications for the habitual interpretation of experience. The focus on basic morphosyntactic categories assures that the linguistic patterns must be taken into account in most utterances in contrast to relatively infrequent or structurally marginal lexical or grammatical forms. The referential nature of the categories allows us to calibrate both the linguistic and nonlinguistic responses of speakers against a common "reality."[1] By working with configurations of meaning, it is possible to formulate qualitative comparisons in terms of different patterns, rather than a quantitative comparison in terms of one language being deficient with respect to the other. Finally, the inherently comparative nature of the linguistic analysis (conducted within a larger cross-linguistic framework) permits a characterization of the patterns of linguistic reference in relatively "neutral" descriptive terms, that is, in terms that do not privilege the categories of either language.

Implications of grammatical number: differential salience of number

The most common denotational correlate of the category of grammatical number is the *number of objects referred to*, that is, whether one or more than one of a given referent is present. In particular, Plural number is signaled with greater regularity and for a wider array of referent types in English than in Yucatec.

First, Plural is signaled more obligatorily in English than in Yucatec. For noun phrases which regularly take Plural in both languages, English speakers will pluralize these noun phrases more often than will Yucatec speakers in similar referential contexts. Thus, in speaking, English speakers must obligatorily attend to, and differentially signal, number where Yucatec speakers need not. If this linguistic pattern translates into a general sensitivity to number (i.e., one versus many) in other cognitive activities, then *English speakers should habitually attend to the number of various objects of reference more than should Yucatec speakers.* This is a simple quantitative prediction.

Second, English speakers routinely pluralize a wider range of noun phrase types than do Yucatec speakers. Specifically, English speakers typically pluralize both Type A [+ animate] and Type B [− animate, + discrete] noun phrases, whereas Yucatec speakers typically pluralize only Type A [+ animate] noun phrases. Thus, in speaking, English speakers attend to, and differentially signal, number for a wider array of referent types than do Yucatec speakers. If this linguistic pattern translates into a general sensitivity to number (i.e., one versus many) in other cognitive activities, then *English speakers should habitually attend to number for a wider array of referent types than should Yucatec speakers.* Specifically, given the notional cores of the three noun phrase types, English speakers should pay attention to number for animals and discrete objects, whereas Yucatec speakers should pay attention to number only for animals.

This second prediction is a qualitative one in that it anticipates specific, *contrasting patterns of response* in the two groups. This permits the development of more diagnostic predictions and frees the assessment tasks from the requirement of establishing equivalent absolute levels of response in the two groups. The expected contrast can be clearly stated in terms of the underlying cross-linguistic regularity proposed in chapter 2. Figure 1 shows the contrast in patterns. The *underlying cross-language regularity* is that Type A noun phrases are pluralized at least as often or more often than Type B noun phrases which in turn are pluralized at least as often or more often than Type C noun phrases: $A \geq B \geq C$. This three-way differentiation of noun phrase types gets collapsed into a two-way formal pattern in English and Yucatec. The *English variant of*

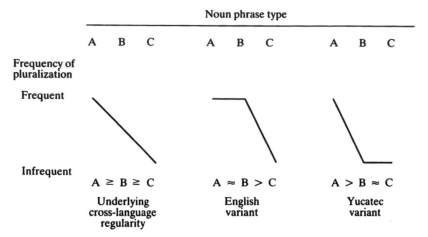

Figure 1   Patterns of pluralization: frequency of pluralization as a function of noun phrase type. Type A noun phrases are [+ animate, + discrete], type B noun phrases are [− animate, + discrete], and type C noun phrases are [− animate, − discrete].

this pattern is to pluralize Type B noun phrases at the same level as Type A noun phrases: $A \approx B > C$. The *Yucatec variant* of this pattern is to pluralize Type B noun phrases at the same level as Type C noun phrases: $A > B \approx C$. Thus, from a global point of view, the two languages agree in pluralizing Type A noun phrases and in not pluralizing Type C noun phrases but *differ dramatically in their treatment of Type B noun phrases*. If attention to number in language has effects on thought, then *these patterns should be reflected in other cognitive activities* with the typical referents of these noun phrase types. One possible attenuation of the contrast might arise from the first, quantitative prediction developed above. Since Yucatec speakers do not pluralize Type A noun phrases at the same *absolute* level as do English speakers, they may exhibit a somewhat lower overall level of attention to number than English speakers. However, the characteristic Yucatec *pattern* ($A > B \approx C$) should emerge nonetheless. In general the emphasis throughout the cognitive assessment will be on the presence or absence of the characteristic qualitative pattern expected for each language group and not on the absolute levels of performance.

Implications of grammatical number: differential salience of shape versus material

It was proposed in chapter 2 that the difference in pluralization patterns between English and Yucatec is connected to a covert difference in the *fundamental semantic structure of lexical items* in the two languages. This difference was reflected most clearly in the sort of constructions necessary to mark Singular. In particular, many English lexical items seem to encode a *presupposable unit* as part of their inherent meaning, whereas corresponding Yucatec lexical items do not. It is difficult, however, to generalize about the concrete denotational correlate of such a contrast in lexical noun meaning because it shifts somewhat across the spectrum of lexical noun types. From a cross-linguistic point of view, judging from the complementary distribution between obligatory pluralization and obligatory unitization which holds for the languages shown in table 17 of chapter 2, the likelihood of a lexical item having a presupposable unit as part of its inherent meaning is stronger for those lexical nouns which head noun phrase types towards the left (Type A) end of the array and weaker for lexical nouns which head noun phrase types towards the right (Type C) end. But since different referential features govern the scope of such presupposition across languages, it is clear that the sort of "unit" being presupposed varies by language. Further, the type of unit being presupposed may shift across lexical types within a single language as well.

However, for those lexical nouns which head Type B noun phrases – where the contrast between the two languages is maximal – certain specific regularities arise from which denotational implications can be drawn. The unit presupposed by English lexical nouns of this type is usually the *form or shape* of an object. Yucatec nouns, lacking such a specification of unit simply refer to the *substance or material composition* of an object. Both means of reference are adequate for differentially signaling objects in most situations. For lexical nouns referring to objects which have a well-defined shape and are composed of a single material, the contrast between the two languages can be especially salient. Use of the English lexical items routinely draws attention to the shape of a referent insofar as its form is the basis for incorporating it under some lexical label. Use of the Yucatec lexical items, by contrast, routinely draws attention to the material composition of a referent insofar as its substance is the basis for incorporating it under some lexical label. Thus, in cases where *English lexical structure routinely draws attention to shape, Yucatec lexical structure routinely draws attention to material.* If these linguistic patterns translate into general sensitivity to these properties of referents, then *English speakers should attend relatively more to the shape of objects* and *Yucatec speakers should attend relatively more to the material composition of objects* in other cognitive activities – with objects of the appropriate type. This constitutes a qualitative prediction of differential habitual preference for certain bases of classification when dealing with a certain range of referents. Development of more general claims for a larger array of referent types, or a general predilection to classify on one basis rather than another, must await a more comprehensive analysis of the range of referential meanings implicated in number marking patterns.

Formal similarity of these hypotheses to Whorf's hypotheses

In Whorf's analyses the crucial claim was that a particular kind of referential element could be incorporated into diverse formal grammatical configurations in different languages (cf. figure 3 in *Language diversity and thought*, chapter 2, on the treatment of cyclic sequences in English and Hopi). In essence, the diverse formal linkages in the languages connected the element in question to different meaning structures. These different connections (corresponding to different structural positions) then affect the meaning value of the element and thereby the interpretation of its typical referents.

The two hypotheses formulated here correspond to this general pattern, but with an important difference. The common referential elements in the present case are the Type B noun phrases. In English they are formally linked with (treated the same as) Type A noun phrases in that they share a pattern of overt plural marking, whereas in Yucatec they are linked with Type C noun phrases in that both lack such plural marking. Further, in English the Type B noun phrases do not require classifier constructions for enumeration, whereas in Yucatec they do. The hypothesis is that these different formal linkages generate implications for the basic meaning structure of the noun phrase heads and for the interpretation of their typical referents. However, unlike Whorf's examples, wherein the formal linkages served merely as bridges for the flow of analogical meaning, in the present case, the formal linkages themselves (for example, applicability of plural marking) are also seen as potentially having direct implications for cognitive activity. Thus, in the present study hypotheses have been proposed at two distinct levels: first, the formal pattern will have a direct effect on cognition (i.e., plural marking patterns will lead to greater attention to number for Type B noun phrases in one language than in the other) and second, the formal pattern will have an indirect effect on the meaning structure of the referential elements (i.e., Type B noun phrase heads and their referents will be interpreted as having a presupposed unit in one language and not in the other).

The analyses here also differ from Whorf's in other respects. First, on the linguistic side, the analysis has been explicitly linked to patterns in other languages and so offers the potential for ready extension to other cases. Second, on the cognitive side, relatively specific, testable predictions about cognitive implications have been made. The analysis does not depend on an analysis of general cultural worldview. Finally, from an analytic point of view, the first hypothesis allows the design of highly diagnostic assessments since it incorporates both commonalities and differences within a single framework: cognitive performance should be relatively similar with respect to the referents of Type A and Type C noun phrases and different only for Type B noun phrases. As will become clear shortly, this offers a number of advantages for developing highly specific predictions.

Locus of cognitive effects

The term cognition can cover a wide range of meanings. As used here cognition refers to a variety of information processing functions, such as remembering and reasoning, which may or may not correspond to specific psychophysiological structural formations. The precise characterization of such functions, and the issue of whether cognitive activity can be segmented into such functional units at all, are topics of considerable dispute within cognitive psychology. A definitive solution for these theoretical problems can not, and should not, be a prerequisite to cross-cultural empirical research, especially since such work can be relevant to the solution of some of these disputes. For example, although many would contend that these processing functions are generalized, that is, not tied to specific informational content, such a view would be challenged by positive findings in the present research.

The general expectation is that language influences of the sort to be discussed here do not affect a speaker's potential ability to see a referent at all or in a certain way, but rather affect a speaker's habitual dispositions towards, or ways of responding to, a referent. These dispositions are assumed to operate across four basic functions which have been assumed in the design of the experiments here: *interpretation*, the application of available perceptual and conceptual schemata or classifications to experience; *remembering*, retrieval of previously processed information; *manipulation*, creation of new categories and category linkages by reasoning and analogy; and *decision*, judging and evaluating cognitive activities by standards of value. Each of these broader functions may be further differentiated (for example, remembering can be divided into recognition and recall). And, any given activity (for example, attending) probably involves multiple functions. Language may have an effect on any of these functions, specific subfunctions, or their mode of systematic interrelation – although its significance need not be the same in all cases. There is, however, no intent to adopt a strong position here regarding the controversies in cognitive psychology concerning the precise differentiation or mode of operation of cognitive functions. The aim is simply to include a variety of tasks, at least some of which involve cognitive functions other than simple interpretation, that is, which involve additional difficulties such as remembering, classifying, making judgments, etc. The hypothesis is that people will appropriate linguistic patterns to guide these processing activities.

Practical techniques of assessment

The cognitive assessment reported here emphasizes controlled comparison even though this necessarily entails some reduction in interpretive validity. (The reasons for this emphasis are given in *Language diversity and thought*, chapter 7.) The comparisons were controlled in that speakers in both languages were asked to perform similar tasks with similar materials. But the emphasis on control was tempered in two ways. First, an effort was made to maximize interpretive validity in the Yucatec context by using simple tasks and familiar materials and by providing some preliminary experience with similar tasks and materials. Second, the procedures were designed to be exploratory in nature. This involved providing relatively rich stimuli and some open-ended tasks so that unanticipated differences between the two groups could emerge, and so that a variety of secondary issues could be explored.[2] It also involved modifying the task procedures when it became clear that the task was going awry for some reason. These "temperings" stem from a conviction that the distortions of spontaneous behavior inherent in all controlled experimental work are often greatly exacerbated in cross-cultural research by the use of inappropriate research instruments. At this stage of our understanding, openness and flexibility seem to be in order even when they lead to some loss of precision in the comparison. More precise contrasts can be undertaken once the main lines of difference are clear and more sensitive procedures have been developed.

The balance of this chapter describes in detail the development of assessment materials and tasks, their administration to groups of English and Yucatec speakers, and the principal findings. The emphasis will be on the general logic of the approach and the main line of results with respect to the two general hypotheses formulated above. To this end, specific details on some issues have been omitted from the main text and provided in appendices. These appendices provide background on the samples; details on the development, pretesting, and content of stimulus materials; information on counterbalancing; and summary sheets of results by individual, task, and stimulus item. These materials have been included so that others attempting to reanalyze, reformulate, or replicate the research reported here will have available a relatively rich array of materials on the design, administration, results, and interpretation of these tasks. The availability of relevant supplementary material will be noted throughout the chapter by reference to the appropriate appendix.

Picture task series

A series of interrelated tasks was constructed to assess cognitive sensitivity to the *number* (i.e., one versus many) of various kinds of objects in the two language groups. Attention and recall memory were assessed by reference to patterns of verbal behavior; classification and recognition memory were assessed by reference to nonverbal responses. Because the stimuli and samples were the same or related across several different tasks, and because the tasks were themselves ordered by design in a specific way, factors relevant to the series as a whole will be described before turning to specific task results.

Design rationale and general procedures

The purpose of this task series is to assess in a controlled way the cognitive significance of number for the two groups. The general expectation is that patterns of sensitivity to number in cognition will follow the patterns of grammatical number marking characteristic of each language as these have been interpreted in the previous section. In order to conduct such an assessment, picture stimuli were created which contained representations of various kinds of objects in different numbers; a variety of cognitive tasks were designed in which patterns of performance might hinge on sensitivity to the number of various kinds of objects in the pictures; and the tasks were administered to a sample of speakers from each language group.

Construction of picture stimuli

Picture stimuli consisting of line drawings were prepared so as to include specific numbers and types of objects relevant to the hypothesis in question. (Reasons for using line drawings are detailed in appendix A.) These pictures were used in all five of the tasks in this series.

Figure 2   Example of picture stimuli depicting typical scenes from Yucatecan village life

Development of original picture sets

General picture content and background.   Because Yucatec performance on pretests was better with familiar objects in appropriate settings,
scenes of everyday Yucatecan village life were used in the pictures. It was
anticipated that the greater overall sophistication of the US respondents
in interpreting pictures would compensate for any difficulty the novel
content might pose for them. Three sets of three pictures each (nine
pictures in all) were constructed. To exemplify the nature of the pictures,
one of the pictures is shown at half size in figure 2. Reduced copies of the
complete set of picture stimuli are available in appendix A.
    The general content of the various pictures is described in table 18. A
primary goal in developing the pictures was to provide a broad sampling
of village settings by including scenes from the domestic sphere (pictures
1.1, 2.3, 3.2), the public/village sphere (pictures 1.3, 2.2, 3.1), and the
agricultural/work sphere (pictures 1.2, 2.1, 3.3). Other possible dimensions of contrast were also represented: open and enclosed areas, scenes
defined by permanent features and by current activities, typical male and
female settings, etc. A fuller discussion of the development and content
of the pictures is given in appendix A.

Incorporation of a set of target objects.   Certain *standard objects* were
systematically incorporated into each picture. Various *Animals* repre-

Table 18. *General content of depicted scenes of Yucatecan village life*

Picture Set 1
1 Kitchen (cooking area of a house)
2 Field (forest being cleared)
3 Truck (waiting to load riders and cargo)

Picture Set 2
1 Garden (cultivated, being irrigated)
2 Town square (typical features)
3 Festival (food preparation at a gathering)

Picture Set 3
1 Store (counter area in a house)
2 Yard (animals and typical features)
3 Bee colony (adjacent to fields in forest)

sented the typical referents of Type A [+ animate] noun phrases, various *Implements* (for example, containers, tools, utensils, etc.) represented the typical referents of Type B [– animate, + discrete] noun phrases, and various material *Substances* represented the typical referents of Type C [– animate, – discrete] noun phrases. Twice as many Implement objects were included for Type B noun phrases since this is the locus of maximum contrast between the two languages. In most cases the standard objects had physical characteristics that assured that they fell unambiguously into one of the classes of referents[3] generated by the linguistic categories of interest in this study. Each of these standard object types was represented in a picture either by a single token or by multiple tokens, and this representation was counterbalanced across pictures and picture sets. The full list of the standard objects and the process by which they were selected and incorporated into the pictures is described in appendix A. From among the standard objects, certain objects were selected as *target objects*. These target objects were the focus of the experimental tasks reported here. The target objects for the various pictures are listed in table 19. The number after each object indicates how many individual tokens of the target object occurred in the given picture.

Development of alternate pictures

Associated with each original picture was a set of *alternate pictures*, that is, pictures which differed from the originals only in the quantity (number or size) of one of the target objects. These pictures are used only in the nonverbal tasks. Each original picture 1 had five such

Table 19. *List of target objects by picture and type*

| Picture ID No. | Object Type | | | |
	Animal	Implement Container	Implement Tool	Substance
1.1	Dog 2	*Tinaja*[a] 1	Candle 2	Corn dough 1
1.2	Human 1	Sack 2	Ax 1	Firewood 6
1.3	Pig 1	Water gourd 1	Machete 2	Cloud 2
2.1	Human 1	Bucket 2	Shovel 1	Smoke 2
2.2	Horse 2	Mesh bag 1	Pulley 2	Puddle 1
2.3	Turkey 3	Gourd 2	Stool 1	Fat/Meat 1
3.1	Chicken 1	Calabash 2	Griddle 2	Fat/Meat 1
3.2	Human 2	Bottle 2	Broom 1	Corn[b] 1
3.3	Bird 2	Barrel 1	Hat[c] 1	Rock 3

Numbers after the object name indicate the number of discrete items of that type represented in each picture.
[a]Ceramic storage vessel for water. [b]Kernels of feed corn. [c]Hat was not being worn.

alternates: **2** with a change in the number of the target Animal; **3** with a change in the number of the target Implement (container); **4** with a change in the number of the target Implement (tool); **5** with a change in the number of representations of the target Substance; and **6** with a change in the amount (indicated by a change of size of the representation in the drawing) of the target Substance. (As explained below, picture **6** was included to provide information on whether the two groups differed in the way they regarded changes in quantity of a nondiscrete type.)

Objects represented by a single token in the original picture were supplemented by a second token in the relevant alternate. Objects represented by two or more tokens in the original picture were reduced to a single token in the relevant alternate. Changes in amount for alternate **6** were always in the same direction as for alternate **5** so that the two could be compared. The changes which were made are deducible, therefore, from the indication in table 19 of number of tokens in the original picture. Thus, for example, in picture set 1.1, picture **1** was the original, **2** deleted one dog, **3** added one *tinaja* (large ceramic water jar), **4** deleted one candle, **5** added a second lump of corn dough, and **6** increased (added to) the size of the lump of corn dough. Reduced copies of the alternate picture stimuli are available in appendix A. As can be seen in table 19, the changes in number were counterbalanced across sets for increases versus decreases of number. This was done to control for any difficulty which might be associated with the two types of change. For example, it might be that it is more difficult to recognize that something is missing from a picture than that something has been added. Thus, for the twelve changes in number associated with each picture set, (i.e., alternates **2, 3, 4,** and **5** for each of three pictures) the changes were counterbalanced so that six were increased and six were decreased.

Administration of the task series

This subsection deals only with some general considerations which were taken into account in the administration of the tasks and their analysis. No attempt is made here to indicate the specific theoretical motivation for each individual task as this will be dealt with later. Background information on the broader cultural context of task administration in Yucatan was provided in chapter 1.

Sequence of tasks

Yucatec respondents were not abundant, so all individuals were asked to perform all tasks. This necessitated an arrangement of the tasks so that they did not interfere with one another in any crucial respect. Also, the Mayans were not very sophisticated with this type of task, so to maximize their performance most were given some preliminary experience with a similar task series (see discussion and table 1 in chapter 1), and the individual tasks in this series were ordered from easiest to most difficult.

The two crucial task parameters being manipulated across the picture series (shown in table 2 in chapter 1) were whether the response depended on memory or not and whether the response was verbal or not (where nonverbal responses involved a selection among the alternate pictures). The rationale for ordering the tasks with respect to these parameters was as follows. The first task required speakers to describe verbally what they saw in a picture. This task was placed first because it allowed respondents to become familiar with the stimuli in the context of a readily understandable procedure. The second task followed the pattern of the first, but was more difficult in that it required that the verbal report be done without the picture in view, that is, on the basis of short-term memory. Only original pictures were used in these two tasks.

The third task involved judging which of the five associated alternate pictures was most similar to an original. It was easier than the second task in that it did not rely on memory, but was more difficult in that it required consideration and judgment among several pictures. This task also served to familiarize the respondents with the notion of alternate pictures. The fourth task involved short-term recognition memory in which each individual was asked to select an original he had seen from an array containing the original and its five alternates. This task combined the difficulty of memory and of judging among multiple pictures. The final task followed the pattern of the previous short-term memory task, but was still more difficult in that the memory period was much longer and the respondents were not forewarned on initial presentation that they would be asked to remember the pictures. However, as these were the pictures which they had described at the outset in the first task, they had already attended to them in some detail. Detail on the ordering of tasks is available in appendix B.

As indicated earlier, the desire for control was tempered by the desire to have the tasks remain interpretively valid. Occasionally, as might be expected in an exploratory study, a problem was encountered that had not been anticipated on the basis of the pilot work and the task administration was adjusted accordingly. These modifications are noted in the section where they are relevant.

Counterbalancing of stimulus presentation

Picture sets were presented in a counterbalanced design as follows. One set of three originals was used in the first task of picture description. A different set of three originals was used in the second task of picture recall. The latter set was used again with its alternates in the third task of similarity judgment. The final set of three originals along with their alternates was used in the fourth task of short-term recognition memory. For the fifth task of longer-term recognition memory, the first set of originals along with their alternates were used. (In this last case, the original described in the first task had to be selected – without seeing it a second time – from among the group of original-plus-five-alternates.) Complete information on counterbalancing of stimuli is given in appendix B.

Statistical considerations

In addition to qualitative judgments as to whether the two groups show the expected patterns of response, it is also desirable, when possible, to assess quantitatively whether the findings are reliable in statistical terms. Although the procedures for analysis and the statistics chosen vary somewhat for each task, it should be emphasized that the same men are performing in all of the tasks and that the results of the various individual tasks cannot therefore be regarded as independent from this point of view. The specific statistics reported in the following sections should be interpreted with this in mind. However, the consequences of this are not especially problematic, since our concern is to characterize the groups not the tasks, and the general hypothesis is that the factors involved in performing the tasks are *not* in fact independent. This issue will be taken up again in the general discussion of the task series.

Sample

Twelve Yucatec men and twelve US men performed each task. The general cultural background of these men was described in chapter 1. The Mayan men ranged in estimated age from 18 to 45+ years (median and rounded mean were both 29 years). (Many of these Yucatecan men, especially the older ones, did not know their exact age.) Ten of the men had at least one year of formal education and some ability to read. Exact amount of school experience is often exaggerated and, in any event, was typically uneven in quality and intermittent in nature. The US men ranged in age from 19 to 27 years (median and rounded mean were both 21 years) and were all college students. An individual listing of attributes for each person is available in appendix B.

As indicated in chapter 1, Mayan men were recruited on the basis of personal relationship with an eye toward even age distribution. They were compensated financially for participating in the tasks. Relative to the general population of Yucatan, these Mayan men are less educated, although they are representative of their village and not atypical of the rural population in Yucatan more generally. Relative to their peers in the village, these Mayan men may be somewhat more adventuresome than most since there were others who chose not to participate.

The US men were also recruited on the basis of personal relationship and were likewise compensated for participation in the tasks. The students are more educated than the general US population. It is likely that the educational difference between the two groups is more significant than the age difference. To minimize the importance of such educational factors, all tasks were designed to be relatively simple, tasks were ordered to maximize understandability as outlined just above, and all respondents were exposed to an analogous series of tasks prior to undertaking this series.

Individual tasks

Verbal description

Speakers are shown a set of original pictures and asked to describe what they see in each picture. The primary goal is to assess attention to number (i.e., one versus many) for various types of objects in verbal description.

Purposes

This task allows a controlled assessment of patterns of verbal response for three purposes. The first goal is to assess the saliency of the different target objects for the two groups by examining the *frequency of mention of the various target object types*. This is important because the objects must be noticed and mentioned before their quantity or number can be indicated. It was expected that Animals would be more salient than Implements and that the latter would, in turn, be more salient than Substances, but that the differences would not be so large as to jeopardize the comparison of attention to number. Further, it was expected that English speakers might mention more objects than Yucatec speakers because of greater familiarity with this type of task.

The second, and primary, purpose of this task is to provide a more precise comparison of the *frequency of indication of number for various object types* by Yucatec Maya and US English speakers. The aim is to see whether the language-specific patterns of pluralization reported in the previous chapter index more general patterns of attention to number actually conveyed in the two languages. The results of the present task are distinct from the linguistic analysis in chapter 2 in two respects. First, the characterizations made in the previous chapter were very global and did not show, except implicitly, how identical referential problems would be solved differently in the two languages. Normal everyday language usage only very rarely produces the sort of situation necessary for a precise comparison along these lines. This experiment provides such a systematic controlled comparison by examining Yucatec and English verbal descriptions of an identical set of stimuli. Second, since a variety of formal means for indicating number will be taken into account here, the task results provide a global estimate of the overall attention to number as a function of object type in the two languages. Thus, the analysis goes beyond an assessment of structural requirements or structural possibilities to a characterization of the informational content regarding number in the two languages. Whereas the linguistic analysis dealt with regularities in linguistic structure, the present task deals with regularities in the information conveyed in actual situations of use. Thus, the results in this experiment stand somewhere between the results of formal linguistic analysis and the results of a nonverbal behavioral assessment – and therefore they provide some insight into the patterns of attention to number characteristic of the two groups.

The third purpose of the experiment is to provide *baseline data and experience* for each group on the stimuli to be used in subsequent tasks. With this baseline data the results of subsequent experiments can be compared to the verbal performance associated with the specific stimuli rather than simply on the general patterns of number marking in the two languages. This is not only useful in testing more precisely the correlation of verbal and nonverbal behavior, but it also allows for tighter analysis of behavior patterns which may have to do with the particular stimuli. As mentioned earlier, a related advantage of placing this task first was that it allowed speakers to become familiar with the stimulus materials on a relatively simple task before proceeding to the more difficult tasks in the series.

Procedures

Informants were told that they would be shown three pictures one by one and then asked to say what they saw in the pictures. Then they were shown the first picture in the set and again asked to describe what they saw. Respondents were given as much time as needed to complete their verbal report. When the first picture was complete, the procedure was repeated for the second and then the third picture. All responses were tape recorded and transcribed. A sample English transcript produced for the stimulus item in figure 2 is given in appendix C.

The descriptions were scored in two ways. First, *mention of target objects* – Animals, Implements, and Substances – was scored either as *explicit mention* (presence of a descriptive nominal form), *implied mention* (presence of a closely related noun or verb), or *no mention*. Details of scoring procedures and the score for each speaker on each target in each picture along with detailed annotation of difficult instances are given in appendix C. *Only cases of explicit mention are analyzed here.* So that each speaker's responses would be given equal weight in characterizing group performance, each speaker's individual perform-ance was classified as to frequency of mention, with mention of two or three objects of a given type (four or more out of six for Implements) being coded as *high mention* and mention of fewer objects of a given type being coded as *low mention*.

Secondly, *indication of number* was scored for target objects that were *explicitly mentioned*. In this task, any and all overt indications of number were tallied so as to get the broadest possible index of attention to number. Overt responses were scored either as *Singular* (indication of singularity by article or numeral), as *Plural* (indication of plurality by nominal or verbal inflection, by modifier agreement, by quantitative adjective [for example, *another*], or by use of a numeral), or as *Unmarked* (no indication of number). However, covert indication of number (by reference to the distributional potential of a lexical item) was not scored. Note, therefore, that English lexical noun phrases with no overt number marking were scored as Unmarked even if number could be deduced by reference to the distributional potential of the lexical head. This convention was adopted to make the scoring more reliable and conceptually equivalent in the two languages. What is striking is that some overt sign of number was usually present somewhere in the protocols for explicitly mentioned nouns in English. Thus, altering the scoring to take into account covert indications of number in English changes the raw response rate only slightly and has absolutely no effect on the qualitative characterization of individual or group patterns of number marking. Details of the coding and scoring procedure for indication of number are available in appendix C.

The measure used in scoring *indication of number* was an index value produced by calculating for each speaker on each object type the ratio of indications of number to objects mentioned:

$$\frac{\text{number of indications of number for target X}}{\text{number of explicit mentions of target X}}$$

If speakers indicated the number of every explicitly mentioned target object of a particular kind, the index value would be 1.0 (or 100%). Throughout the scoring of both mention of objects and indication of number, the two types of Implements (containers and tools) were analyzed as a single object type and the score for each respondent adjusted accordingly. So that each speaker's responses would be given equal weight in characterizing group performance, each speaker's individual performance was classified as to frequency of indication of number. Speakers indicating number for 50% or more of their explicit mentions of a given type of target object were scored as exhibiting *high indication* of number, and speakers indicating number for less than 50% their explicit mentions were scored as exhibiting *low indication* of number. Details of scoring procedures and the index value for each speaker on each target in each picture along with detailed annotation of difficult instances are given in appendix C.

Table 20. *Mention of target objects by English and Yucatec speakers in picture description task*

Group	Animal		Implement		Substance
			Object type[a]		
English	11	>	8	≈	8
Yucatec	12	>	4	≈	6
Difference[b]	1		4		2

Values in the cells for each group indicate the number of speakers exhibiting "high mention" for each object type. "High mention" consisted of mentioning a given object type in two-thirds of the possible cases. Maximum in each cell is 12.
[a]Using data from *both* groups, Animals are reliably distinguishable from Implements ($p < .002$, $n = 9$) and Substances ($p < .001$, $n = 11$) by one-tailed sign tests.
[b]Group differences are not statistically significant by the Fisher exact test.

Results

In general, men in both groups found the task relatively easy and straightforward. Obviously, a great deal of information is available in the transcripts. In the present context, only two kinds of responses will be analyzed: frequency of mention of target objects and frequency of indication of number.

Mention of target objects.   Table 20 shows the number of speakers in each group showing high mention for each object type. Nearly all speakers in both groups exhibited high mention of Animals. About two-thirds of the English speakers exhibited high mention for the other object types – slightly more than the number of Yucatec speakers showing high mention in these cases. Despite these absolute differences, the two groups again show *similar overall patterns of mention*. The similarity of the patterns in the two groups is highlighted in the table by the use of signs of approximate equality (≈) and signs of inequality (>) between columns.

Combining the data for both Yucatec and English samples to achieve a sufficient number of cases, a one-tailed sign test for the difference in related samples between the mention of Animals and mention of the other two object types is statistically reliable: $p < .002$ ($n = 9$) for the Animal–Substance difference and $p < .001$ ($n = 11$) for the Animal–Implement difference. The Implement–Substance difference $p < .891$ ($n = 6$) is not reliable. English speakers mention more of the non-Animal object types than do the Yucatec speakers, but these absolute differences between the two groups are not statistically reliable by a one-tailed Fisher test.

Indication of number.   Table 21 shows the number of speakers in each group exhibiting high indication of number for each object type. As expected, all English speakers indicate number for Animals and Implements and only about half of them indicate number for Substances. Yucatec speakers indicate number somewhat less overall, but about two-thirds of them indicate number for Animates as compared with only about one-third for Implements and Substances. Thus the two groups of speakers show *contrasting overall patterns of indication of number*. Again, the general structure of the patterns in the two groups is highlighted in the table by the use of signs of approximate equality ($\approx$) and signs of inequality ($>$) between columns.

For the English sample, the difference in indication of number for Implements and Substances is statistically reliable in a sign test for differences in related samples: $p < .016$ ($n = 6$). For the Yucatec sample, the difference in indication of number for Animals and Implements approaches statistical reliability in a sign test for differences in related samples: $p < .062$ ($n = 7$). In addition to these differences in the treatment of object types within the two languages, there were also reliable differences between the two languages in the indication of number for Animals ($p < .05$, $n = 12$, one-tailed Fisher test) and for Implements ($p < .005$, $n = 12$, one-tailed Fisher test). The difference for Substances was not significant. By far the most dramatic difference between groups, as expected, is in the Implement category.

Discussion

Mention of objects by type.   Speakers in both groups tended to mention Animals more than either Implements or Substances. This suggests that Animals are more salient in the pictures. Since the Animals were counterbalanced in various ways and not larger in size or more centrally placed in the picture than other object types, this may be regarded as a reflection of the greater general saliency of this object type. In fact, across the two groups, the difference between Animals and other object types was statistically reliable. Further, since both groups showed the same basic underlying pattern, this unevenness in saliency should not pose a problem in comparing the two groups. Although the response level of the English speakers was, as expected, somewhat higher than that of the Yucatec speakers, the difference between response levels was not significant. However, objects of all three types were mentioned with

Table 21. *Indication of number for target objects by English and Yucatec speakers in picture description task*

Group	Object Type					
	Animal		Implement		Substance	
English	12	≈	12	>[†]	6	
Yucatec	8	>*	4	≈	4	
Difference	4**		8[††]		2	

Values in the cells for each group indicate the number of speakers exhibiting "high indication of number" for each object type. "High indication of number" consisted of indicating number for at least half of the target objects of a given type explicitly mentioned.
*$p < .062$ ($n = 7$) one-tailed sign test. **$p < .05$ ($n = 12$) one-tailed Fisher test.
[†]$p < .016$ ($n = 6$) one-tailed sign test. [††]$p < .005$ ($n = 12$) one-tailed Fisher test.

sufficient frequency to provide a basis for evaluating differences in indication of number.

Indications of number.   The results with this referential task involving a controlled set of stimuli fit perfectly with the general predictions made on the basis of more global linguistic analyses. English speakers indicate number in one way or another for almost every Animal and Implement explicitly mentioned – just as we would expect from the structural analysis of number marking patterns in English. They indicate the number of the Substance type objects significantly less frequently – again, in conformity with their number marking patterns. By contrast, Yucatec speakers indicate number much less often overall. Further, within this lower level of specification, Yucatec speakers indicate number relatively frequently for the Animals, and significantly less frequently for the Implements and Substances.

We may summarize the contrast of *patterns* – ignoring the differing *levels* of response – by saying that both groups indicate number relatively often for Animals, both groups indicate number relatively infrequently for Substances, and the two groups diverge in their treatment of Implements. If we hypothesize that the three object types exhibit an ordered salience with respect to likelihood of number marking in languages, then we can regard the deflections of the number marking pattern for Implements towards the level for Animals in English and towards the level for Substances in Yucatec as deflections towards linguistically specific configurations. Locating such a difference in pattern is more useful than locating a simple difference in overall response level because the latter is much more likely to be accounted for by reference to general Yucatec difficulties with the materials or tasks.

The pattern of results corroborates in a specific, controlled test the expectations based on general linguistic analysis and it shows how similar referents would be construed. Further, the task shows that the differences in linguistic structure in the form of regular patterns of morphosyntactic marking index clear differences in informational content with respect to number as a function of object type in these two languages. Although the structural analysis and the information content analysis are closely related – this is precisely the point the experiment seeks to verify – they are by no means the same regularity. For example, Yucatec speakers use plural marking relatively infrequently, but apply it most often to Type A noun phrases when it is used. In the present task, most of the number marking in Yucatec did not take the form of plural marking at all, but these speakers nonetheless showed a strong inclination to indicate the number of the Animal targets in other ways such as adjectival modification. Thus the plural marking pattern indexes, and may even give rise to, the general pattern, but it is not equivalent to it.

Provision of baseline data and experience.   This pattern of findings shows how the linguistic patterns identified through traditional methods of analysis operate with this specific set of stimuli in a controlled referential situation. This provides a baseline against which to interpret the subsequent experiments. For example, one can rule out that a certain object type was not sufficiently salient or one can judge whether a certain pattern of responses might be due to differences in pattern of mention rather than differences in patterns of number marking.

It is worth noting, finally, that, although the values of the scores for the indication of number are independent of the scores for mention of objects, the reliability of the scores as estimates of actual rates is not. The less often an object is mentioned, the fewer instances there are to test for the indication of number and the more unreliable is the estimate. This means that the estimates for indication of number for Substance type objects must be regarded as somewhat less reliable than those for Implements which in turn are less reliable than those for Animals. Likewise, estimates for Yucatec indication of number must be regarded as less reliable than English scores in general.

Verbal recall

Speakers are shown a set of original pictures one at a time. After viewing each picture, they are asked to wait an interval of time. Then they are asked to describe what they saw in the picture. The primary goal is to assess recall of number (i.e., one versus many) for various types of objects as reflected in verbal report.

Purposes

Like the description task, this task explores the frequency of mention and the frequency of indication of number for the various target object types. However, this task modifies the procedure of the previous task by asking speakers to report on picture content indirectly from memory rather than directly from the pictures themselves. This alteration serves two purposes. First, since the data are verbal, they provide a second case of *controlled linguistic comparison* of Yucatec and English. In fact, the reports in this task should correspond more closely with everyday patterns of speaking, since it is more common for people to report in detail about things which they have previously seen, than it is for them to give an exhaustive inventory or account of something immediately visible in the environment. In particular, it is expected that elements of the pictured scenes which are described may be more fully specified from a semantic point of view on categories such as number since the picture is not co-present.

Second, since the responses depend on memory, they may give some insight into *patterns of memory* characteristic of the two groups – at least insofar as any drop in performance relative to the description task is selective rather than random. If the memory patterns in each group are selective and the patterns of selectivity correlate with the groups' characteristic language patterns, then this may indicate that these language patterns influence or play a role in memory. However, this is a difficult claim to establish with any certainty when language itself constitutes the overt response mode, since any decline in performance under the recall condition can stem either from failure to remember or from failure to report. This can be true both for the mention of an object and for indication of number: selective declines in performance paralleling language patterns may stem from decontextualized reporting strategies rather than from memory.[4] These alternatives can be operationally separated by using a nonverbal response mode, and this is one motivation for using such tasks below. However, any increase in performance under the recall condition, all other things being equal, can fairly reliably be attributed to a verbal reporting strategy.

Procedures

This task immediately followed the description task. Each speaker was shown the first picture and was told that he should look at it for one minute. At the end of that time we would wait an additional minute. This period could be filled either with silence or idle chatter at the speaker's discretion. Then the speaker was asked to tell me what he had seen in the picture – just as he had in the first task. The men were given as much time as needed to complete their verbal report. When the first picture was complete, the procedure was repeated for the second and then the third picture, repeating the instructions if necessary. All responses were tape recorded and transcribed. A sample English transcript produced for the stimulus item in figure 2 is given in appendix C.

There were some slight differences among the individuals in details of administration. These are indicated in appendix B. For example, some of the Yucatecan men were asked questions after having given their responses to ascertain whether an object had in fact been remembered but not reported. The results of these probes were so ambiguous (for example, speakers would assent to having seen things not in the picture) that the procedure was abandoned.

The descriptions were transcribed and coded in exactly the same way as in the verbal description task. Details of scoring procedures and the scores for each speaker on each target in each picture are given in appendix C.

Results

In general, men in both groups found the task relatively easy. I had some difficulty in getting the Mayan men to wait the full time period before beginning their report, but most did so after being reminded. As in the previous task, only two kinds of responses were considered: frequency of mention of target objects and frequency of indication of number. These were scored and compared in the same ways as in the verbal description task. In addition, results from the two tasks were compared.

Mention of target objects.   Table 22 shows the number of speakers in each group showing high mention for each object type. Animals are mentioned more than the other two object types and this is statistically reliable for both groups (English $p < .031$, $n = 5$, Yucatec $p < .001$, $n = 11$, one-tailed sign tests). Further, the contrast in between the two languages in the Implement category is even more pronounced and is statistically reliable ($p < .005$, $n = 12$, one-tailed Fisher test). The two groups show *similar overall patterns of mention* (highlighted in the table again by the marks of approximate equality and inequality) but the approximate equality between Implements and Substances is less clear in the Yucatec case.

Table 22. *Mention of target objects by English and Yucatec speakers in picture recall task*

	Object type		
Group	*Animal*	*Implement*	*Substance*
English	12 >*	7 ≈	5
Yucatec	11 >†	0 ≈	4
Difference	1	7**	1

Values in the cells for each group indicate the number of speakers exhibiting "high mention" for each object type. "High mention" consisted of mentioning a given object type in two-thirds of the possible cases. Maximum in each cell is 12. *$p < .031$ ($n = 5$) one-tailed sign test. **$p < .005$ ($n = 12$) one-tailed Fisher test. †$p < .001$ ($n = 11$) one-tailed sign test.

The low rate of Yucatec mention for the Implement category in this recall task was not expected. It may suggest that Implement targets are less well remembered by Yucatec speakers. By contrasting these recall data with the description data reported earlier, we can isolate the source of the difference in memory pattern. Table 23 displays the change in scores between the description task (table 19) and the recall task (table 22).

Overall, speakers mentioned slightly fewer objects in the recall condition as indicated by the negative signs associated with the numbers. English speakers' changes under the recall condition were most marked for Substances, whereas Yucatec speakers' changes under the recall condition were most marked for Implements. Thus the groups showed slightly asymmetric declines in mention. The weakening of the similarity in patterns of mention exhibited in the description task is due, then, to changes in both groups. The asymmetric decline results in a close alignment of the *absolute* mention of Animals and Substances so that the entire difference between the two groups is localized in the Implement category.

Table 23. *Change in mention of target objects between picture description and picture recall tasks*

	Object type		
Group	*Animal*	*Implement*	*Substance*
English	+1	−1	−3
Yucatec	−1	−4	−2

Table 24. *Indication of number for target objects by English and Yucatec speakers in picture recall task*

	Object type					
Group	Animal		Implement			Substance
English	12	≈	11	>**		4
Yucatec	12	>**	5	≈		2
Difference	0		6*			2

Values in the cells for each group indicate the number of speakers exhibiting "high indication of number" for each object type. "High indication of number" consisted of indicating number for at least half of the target objects of a given type explicitly mentioned.
*$p < .025$ ($n = 12$) one-tailed Fisher test. **$p < .008$ ($n = 7$) one-tailed sign test.

Indication of number.   Table 24 shows the number of speakers in each group exhibiting high indication of number for each object type. *Both the English and Yucatec patterns follow the linguistic predictions and are statistically reliable.* The patterns are highlighted in the table again by the marks of approximate equality and inequality. English speakers indicate number for the Animals and Implements but not for Substances ($p < .008$, $n = 7$, one-tailed sign test) whereas Yucatec speakers indicate number for Animals but not for Implements and Substances ($p < .008$, $n = 7$, one-tailed sign test). (Yucatec speakers do, however, indicate number slightly more often for Implements than Substances.) Further, the difference between the two groups in the Implement category is statistically reliable ($p < .025$, $n = 12$, one-tailed Fisher test).

These recall results for indication of number differ from the description results as shown in table 25. English speakers exhibit a slightly lower indication of number in the Substance category (-2 individuals or -33% relative to the description tasks). Yucatec speakers too show a slight decline in the Substance category (-2 or -50%) but, more strikingly, they also exhibit a higher indication of number in the Animal category ($+4$ or $+50\%$). This suggests that indicating number for Animals is more important when the referent is not in view. *The overall effect of these changes is to reinforce the contrasting characteristic patterns found in the description task.* However, given the lower rate of mention of Implements in this task by Yucatec speakers, the reliability of the estimate of Yucatec performance should be regarded as somewhat lower.

Table 25. *Change in indication of number of target objects between picture description and picture recall tasks*

	Object type		
Group	*Animal*	*Implement*	*Substance*
English	0	−1	−2
Yucatec	+4	+1	−2

Discussion

Mention of objects by type.   The overall level of mention in this recall condition declined somewhat less than one might expect, suggesting that the task did not tax the subjects greatly. The decline in the rate of mention was least for the Animal targets. The changes in response were confined largely to the Implement and Substance targets, with the English speakers mentioning fewer Substances, and Yucatec speakers mentioning fewer Implements. This differential pattern of decline resulted in diverging overall patterns of mention in the two languages. In particular, under the recall condition, frequency of mention of the two object types at the extremes – Animals and Substances – looked virtually identical, whereas the middle object type – Implements – showed a statistically reliable difference. This differential cannot be accounted for by reference to some common factor, but must have its origin in some difference between the two groups either in memory or in verbal report strategies. I see no linguistic basis for the pattern at present.

Indications of number.   The frequency of indication of number in this recall condition showed the same overall pattern as in the description condition. Both English and Yucatec speakers tended to indicate number somewhat less often for Substances. But the most notable difference was a substantial rise in Yucatec indication of number for Animals. Although English speakers do not show the same increase in indication of number for Animals, this may be due to a ceiling effect in the measure – the English response level was already nearly at maximum. These shifts in indication of number in the recall task (particularly the increase in the Yucatec case) may arise from the norms or requirements of out-of-context verbal report. (From a descriptive linguistic point of view, we might want to indicate that number marking is contingent on context. Certainly this makes sense when we recall that

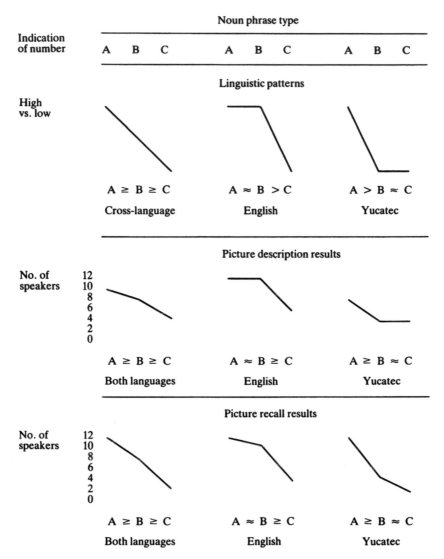

Figure 3   Comparison of patterns of number marking (pluralization) with indication of number in verbal description and verbal recall tasks. (Cf. figure 1.)

mentioning singularity is involved in establishing indefinite reference in the two languages. In the present case, however, the increase in overt number marking in the Yucatec sample was equally divided between additional Singular marking and additional Plural marking.) Because changes in performance observed under the recall condition may be due to such shifts in the context of report, it is difficult to conclude that memory *per se* is being affected. However, it is clear that the pattern of response directly follows the expectations based on the linguistic analysis, and this suggests that the potential for language effects on memory is definitely present. In fact, it is precisely the differential conventional requirements for indicating number in the two languages that one would expect to give rise to anticipatory effects on attention (description task) and memory (recall) task. Figure 3 portrays graphically the fit between the original expectations (from figure 1) based on the grammatical patterns and the observed number marking patterns in these first two tasks.

Baseline for the nonverbal tasks.   We now have strong evidence that the contrast in number marking patterns predicted on the basis of linguistic analysis does in fact hold up under controlled conditions and with the specific stimuli to be used in the remaining experiments. One unanticipated finding, however, complicates the situation and warrants special comment: the frequency of mention was not evenly distributed across object types. On the one hand, this affects the reliability of the estimates of rate of indication of number. The rate of mention, however, at the level of actual individual responses seems high enough to provide a reasonable estimate for each object type. (It is important to emphasize here that there are twice as many Implement targets on which to base the estimate for this object type since this is the point of key contrast.) On the other hand, differences in performance as a function of object type may stem from simple failure to notice the object rather than from inattention to its number. This problem is minimal in the description task, since both languages showed the same unevenness, and no difference between the two languages can be accounted for by this common pattern.

The pattern of response in the recall task, however, presents a more significant difficulty since the two languages differed in rate of mention as a function of object type. Further, the pattern of mention in this memory condition mimicked the pattern of indication of number in an important respect. The two language groups both mentioned Animals at a high rate and Substances at a low rate, but differed in their treatment of Implements. This, of course, was the crucial design feature of the original hypothesis about number marking: prediction of a common rate of response to contrasting high and low end points so as to establish that the two groups of speakers are engaged in the same task and performing similarly, coupled with a prediction of a divergent rate of response to a middle category where language-specific patterns are decisive.

Three points need to be kept in mind about this pattern of mention when weighing it as an alternative predictor of nonverbal behavior patterns. First, it only applies if attending to number requires first singling out (behaviorally "mentioning") an object. Second, it apparently only applies if the task is based on memory, since the pattern for simple verbal description in context is different and poses no special problem. Third, and most crucially, the pattern of mention is distinguishable from the pattern for indication of number in important respects (cf. tables 20 and 22) and each predicts different patterns of response. *The English number marking pattern predicts* that the rate of response (or nonresponse) for the Animal and Implement object types should be roughly equivalent (for example, both high) and different from the rate for the Substance object type. By contrast, *the English pattern of mention predicts* that the rate of response (or nonresponse) for Animal and Implement object types should differ and that Implement and Substance object types should be roughly equivalent (for example, both low). (Notice that the English pattern of mention essentially predicts a pattern of response similar to the Yucatec number marking prediction!) *The Yucatec number marking pattern predicts* that the rate of response (or nonresponse) for the Implement and Substance object types should be roughly equivalent (for example, both low) and different from the rate for the Animal object type. By contrast, *the Yucatec pattern of mention predicts* that the rate of response (or nonresponse) for Animal, Implement, and Substance object types should all differ and that, in particular, the Animal and Implement object types should have maximally opposing values (for example, one high and one low) with Substance object types somewhere in between and nearer the Implements. In short, although both frequency of mention and frequency of number marking predict a similar pattern of *contrast* between the two languages, *they predict dramatically different patterns of response within each language.* This contrast of within language predictions provides a basis for deciding which factor – mention of object or indication of number – is likely to be governing nonverbal behavior patterns that might plausibly stem from either one.

Nonverbal similarity judgment

Speakers are shown original pictures and asked to judge which of several alternate versions of each picture is most similar to its original. The alternate versions differ only in the number of some target object. The goal is to assess by nonverbal means the salience of the number of various types of objects as a basis for classification.

Purposes

The primary purpose of this task, and of the two which follow, was to provide evidence that cognitive responses in a task correlate with linguistic patterns even when language is not involved as a mode of response. Under the hypothesis of linguistic influence, these nonverbal responses should follow the distinctive qualitative patterns implied by the number marking patterns for noun phrase types in each language ($A \approx B > C$ for English, and $A > B \approx C$ for Yucatec). As mentioned earlier, a close association of nonverbal response pattern with these distinctive patterns constitutes evidence in favor of language structure having a shaping influence on cognition.

The specific task explores how changes in the number (i.e., one versus many) of the various target objects in alternate versions of a picture affects judgments about the similarity of those alternate pictures to the original. For example, does a change in the number of an Animal target in an alternate picture lead speakers to regard the picture as more different from the original than an alternate with a change in the number of an Implement target? For the results to clearly implicate specific languages as a shaping factor, the pattern of similarity judgments for each group of speakers must follow the characteristic number marking pattern in each language.

A secondary purpose of this task was to explore whether any nonverbal evidence could be found for underlying commonalities between the two groups. This involved seeing whether the differential, ordered sensitivity to changes in number of different referent types (i.e., Animals $\geq$ Implements > Substances) corresponds to the cross-linguistic likelihood of plural marking as a function of noun phrase type (i.e., $A \geq B \geq C$). The discovery of such a pattern would provide a framework within which divergent nonverbal behavior patterns could be characterized and evaluated – on analogy with the cross-linguistically based characterization of morphosyntactic patterns. Such commonalities may indicate the operation of cognitive universals in interaction with universal functional demands of speech.

A related concern was whether the groups were alike in their sensitivity to different types of changes in quantity. This was tested by including two different types of quantitative changes in the Substance target. That there might be a difference is suggested by the fact that English quantitative modifiers draw distinctions that Yucatec modifiers do not; for example, English distinguishes *many* from *much* where Yucatec uses a single form *yá'ab'*. This raised the possibility that continuous and discontinuous changes in quantity might be differently regarded by the two groups.

Procedures

An original picture (1) and its five alternates (2 with a change in the number of the Animal target; 3 and 4 with changes in the number of the Implement targets; 5 and 6 with a change in the quantity of the Substance target) were placed on a table immediately in front of each respondent in one or two horizontal rows. Each man was told that each picture differed from the original in some way. They were then allowed to examine the pictures until the differences were all recognized. Any differences which were not noticed were pointed out so that *each respondent was aware of all five differences*.

Then the men were asked to indicate which of the five was "most like" the original. Originally, the task had been designed to get a rank ordering of the five alternates as to degree of similarity to the original so as to be able to compare in detail the importance of changes in number of various object types for each speaker and each group. However, many Yucatec speakers had difficulty with this task – apparently because there were simply too many alternatives to weigh simultaneously. Men who had difficulty were encouraged either by repetition of the instructions or by suggestions as to how to break the task down into more manageable units. For example, some found it helpful to focus on selecting two or three "like" the original and then weigh which of these in turn was "most like" the original. Many found it easier to begin by making judgments of which pictures were "most different" rather than most similar. In the end it was possible to get decisions for each Yucatecan man as to which pictures were "most like" and "second most like" the original, but it was not possible to get a complete ordering of the entire set of five alternates. (This failure led to a somewhat awkward scoring situation which is described below.) US informants were asked to give an ordering of the entire set of five alternates and performed this task without much difficulty, although the exact placement of individual pictures was not always easy.

The principal measure, then, was each man's selection of the alternate that he regarded as "most like" the original. Since each man saw three picture sets, he had three opportunities to select such an alternate. The modal value of these three scores was used to characterize each individual's response pattern as favoring Animals (2), Implements (3 and 4), or Substances (5 and 6). One tie was broken by looking at the respondent's second choices. This scoring procedure may underestimate the absolute tendency to choose Animals since there is only one picture representing a change in this type of target whereas there are two pictures representing changes in the other two categories. But the scoring procedure has no substantial effect on the group comparison both

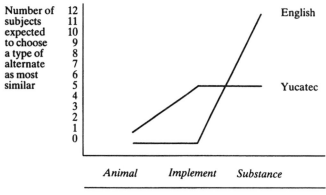

Number of subjects expected to choose a type of alternate as most similar

12
11
10
9
8
7
6
5
4
3
2
1
0

English

Yucatec

Animal   *Implement*   *Substance*

Target object type changed in alternate

Figure 4   Comparison of language-based predictions for English and Yucatec speakers on similarity judgment task. (Specific numbers in this figure are for illustration only.)

because the two groups were scored identically and because alternate **2** was infrequently chosen.

The language-based prediction for the English speakers was that they would regard changes in the number of an Animal or Implement target as significant, but would not regard changes in the number of a Substance target as noteworthy. Thus, English speakers should choose an alternate with a change in the Substance target as "most like" the original – that is, alternates **5** or **6**. The language-based prediction for the Yucatec speakers was that they would regard changes in the number of an Animal target as significant, but would not regard changes in the number of an Implement or Substance target as noteworthy. Thus, Yucatec speakers should choose an alternate with a change in one of the latter types of object as "most like" the original – that is, alternates **3, 4, 5,** or **6**. Further, Yucatec speakers should distribute their selections *evenly* between the Implement and Substance alternates. This prediction can be further refined if we take into account that Yucatec speakers do not obligatorily signal number even for Animal targets. We can adjust the prediction to incorporate a low level of response for the alternates containing a change of Animal target. Figure 4 displays the predicted patterns graphically. (Numbers are for illustration only – it is the pattern that is crucial.)

Results

The observed patterns of results shown in table 26 match the linguistically based expectations (even down to the occasional Yucatec speaker

Table 26. *Speaker evaluation of the importance of changes in number of target objects of different types on similarity judgment task: first choices only*

Group[a]	Object type changed in number				
	Animal *(2)*		*Implement* *(3 and 4)*		*Substance* *(5 and 6)*
English	0	≈	0	<	12
Yucatec	1	<	5	≈	6

Numbers in cells indicate the number of subjects selecting a given picture alternate (i.e., **2**, **3**, **4**, **5**, or **6**) with a change of a given object type as "most like the original." Number of speakers in each group was 12. The marks of inequality (<) and approximate equality (≈) do not indicate statistical evaluations. However, see note *a*.
[a]English versus Yucatec: $p < .01$ ($n = 12$), one-tailed Fisher test for combined Animals and Implements versus Substances.

preferring selections showing a change in number of a target Animal). The patterns are highlighted as in previous tables by the use of the marks of approximate equality (≈) and inequality (<). Further, the English and Yucatec results are reliably different from one another ($p < .01$, $n = 12$, one-tailed Fisher test for Animals and Implements versus Substances). (The expected frequency for the Animal's category is too small to permit using a chi square test across all three categories. If a chi square value is calculated anyway, it produces the same value as the Fisher test.) It is worth noting that this statistical difference emerges no matter which of several alternative scoring methods is used.

Each speaker also made a selection of a picture second "most like" the original. Including these scores in the analysis should weaken the group differences since it will increase the opportunities for overlap between the two groups. Including two responses in the analysis should reveal certain commonalities of response between the two groups and present the opportunity to confirm the postulated cross-linguistic ordering of the target types. The desirable outcome with respect to this hypothesis would be that the two groups converge with one another, but continue to differ from a pattern expectable by chance.

Unfortunately, because not all the alternate pictures are assigned a value by each speaker and because second choices are necessarily contingent on first choices, it is very difficult to create a simple composite measure for each speaker so that such a convergence can be evaluated statistically. Nonetheless, the data were examined qualitatively using

Table 27. *Speaker evaluation of the importance of changes in number of target objects of different types on similarity judgment task: first and second choices combined*

Group	Object type changed in number					
	Animal (2)		*Implement* (3 and 4)		*Substance* (5 and 6)	
	Summed modal scores[a]					
English	0	≈	6	<	18	
Yucatec	1	<	10	≈	13	
	Summed raw scores[b]					
English	2	<	21	<	49	
Yucatec	9	<	27	<	36	

Numbers in cells indicate the number of selections of a given picture alternate (i.e., **2, 3, 4, 5,** or **6**) with a change of a given object type as "most like original." The marks of inequality (<) and approximate equality (≈) do not indicate statistical evaluations.
[a]This scoring method is described in the text. Total number of selections for each group under this scoring method was 24.
[b]This scoring method is described in the text. Total number of selections for each group under this scoring method was 72.

two very crude measures to see if the expected pattern emerged. The first measure simply scored the second choices for a modal value just as if they were a new set of first choices. This new set of modal values was then added to the first (simulating 24 independent responses) to create a composite picture of each group. The second measure summed all the first and second choices for each group independently, that is, each subject's three first choices and three second choices were directly added as if there were 72 independent responses for each group. Table 27 shows the results of these two measures.

The first measure shows the expected rank order in rate of selection among the three categories: Animal ≤ Implement ≤ Substance. However, the language-specific patterns are still clearly visible and have been highlighted as in previous tables by the use of the marks of approximate equality (≈) and inequality (<). This is a startling finding. If two out of three of a respondent's first choices fall into a given category, it is much more difficult to have the two out of three of the second choices fall in that category because fewer of the relevant alternates are available. The second measure shows the expected rank ordering somewhat more clearly, but also shows noticeable deviations toward the language-specific patterns. Under either measure it is clear that the men are not responding randomly. We can conclude, conservatively, that when we take second choices into account there is some evidence for a common, nonrandom pattern of response across the two groups, but that language-specific patterns are still clear. It bears repeating, however, that these are crude measures and that there is no simple way with the present materials to generate a valid index of individual performance or to show that these particular group patterns are statistically reliable.

The comparison of rate of selection of alternate **5** versus alternate **6**, which was designed to contrast sensitivity to different types of changes in quantity, did not yield interesting differences in overall pattern. Comparing absolute number of selections of a given type, both groups selected alternate **6** as most like the original more often than they selected alternate **5**. This suggests that both groups regard the introduction or deletion of an additional object as more noteworthy than an increase or decrease in the size of an existing object. Although the English speakers selected alternate **6** more often than did the Yucatec speakers (23 as opposed to 16 times), they did so in slightly smaller proportion (i.e., in ratio to choices of alternate **5**), that is, contrary to expectation, it was the English speakers who treated the two alternates as most similar.

Discussion

For first choices in this similarity judgment task *the patterns of response follow the language-based expectations for each group.* English speakers regarded alternates containing changes in the number of Substance targets to be most like the originals, and treated changes in the number of both Animals and Implements as significant. Yucatec speakers regarded alternates containing changes in either the number of Substance targets or Implement targets to be most like the originals, and treated only changes in the number of Animals as significant. Notice in particular that *each individual saw all the changes in number, so the results cannot be a function of failure to notice the relevant target objects or the changes effected on them.* Notice further that the responses were nonverbal in nature so that *the results cannot be due to immediate verbal reporting conventions but must reflect a more general cognitive disposition.*

As indicated above, the original goal of the experiment was to have all the alternates ordered by each group so that both similarities and differences in judgment could be assessed. The second choices made by each subject were all that remained of this aspect of the design. If we aggregate both first and second choices so that group differences are attenuated, we see that *there is some evidence of a common underlying ordering of the importance of number in the targets: Animal ≥ Implement ≥ Substance*. It is reasonable to take this as preliminary evidence of an underlying, cross-linguistic similarity in saliency of the various changes in number as a function of object type and to conceptualize the cognitive response patterns of the two groups as deflections of this pattern in language-specific ways. The comparison of alternates 5 and 6 also suggests that the two groups of speakers are regarding the target objects in similar ways at a perceptual level. These various commonalities accentuate the significance of the group differences paralleling number marking patterns, since they suggest that in other respects the two groups are performing similarly.

Several possible problems with the analysis of these data require further comment. First, a considerable amount of information has been lost by the grouping together of pictures 3 with 4 and 5 with 6 and this could possibly affect the results. However, if the analysis is redone with a five-way analysis, that is, treating each picture alternate independently, the results still follow the predictions and the two groups still differ from one another reliably. Further information has been lost by reducing each person's three responses to a single modal value. By a more detailed analysis it can be established that *relative to his group* each individual's response to each picture was independent of (i.e., not directly predictable from) his previous response. Using this fact to justify an overall reanalysis using all three individual scores, a separate statistical analysis produces essentially the same results on both the three- and five-way analyses. In brief, the various category groupings and scoring assumptions used in the present analysis do not seem to have resulted in any fundamental loss of information or to have concealed conflicting patterns in the data.

A second possible problem, given the small sample size, is that the prediction for the Yucatec group is close to the pattern of response that might be expected by chance, that is, it might be contended that Yucatec speakers were responding randomly. This problem arose because the design of the experiment was altered to accommodate to the fact that Yucatec speakers were not able to give a comprehensive ordering of the entire picture set. Two factors suggest that the Yucatec speakers' responses were not random. First, most of Yucatec men clearly and overtly engaged in the task – weighing alternative pictures, discarding some as clearly different and keeping others as candidates for being most like the original. Second, if we take account of the maximum amount of information in the data by using the five-way analysis of each individual's three choices (regarded, on the basis of the analysis mentioned above, as being independent within each group), then the data are, in fact, clearly distinct from the pattern expected by chance ($p < .01$ for both groups on a two-tailed chi square test). These two factors together suggest that the Yucatec pattern is not the result of random selection among the alternates. Ultimately, however, given the reality of the Yucatec speakers inability to order the complete set of pictures, the experiment needs to be redesigned to produce a more distinctive prediction.

A third possible problem involves the inclusion of alternate 6 which was structurally somewhat different from the other four alternates. It is possible that the inclusion of this item skewed the data in favor of the Substance category, since English speakers favored this choice more in absolute terms than did Yucatec speakers. This seems unlikely since, in fact, the English speakers actually selected alternates 5 and 6 in a closer ratio than did Yucatec speakers. This possibility of skewing can be further evaluated by looking at the distribution of second choices since these choices suggest what picture the speakers would have chosen if alternate 6 had not been available. For individuals choosing alternate 6 as most like the original, roughly half in each group selected alternate 5 as their second choice. Reanalyzed and properly rescaled (to accommodate to the elimination of one alternate), the data show English speakers choosing Substances at nearly two times the rate expected by chance (with Animals and Implements being selected well below chance levels) and Yucatec speakers choosing Implements and Substances at slightly above chance levels (with Animals being selected below chance level). This reanalysis suggests that even if alternate 6 had been removed from the task, the basic pattern of results would have been essentially the same. Confirmation of this will have to await further research.

Nonverbal recognition memory I (shorter term)

Speakers are shown pictures and after a short interval of time they are asked to select the original picture that they saw from among an array of pictures that contains the original and some similar alternate pictures. The goal is to assess nonverbally the salience of the number of various types of objects in short-term recognition memory.

Purposes

The general purpose of this task was the same as of the previous similarity judgment task, namely, to provide evidence that responses in a cognitive task correlate with linguistic patterns even when language is not overtly involved as a response mode.

In the present case, the task involved short-term recognition memory. The specific goal was to see whether changes in the number (i.e., one versus many) of various kinds of objects affected the likelihood that a picture would be mistaken for the original when a selection based on memory had to be made. For language to be clearly implicated as a shaping factor, the responses of the two groups must follow the pattern of number marking in the languages – differing where the languages differ and agreeing where the languages agree.

Procedures

This task immediately followed the similarity judgment task, so the men were familiar with the notion of an original picture and several alternates. Each man was told that he would be shown a picture and that they were to look at it for one minute. Then they would have to wait one minute without seeing the picture as they had done with the earlier (recall) task. And then they would be asked to select the picture they had seen from an array of pictures. One picture in the array would be the one they had seen and the others would differ in some respect.

Then the first picture was displayed for one minute. During the subsequent one minute waiting period, while the informant watched, the original was added to the stack of alternates and the set shuffled, so he could be quite certain that the original was included in the set of six pictures. Either silence or idle chatter about a topic other than the pictures was permitted during the waiting period. Then he was presented with the set of pictures from which to select the original that he had seen. Respondents were given as much time as they needed for their selection.

For the Yucatec sample, the six pictures were initially laid out on the table in an array two deep and three wide. However, the men were allowed to move the pictures around as they wished: some chose to put aside those they were sure were not originals, and some chose to make some two-by-two comparisons when they could not see any difference between two pictures.

For the English speaker the presentation procedure was modified to minimize the possibility of deducing the identity of the original by careful comparison of the six pictures.[5] The pictures were handed to the men in a stack and they were asked to make a judgment as to whether each picture in turn was the original or not. If more than one picture was chosen as an original, men were allowed to make a second (or, rarely, a third) pass through these pictures (again arrayed in a stack), until they had made a decision. Although it was clear that some English speakers still tried to use deductive strategies, most did not and those who did so were hampered by having to rely on memory. For both groups, notes were kept on their comments and on the pictures which presented difficulties. For the English sample, the judgments made for each pass through the stack were recorded. For purposes of comparison of the two groups, only the results of the first pass by English informants were used so as to minimize the influence of any use of deductive strategies.

Not all responses to this task provide an equivalent amount of data regarding the hypothesis. Although the ratio of correct to incorrect selections gives information about general memory skills, and perhaps about the overall sensitivity to quantitative changes in objects, patterns in the error data were much more illuminating with respect to differences in attention to the number of various object types. If an individual selects the original picture, we learn little about his differential memory for the number of various kinds of objects. Only the erroneous selection of an alternate provides insight into what differences were not noticed originally or were not significant enough to be remembered. An alternative design which makes all data informative in this way involves omitting the original picture from the final set of alternatives to choose from. This approach was rejected because it either involved deception (which was rejected on ethical grounds) or it involved trying to instruct Yucatec speakers to make a judgment on the basis of memory as to which picture was "most like" the one seen earlier (which was rejected as too complicated a procedure to convey to Yucatec speakers and therefore likely to go seriously awry).

As it turned out, the recognition task was quite difficult for both groups of speakers and there were in fact plenty of errors. Many individuals were unable to identify the original picture in the array, although they were usually able to narrow the field of candidates and this field usually included the original. Each response then consists of an individual's set of candidates for each of three trials. Given the difficulty of the task and the related likelihood of random error it was desirable to preserve as much information in the scoring as possible. To accomplish this a composite score was constructed for each man which gave equal weight to his three recognition opportunities and equal weight to the various specific choices (which could consist of between one and six pictures and might or might not include the original) made in each opportunity.

A weighted index was constructed for each individual showing how many *correct selections* he made relative to his total set of selections. For correctly selecting the original and only the original from the array of alternatives, a speaker was assigned six points. If he could not distinguish between the original and one other alternate, three points were assigned to the original and three to the alternate. If an original and two alternates were selected, then each received two points, and so forth for all the possibilities. If the original was not chosen, the points were distributed evenly among the alternates selected and zero points were given to the original. Since each participant made three such selections, a total of 18 points was possible for each person. The total score for each man was therefore divided by 18 to give an index value ranging from zero to one. Summing index values across the twelve men in each group then provided an index of the proportion of correct responses for the group as a whole. Notice that each respondent and each of his three responses are equally represented in the final result under this procedure.

Finally, a similar set of weighted values was constructed to provide an index of each respondent's *pattern of errors*, that is, which of the alternates he tended to confuse with the original. Since the *rate* of error differed slightly for the two groups, these values were calculated on the error data alone, thereby equating the estimates for the two samples. Further, the scoring procedure equalized the likelihood of falling into each of the three target object categories by chance.

Results

As indicated above, the task was difficult for most of the men in both groups and, in most cases, rather than being able to make a single choice, respondents were only able to narrow the field. Two sets of results are important: whether the two groups were correct equally often and what alternate pictures generated the most errors.

Proportion of correct choices.   First, the proportion of correct choices for each group was examined. Using the index value for correct selections just described we find that the two groups performed very similarly: about 30% of the selections of both groups were of the original. The exact figures are shown in table 28. Thus, *the two groups do not differ in terms of their relative probability of choosing the original.* This is important because differences in error pattern between the two groups cannot, therefore, be accounted for by reference to poorer levels of accuracy on the part of Yucatec speakers. This rough equivalence also suggests that the alteration of the procedure for the English sample produced a task of equivalent difficulty. The value expected by chance is also included in table 28 and number of correct responses for both groups exceeds this level.

Distribution of errors.   The second concern is with distribution of errors for the two groups among the various alternates. For each

Table 28. *Weighted distribution of correct and incorrect responses on short-term recognition memory task*

Group	Weighted responses	
	Correct (*= Original*)	*Incorrect* (*= Alternates*)
	%	%
English	33	67
Yucatec	29	71
Chance	17	83

Procedure for calculating the weighted score is given in the text.

speaker's three recognition opportunities a weighted value was constructed indexing the alternate pictures that were confused with the original. These values were directly summed to produce an estimate of the pattern of errors characteristic of each group. (This produces a very conservative measure since it treats all errors alike.) Table 29 shows the distribution which emerges from this direct summing of scores.

As is clear from the table, English speakers often mistake alternates that contain a change in the number of a Substance for the original. They mistake alternates that show changes in the number of an Implement or an Animal for the original much less often. Yucatec speakers, by contrast, mistake alternates that contain a change in the number of an Implement or a Substance for the original about equally often, and

Table 29. *Weighted distribution of errors due to changes in number of target objects on short-term recognition memory task*

Group	Object type changed in number[a]				
	Animal (*2*)		*Implement* (*3 and 4*)		*Substance* (*5 and 6*)
	%		%		%
English	8	$\approx$	24	$<$	68
Yucatec	17	$<$	44	$\approx$	39

[a]Numbers in cells indicate percentage of selections of a given picture alternate (i.e., **2, 3, 4, 5**, or **6**) with a change of a given object type as "most like original." The marks of inequality ($<$) and approximate equality ($\approx$) do not indicate statistical evaluations.

mistake alternates that contain a change in the number of an Animal for the original only occasionally. In short *there is a very good match with the predictions* especially when we consider the much greater difficulty of the task.

Discussion

When the results are compared with the predictions (see figure 4), *the patterns of response generally follow the language-based expectations for each group.* The one possible exception is that English speakers select alternates **3** and **4** more than might be expected but given the difficulty of the task, such a development is not surprising. Further, since the responses were nonverbal in nature, the *results cannot be due to immediate verbal reporting conventions, but must reflect a more general indirect influence of those conventions on other cognitive behaviors.*

Although the percentages reported here are not equivalent to individual scores, the pattern of results is quite close to those found in the similarity judgment task (cf. tables 26 and 27). Figure 5 shows graphically the parallelism between the original expectations (from figure 4) and the patterns of results observed in these two tasks. This match with the results on the previous task is important in helping to weaken some possible alternative interpretations of the results. First, to the extent the patterns are due to genuine *failure to remember*, then it is possible that this failure stems from not noticing the target object in the first place. If this failure to notice is a function of target object type rather than number then this might also account for the results. Thus, the possible differential salience of the target objects themselves which was encountered earlier in the verbal tasks re-emerges as a possible alternative here. However, the close correspondence of the results here with the similarity judgment task (where notice of the targets was not an issue) suggests that the operative factor in memory is, in fact, the number of the targets and not the notice (or nonverbal "mention") of the targets in the first place. Further evidence in this direction comes from comparing the results in this task with those arising from the pattern of mention in the verbal recall task. If the latter provides an index of actual memory patterns, then the prediction would be that English speakers would choose Implements and Substances at roughly equal rates – which they do not – and that Yucatec speakers would choose Implements at by far the highest rate – which they do not. The best conclusion in this context is that actual forgetting of the various object types distributes evenly across the alternatives and does not produce the observed language characteristic patterns.

Second, not all of the difficulty respondents had with this task can be

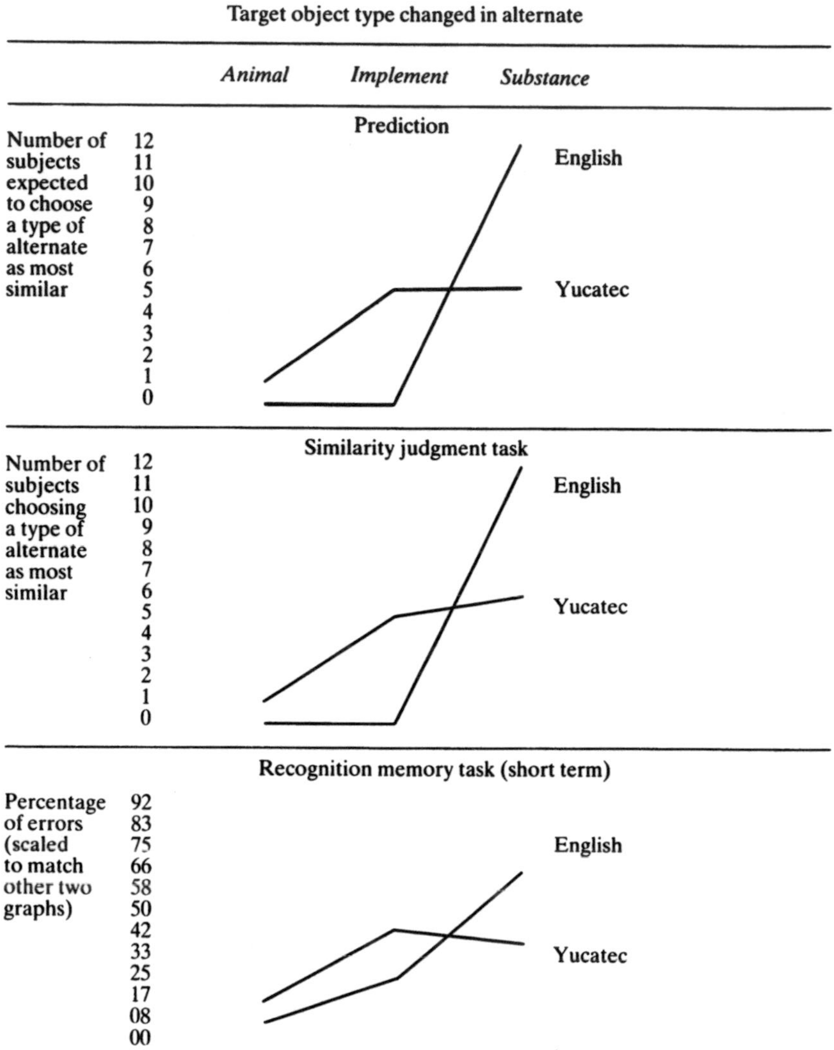

Target object type changed in alternate

	Animal	*Implement*	*Substance*

Prediction

Number of 12
subjects 11
expected 10
to choose 9
a type of 8
alternate 7
as most 6
similar 5
4
3
2
1
0

English

Yucatec

Similarity judgment task

Number of 12
subjects 11
choosing 10
a type of 9
alternate 8
as most 7
similar 6
5
4
3
2
1
0

English

Yucatec

Recognition memory task (short term)

Percentage 92
of errors 83
(scaled 75
to match 66
other two 58
graphs) 50
42
33
25
17
08
00

English

Yucatec

Figure 5   Comparison of predicted response patterns with results on similarity judgment and short-term recognition memory task. (Cf. figure 4.)

assigned to memory for number. Although in some cases speakers saw differences but could not recall the relevant details of the original picture, in other cases *speakers could not see any difference* among some of the pictures or, at least, would not make any further effort to discover them. Thus, for both groups, their responses are not purely memory-based, but also depend to some extent on ability to recognize differences in the alternative pictures from what they remember. If patterns of noticing differences was a function of target object type then this might also account for the results. It is in this context that parallels between these results and those in the similarity judgment task again become important: since in the previous task the issue of locating the differences was eliminated, the parallel here suggests that change in number is again the operative factor. Further evidence along these lines can be derived from the verbal description task. In that task speakers showed some preference for noticing Animal targets – but this cannot account for the difference between groups in the Implement and Substance categories. The best conclusion in this context is that difficulties in noticing any given feature of an alternate picture distributes sufficiently evenly so as to not produce the characteristic group patterns.

The three problems mentioned in regard to the similarity judgment task also emerge with the present task. Various recalculations of the results using various groupings of the data again appear to have no significant impact on the findings. The problem of the closeness of the Yucatec prediction to chance is also present once more. Again, informal observation confirms that speakers in both groups engaged in the task and were not performing randomly in this respect. In this task, however, the strategy used earlier, of trying to show that each individual's three responses were independent, did not seem worth pursuing since each response was itself a complex weighted score. However, the similarity in the number of *correct* choices between the two groups, and the general *match of error patterns* with the patterns in the previous task, suggest that speakers were not responding randomly.

Finally, questions can be raised again about the inclusion of alternate **6** affecting the estimate for the Substance category. For example, English speakers erred most often by selecting alternate **6**, whereas Yucatec speakers, by contrast, erred more often by choosing alternate **5** than **6**. However, unlike the previous experiment, it was possible to select alternate **6** and another alternate at the same time, so the net impact of including this alternate among the choices was much less. Further, it is possible to recalculate the pattern of errors omitting alternate **6**. When this is done, the pattern of results is much the same. In particular, for the English group where the impact should be greatest, the basic rank order among the three target types is maintained, although the absolute difference between the Implement and Substance categories for this group is somewhat weaker (36% and 51% respectively). This suggests that even if alternate **6** had been removed from the task, the basic pattern of results would have been similar.

Nonverbal recognition memory II (longer term)

Speakers are shown a set of pictures, and after a relatively long interval of time they are asked to select each of these original pictures from an array of pictures containing the original and some similar alternate pictures. The goal is to assess nonverbally the salience of the number of various types of objects in longer-term recognition memory.

Purposes

The general purpose of this task was the same as that in the previous recognition memory task. However, by introducing a longer interval between initial presentation and eventual opportunity for recognition, and by not forewarning speakers that they would later be asked to identify the picture, the task was effectively made much more difficult. The specific goal was to see whether under these more demanding conditions the relation of response pattern to language would become more pronounced. Such an influence should affect both the absolute number of correct responses and the relative patterns of errors for each language group. Further, the conditions of this task, such as lack of forewarning and substantial time interval before having to recognize, were felt to approximate some everyday conditions of remembering more closely than the previous task.

Procedures

Following the shorter-term recognition memory task, the men were told that once more they were going to be asked to locate an original picture from among a set of alternates. However, this time, the pictures they were to locate would be those they had described when the series of tasks was begun. Speakers were then shown the first set of six pictures they were to choose from. As in the previous task, the method of actual presentation differed for the two groups – Yucatec speakers saw all six pictures laid out at once in an array and English speakers saw the pictures one at a time in a stack (with the possibility of multiple passes being made). Again, notes were kept on incidental comments and sequence of elimination for both groups. The amount of time between the beginning of the task series and the beginning of this recognition procedure was between one and one-and-a-half hours.

Table 30. *Weighted distribution of correct and incorrect responses on long-term recognition memory task*

	Weighted responses	
Group	Correct (=Original)	Incorrect (=Alternates)
	%	%
English	37	63
Yucatec	17	83
Chance	17	83

Procedure for calculating the weighted score given in the text.

Results

Most of the men found the task difficult. Many men in both groups expressed dismay when they realized the nature of the task. Many in both groups were unable to identify the original picture in the array, although they were able to narrow the field of candidates and this field usually included the original. So again, most responses consisted of multiple choices for each of the three trials presenting the same problems for analysis as the previous task. Again, two sets of results were important: whether the two groups were correct equally often and what alternate pictures generated the most errors.

Proportion of correct choices.   In terms of the weighted index value for correct selections, the two groups performed somewhat differently. As shown in table 30, English speakers were more accurate than Yucatec speakers in locating the original. Further, Yucatec speakers did no better than would be expected by chance.

Distribution of errors.   The second concern was with the distribution of errors for the two groups. The same weighted measure of error distribution used in the previous task was employed here. Table 31 shows the distribution of errors and marks the patterns of approximate equality and inequality in the usual way.

Again, English speakers often mistake alternates that contain a change in the number of a Substance for the original. They mistake alternates that show a change in the number of an Implement for the original much less often. Yucatec speakers, by contrast, mistake alternates that contain

Table 31. *Weighted distribution of errors due to changes in number of target objects on long-term recognition memory task*

Group	Object type changed in number				
	Animal (2)		Implement (3 and 4)		Substance (5 and 6)
	%		%		%
English	19	≈	23	<	58
Yucatec	28	≈	34	≈	38

Numbers in cells indicate percentage of selections of a given picture alternate (i.e., **2**, **3**, **4**, **5**, or **6**) with a change of a given object type as "most like original." The marks of inequality (<) and approximate equality (≈) do not indicate statistical evaluations.

a change in the number of an Implement or a Substance for the original about equally often. Thus, there is a clear contrast between the two groups and it generally matches the predictions. However, both groups also mistakenly choose alternates that contain a change in the number of an Animal more often than expected. This posed no problem for the English sample since their overall pattern remains quite distinctive; however, the rate of selection of this alternate in the Yucatec case brought the distribution closely into alignment with chance. Coupled with the close match to chance on overall selection of the original (cf. table 30), this pattern suggests that the Yucatec group may indeed be responding randomly.

Discussion

English speakers showed no decline in recognition accuracy and their pattern of errors continued to follow the language-based prediction, although the pattern was attenuated relative to the previous task. Yucatec speakers showed a similar attenuation in characteristic error pattern relative to the previous task. But since the Yucatec prediction was less distinctive in the first place, this attenuation of error pattern brought the results very close to what would be expected from a random pattern of response. Yucatec speakers also showed a decline in overall accuracy that suggests a random pattern of response. They may be performing the task with such a low level of success that any potential linguistic influences simply cannot emerge. Thus, although the observed

Yucatec error pattern is not inconsistent with the prediction, it is best to regard the Yucatec results in this task as unreliable.

The interval between seeing the original and seeking it among the alternate pictures was considerably longer than in the short term task, and this feature of the task design provides the most straightforward explanation for the changes in performance. In particular, we can conclude that Yucatec responses probably reflect a general decline in memory for the original pictures. However, two other factors that might have affected the results warrant mention. First, the original pictures were described rather than simply observed. This should, if anything, improve performance relative to the hypothesis and so is unlikely to account for the attenuation in both groups. Second, at the time the original pictures were seen, respondents did not know that they would have to remember them, so anticipatory (or voluntary) memory strategies were probably not employed. This would make it likely that any recognition patterns in the long-term task have to do with passive or semi-automatic memory rather than with the active use of specialized strategies. If this difference between the two conditions played a role in the change in response patterns, then it would suggest that language patterns play a more important role in strategic memory than in semi-automatic memory. This possibility can only be evaluated by administering a long-term task explicitly construed as a memory task from the outset.

As noted in the previous discussion, it is unlikely that differences in pattern between the groups are due to differential memory for the various types of objects themselves or difficulty detecting differences in the various pictures. Nor is it likely that the methods of scoring and grouping themselves produce the results. The preference for alternate **6** re-emerges again for English speakers but it is not nearly as strong. The distribution of errors remains essentially unchanged under a reanalysis omitting consideration of alternate **6**.

Summary of picture task series

The results in these exploratory studies of psychological functioning show the divergent patterns in English and Yucatec speakers predicted by the analyses of grammatical patterns in the two languages. The central expectation was that language-specific patterns of grammatical number marking (i.e., one versus many) would correspond to more general cognitive dispositions toward number among speakers of the languages. Although each individual task taken alone shows some ambiguities, the overall configuration of results across the five tasks indicates a basic and reliable difference between the two groups. Any alternative hypothesis for the results of any one task must provide an equally cogent account of the specific patterning of the data across the entire task series.

The first two tasks were designed to show that the different patterns of grammatical number marking actually corresponded to global differences in the signaling of information content related to number (i.e., one versus many). Both the verbal description and verbal recall tasks showed English speakers providing more information about number overall. Further, within each language, information about number varied as a function of object type in the expected ways: English speakers provided relatively more information about the number of Animals and Implements than of Substances, and Yucatec speakers provided relatively more information about the number of Animals than of Implements and Substances. These results are distinct from the grammatical analysis *per se* in an important respect: the grammatical analysis dealt with formal patterns of marking (for example, what nouns take a plural, whether plural marking is facultative or obligatory, etc.) whereas the experimental analysis deals with what informational content is actually conveyed in referentially equivalent contexts. The two analyses are clearly related – this is the claim established by these two experiments – but they are not identical or necessarily related. Quite diverse grammatical structures can achieve similar referential results and, conceivably, convey equivalent informational content. But, in the present case, the grammatical patterns actually index the existence of different levels of informativeness about number in the two languages.

One pattern that emerged in these first two tasks was a differential rate of mention for the three object types – in particular, a higher rate of mention of Animal targets. The differential pattern of mention is more or less the same under both conditions and for both language groups, suggesting that it is independent of memory and of the patterns of each specific language. This regularity had no direct effect on the assessment of indication of number, since the scoring of the latter was operationally independent of the rate of mention. However, this differential rate might provide an alternative account of the differences observed in the nonverbal tasks. For example, the greater verbal mention of Animals might lead to a higher rate of memory for them, and a higher rate of recognition of them, quite independently of number.

Three arguments can be made against such an interpretation in the present context. First, a *common* pattern of mention cannot account for language-specific *differences* in nonverbal performance. Second, and relatedly, the number marking results provide a closer approximation of the pattern of nonverbal results than do the rate of mention results even if we use the most contrastive, most distinctive, patterns of mention as our predictor (i.e., verbal recall). Third, this hypothesis cannot efficiently account for the similarity judgment data because all the differences among pictures were indicated to the respondents – that is, differences in saliency were minimized and differences in number foregrounded.

At a deeper level, however, there is probably some relationship between the rate of mention of certain types of objects in speech and the likelihood of number being indicated in speech. For example, the appearance of a second token of an object typically mentioned can be effectively and efficiently signaled by pluralization or change in numeral modification. This would represent another way in which definiteness and number marking intersect, and this relationship deserves further exploration. Relevant issues would include the extent to which different objects get independently mentioned (versus incorporated into verbs), the scope of number marking, and cultural differences in the importance of various kinds of objects.

The nonverbal tasks showed that the group differences in attention to number in speech also emerged in other response modes. Both in the similarity judgment and in the recognition memory tasks, English speakers showed a greater sensitivity to changes in the number of an Animal or Implement than to changes in the number of a Substance, whereas Yucatec speakers showed a greater sensitivity to changes in the number of an Animal than to changes in the number of an Implement or a Substance. These patterns were clearest in the similarity judgment task which involved informants' considered judgments and interpretations. The patterns were also clear in the short-term recognition task despite the more difficult nature of the task. The results in the long-term recognition task were less distinctive but still consistent with expectations. In short, the nonverbal response patterns follow the linguistically based predictions on these controlled tasks and suggest that at least some language patterns can play a shaping role in thought.

Evidence was also sought for underlying commonalities in nonverbal response pattern in the two groups against which the group differences could be more precisely defined. In the similarity judgment task some evidence of common underlying pattern of salience for the various object types was found when the analysis included second choices, but even here the basic pattern of differences between the two groups was still visible. The inclusion of third choices probably would have been sufficient to lead to a complete convergence of the two group patterns. In the short-term recognition task the point of commonality was in the overall rate of error. It was against this common rate of error that the differences in the distribution of errors became meaningful.

Finally, in all three nonverbal tasks specific attention was paid to differences in sensitivity to continuous (alternate **6**) and discontinuous (alternate **5**) changes in quantity. The results here were equivocal. As expected, English speakers always saw an increase in size as less significant than a change in number of discrete tokens of an object. Yucatec speakers showed this same pattern (even more strongly) in the similarity judgment task, but showed no evidence of preference for either type of change in the two recognition memory tasks. This may suggest that Yucatec speakers had difficulty recognizing the size changes, but judged them in the same way as English speakers when they were in fact recognized. Further work will be required to see whether English speakers in fact show greater sensitivity to changes in quantity due to adding or deleting tokens. (In the present context, it is important to emphasize that reanalyses in each case showed that the inclusion of alternate **6** did not, in itself, generate the overall pattern of results.)

One weakness of these nonverbal tasks was that the prediction for the Yucatec group was close to what might be expected by chance. This was a particular problem in these exploratory studies because of the small sample size and the loss of data incurred by various alterations in the original design. Since this difficulty will always arise where the language prediction indicates a relatively undifferentiated response pattern, it will be important in future work to design new tasks that contain highly characteristic predictions or some ancillary means of checking for participant engagement. In the present case, arguments have already been given to support the contention that Yucatec speakers were not responding randomly. An important additional piece of evidence comes from surveying the overall configuration of results. The same basic pattern of Yucatec results was visible across all three nonverbal tasks – even in the highly attenuated long-term condition. Coupled with the corresponding consistency of the English response patterns, the configuration of results strongly implicates grammatical structure as the operative factor influencing cognitive activity in these tasks.

Object task

Speakers are asked to make judgments of similarity among triads of objects. The goal is to assess the relative cognitive salience of shape versus material as bases for classification in the two language groups.

Purposes

The main purpose of this task was to seek further nonverbal evidence for an effect of language-specific morphosyntactic patterns on cognition.

The specific focus was on whether differences in the fundamental lexical structure of the heads of Type B noun phrases influence the interpretation of the objects typically referred to by those lexical items. English lexical nouns of the relevant type differentially signal referents on the basis of characteristic unit or shape, whereas Yucatec lexical nouns differentially signal referents on the basis of characteristic material. The contrast between the two languages indicates that there is nothing in the objects themselves that requires adopting one basis of reference rather than the other. The differences stem from the general morphosyntactic treatment of referents of that type in the two languages.

The hypothesis was that these differences in the structure of linguistic reference would lead speakers to interpret and classify objects in terms of shape or material depending on which signaling pattern their language favored. Specifically, English speakers should prefer to classify objects on the basis of shape, and Yucatec speakers should prefer to classify objects on the basis of material. These preferences should lead to completely opposite classificatory strategies when shape and material are the only two classification options. Likewise, characteristic differences should appear when shape and material are each contrasted with other possible dimensions of classification.

Procedures

Sample

Ten Mayan men and thirteen US men performed the task. Four of the Mayan men and twelve of the US men had also performed the picture task series. (Further individual details are given in appendix B.)

Stimuli

Stimuli consisted of seventeen sets of three inanimate physical objects each. Each "object" consisted of a single item (either a physically contiguous whole or some fragment of such a whole) or of a discrete collection of items (either systematically arranged or simply gathered together). All were everyday items familiar to the Maya and, for the most part, to the US speakers as well.

Each triad contained one *original object* and two *alternate objects*. For example, one triad consisted of a cardboard box as the original, a plastic box as the first alternate, and a piece of cardboard as the second alternate. Each object can be regarded as consisting of a collection of attributes which can potentially function as features of reference. Each

Table 32. *Triad sets used to directly contrast shape and material as bases of classification*

Triad number	Triad objects		
	Original	*Shape alternate*	*Material alternate*
1.1	sheet of paper	sheet of plastic	book
1.2	strip of cloth	strip of paper	shirt
1.3	stick of wood	candle stick	block of wood
1.4	cardboard box	plastic box	piece of cardboard
1.5	length of vine	length of string	woven ring of vine
1.6	grains of corn	beans	tortilla
1.7	half gourd	half calabash	gourd with opening
1.8	ceramic bowl	metal bowl[a]	ceramic plate

[a]A plastic bowl was used with the English sample.

triad was constructed around two such attributes so that each original object had both attributes and each alternate contained one of the two attributes but not the other. In the example just given, the two attributes characterizing the original were the box shape and the cardboard material. The first alternate was similar in that it had a box shape but was made of a different material (i.e., plastic). The second alternate was similar in that it was made of cardboard but it had a different shape (i.e., a flat square). Other attributes were kept constant within each set to the degree possible with everyday objects. The potential importance of any such other attributes was minimized by the use of an array of different triads.

The relative salience of several different attributes was addressed in the set of seventeen triads. The first eight triads, listed in table 32, involved *direct contrasts* of shape and material as bases of classification. The original was an object with a distinct shape and material composition. The shape alternate was an object that had the same shape as the original object. The material alternate was an object composed of the same material as the original object. The goal of the experiment was to see which of these alternates was regarded as "most like" the original. These triads were the most difficult to construct, but were also the most directly relevant to the hypothesis that the two groups of speakers should differ in their preference for shape or material as a basis of classification. These first eight triad sets were counterbalanced as to the linguistic labels that might be applied to them, for example, whether they were typically referred to by the same terms or not, by Mayan or Spanish lexical forms, etc.

Table 33. *Triad sets used to indirectly contrast shape and material as bases of classification*

Triad number	Original	First alternate	Second alternate
		Triad objects	
		Shape and Material	Number
2.1	three chiles	two chiles	three beans
2.2	one AA battery	two AA batteries	one pen
2.3	two nails	three nails	two spoons
		Material	Number
3.1	three corn kernels	lump of corn dough	three beans
3.2	three small paper squares	one large paper square	three small cardboard squares
3.3	three small rocks	one large rock	three small shards
		Configuration	Number
4.1	circle of six beans	circle of five beans	line of six beans
4.2	triangle of three coins	triangle of five coins	line of three coins
4.3	circle of eight small rocks	circle of six small rocks	double row of eight small rocks

The next nine triads, listed in table 33, involved *indirect contrasts* of shape and material by contrasting these attributes with number as a basis of classification. An original object in some distinct number was contrasted in each case with an alternate consisting of either the same object in a different number or a different object with the same number. The key goal of the experiment again was to see which of these alternates was regarded as "most like" the original.

"Number" here does not refer to the distinction of one versus many explored in the picture task, but to specific numerical values such as two, three, four, etc. Number was pitted against material (set 3), shape or configuration (set 4), or both (set 2). When number was pitted against material in set 3, the shapes of the new items in the number alternate were kept somewhat similar to the items in the original so that number would be the salient difference and not an incidental change in shape. When the number was pitted against shape as in set 4, the material composition of the new items in the number alternate were kept identical so that number would be the salient difference and not an incidental change in material. Finally, the change in shape in set 4 was actually at a different level than in the other triads as it involved a configuration among individual items rather than the shape of a contiguous whole.

Administration

For all of the English men and four of the Yucatec men, the triads task was administered immediately after the completion of the picture task series. The remaining Yucatec men executed the task at the end of sessions devoted to recording traditional Yucatec stories. Each man sat at a table and was shown the seventeen triads one at a time. For the first few triads, the original was indicated and the respondent was asked whether the original was "more like this one [pointing to first alternate] or this one [pointing to second alternate]." Instructions were repeated and/or modified slightly for the few men who didn't understand the initial question. After the first few triads, most men continued through the series without further instruction.

Results

Direct contrast of shape and material

The first eight triads directly contrasted shape and material as bases of classification. Each speaker made eight selections. Speakers who chose the shape alternate four or more times were scored as preferring to classify on the basis of shape; the remaining speakers were scored as preferring to classify on the basis of material. This procedure effectively assigned ties to the group classifying on the basis of shape. The English–Yucatec differences which are reported below remain statistically reliable even if the ties are assigned to the other group.

Table 34 shows the pattern of selection across these eight triads for the two groups of speakers. The results differ from chance (English $p < .005$, $n = 13$, and Yucatec $p < .025$, $n = 10$, one-tailed binomial tests) and are strongly in the expected direction: the English speakers prefer to classify on the basis of shape and the Yucatec speakers on the basis of material. The group difference is also reliable ($p < .0007$, one-tailed Fisher exact test). Table 35 shows how the eight triads were viewed by the two groups. Yucatec speakers resolve all of the triads by reference to material ($p < .0018$, $n = 8$, one-tailed binomial test where P = .50 for shape, Q = .50 for material), whereas English speakers resolve most of the triads by reference to shape ($p < .145$, $n = 8$, one-tailed binomial test

Table 34. *English and Yucatec preferences for shape or material as a basis for object classification in a triads task: direct contrasts*

	Preference	
Group***	Shape	Material
English**	12	1
Yucatec*	2	8

*Yucatec versus Chance: $p < .025$, $n = 10$, one-tailed binomial test ($P = .56$ for shape, $Q = .44$ for material).
**English versus Chance: $p < .005$, $n = 13$, one-tailed binomial test ($P = .56$ for shape, $Q = .44$ for material).
***English versus Yucatec: $p < .0007$, one-tailed Fisher exact.

where $P = .55$ for shape, $Q = .45$ for material). Again, the group difference is reliable ($p < .0035$, one-tailed Fisher exact test).

Indirect contrast of shape and material

Further information on preference for shape versus material as a basis for classification is available from the nine triads that indirectly contrast shape and material. The general strategy – somewhat exploratory in nature – was to pit shape and material each against a third alternative attribute: number. (It may be useful to consult the list of triads in table 33 at this point.) The first set of indirect triads (items 2.1, 2.2, and 2.3) provided a control case by isolating number as a basis of classification. In these triads the original was to be matched either with an alternate that was exactly the same in shape and material as the original object (but different in number) or with an alternate that was the same in number (but different in shape and material). Thus *both* shape- and material-based matches should lead to selecting the first alternate. Selection of the second alternate can only be based on number and thus provides an indication of how strong number alone is as a basis of classification. If the English speakers classified on the basis of shape and the Yucatec speakers classified on the basis of substance, they should perform alike on this triad set. The results show precisely this pattern as shown in the first two rows of table 36. Both groups' selections differ from chance (English $p < .001$, $n = 13$, and Yucatec $p < .055$, $n = 10$, one-tailed binomial tests), but not from each other. This suggests that neither group regards number alone as a strong basis for classification.

Table 35. *English and Yucatec construal of direct contrast triad sets by shape or material*

	Preference	
Group*	*Shape*	*Material*
English	6	2
Yucatec**	0	8

*English versus Yucatec: $p < .0035$, one-tailed Fisher exact.
**Yucatec versus Chance: $p < .0018$, $n = 8$, one-tailed binomial test ($P = .50$ for shape, $Q = .50$ for material).

The second set of indirect triads (items 3.1, 3.2, and 3.3) pitted material against number. In these triads the original was to be matched either with an alternate that was exactly the same in material as the original object (but different in number) or with an alternate that was the same in number (but different in material). To the extent possible, shape was held constant. The language-based expectation was that Yucatec speakers would select the material alternate. By contrast English speakers should select the number alternate relatively often since the shape attribute favored by their language was not available. The results are shown in the middle two rows of table 36. Yucatec speakers' selections fit the prediction – they classify on the basis of material ($p < .055$, $n = 10$, one-tailed binomial test). English speakers do not choose either alternate at better than a chance rate but show some tendency to favor material over number. This suggests that both groups regard material as a stronger basis for classification than number but that Yucatec speakers favor it more than do English speakers.

The third set of indirect triads (items 4.1, 4.2, and 4.3) pitted configurational shape against number. In these triads the original was to be matched either with an alternate that was exactly the same in shape configuration as the original object (but different in number) or with an alternate that was the same in number (but different in shape configuration). Material was held constant. The language-based expectation was that English speakers would select the configuration or shape alternate. By contrast Yucatec speakers should select the number alternate relatively often since the material feature favored by their language was not available. The results shown in the last two rows of table 36 fit the prediction. English speakers reliably favor shape configuration over number ($p < .001$, $n = 13$, one-tailed binomial test) and Yucatec speakers favor number over shape configuration ($p < .055$, $n = 10$, one-tailed

Table 36. *English and Yucatec preferences for shape or material as a basis for object classification in a triads task: indirect contrasts involving number*

| | Preference | |
| | First | Second |
Group	alternate	alternate
	Shape and Material	Number
English**	13	0
Yucatec*	8	2
	Material	Number
English	9	4
Yucatec*	8	2
	Configuration	Number
English**/***	13	0
Yucatec*	2	8

*Yucatec versus Chance: $p < .055$, $n = 10$, one-tailed binomial test.
**English versus Chance: $p < .001$, $n = 13$, one-tailed binomial test.
***English versus Yucatec: $p < .00009$, one-tailed Fisher exact.

binomial test). The groups also differ reliably from each other ($p < .00009$, one-tailed Fisher exact text).

Two of the three indirect contrasts follow the expectation based on the language analysis and the third does not directly contradict it since the English results do not differ from chance. These results have been brought together graphically, along with the direct contrast results, in figure 6 to show more clearly the overall pattern of the responses. The direct contrast results have been plotted twice – once to the left with material on top and once to the right with shape on top – so as to indicate the continuity of each group's response pattern. Whenever material is available as an option, 80% of Yucatec speakers prefer it as a basis of classification; given a choice between shape and number alone, they choose number by the same proportion. Whenever shape is available as an option, 90% to 100% of English speakers prefer it as a basis of classification; given a choice between material and number alone, some English speakers shift to number, although the reversal is not so dramatic as with the Yucatec speakers given a choice between shape and number. In short, evidence for English speakers favoring shape and Yucatec speakers favoring material shows up across all the various triad types.

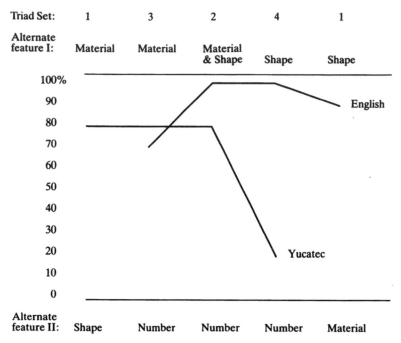

Triad Set: 1   3   2   4   1

Alternate
feature I: Material   Material   Material   Shape   Shape
                                        & Shape

Figure 6   Percentage of English and Yucatec speakers preferring shape,
material, and number as bases of classification in various triad combinations

Discussion

The results of the triad task generally show the predicted patterns.
Yucatec speakers show a strong tendency to group objects on the basis of
common material composition, and English speakers show a strong
tendency to group objects on the basis of common shape. The response
patterns are distinct for the two language groups and clearly are not
random. These patterns suggest strongly that the underlying lexical
structures associated with the overt number marking patterns in the two
languages have an influence on the nonverbal interpretation of objects.

This experiment also foregrounds a number of important issues raised
in the course of the earlier discussions. First, it indicates the complexity
of possible linguistic effects on cognition. It was emphasized earlier that
in the analysis of number marking no firm line could be drawn between
lexical and syntactic facts. The results of this classification task suggest
that the grammatical contribution to lexical reference can affect the
interpretation of the referents of those lexical items. And the task
suggests that a covert lexical structure – which, from one point of view,

underlies and accounts for the overt differences in number marking patterns – can have direct effects on cognition. Although this triads task and the picture task series reported earlier look quite different both in procedures and in content, they deal in fact with two aspects of a single, integrated morphosyntactic configuration in each language. Since each experiment isolates only a single element of the configuration for examination, multiple studies are necessary to assess the full impact of the linguistic differences.

Second, the triads task achieves several desirable methodological goals, but at some cost. It uses actual objects rather than pictorial representations. This eliminates difficulties due to the mode of representation (cf. appendix A). The task also successfully isolates a series of specific contrasts and thus provides for exceptionally well controlled comparison. Both of these features represent advantages over the more complex picture tasks. What is forfeited relative to these earlier tasks, however, is the embeddedness of referents in some context more closely simulating everyday conditions. It remains to be seen how widespread this pattern of favoring shape or material (form or substance) might be, both in other situations simulating everyday conditions or with other kinds of referents (for example, animates).

Informal observation suggests that the interpretive pattern may be operative outside of this experimental context. To take a particularly striking case, new objects introduced into the local Mayan context from the Mexican national culture are often referred to with lexical items indicating their material composition. Some of these have become quite general (for example, cardboard boxes are referred to with Spanish *cartón* 'cardboard' rather than *caja* 'box'). Others are clearly *ad hoc* individual creations (for example, one man wanting to borrow my kerosene lamp referred to it as *'a-gas* 'your gas [kerosene]'). There are other suggestive patterns in the culture beyond these simple linguistic clues, but a major ethnographic investigation would be necessary to establish distinctive contrasting patterns in the two cultures given the tremendous number of cultural differences. Perhaps the more important point in the present context is that one would not even consider looking for such differences without the evidence that linguistic patterns correlate with other behaviors. (Recall in this regard Hoijer's concerns that much of cultural comparison is based too heavily on superficial contrasts.)

Third, the shape versus material (or form versus substance) opposition has a special historical significance. It has emerged in one way or another in virtually every empirical study of the linguistic relativity issue outside of the color tradition. It played a central role in the empirical work of Whorf, Lee, Mathiot, Friedrich, Brown, Maclay, and Carroll and

Casagrande, and emerged as a secondary issue in the work of Hoijer and Bloom. This concentration of interest on the form–substance opposition offers an opportunity to compare directly the approach taken here with these earlier approaches. For example, under the present interpretation, languages which have numeral classifiers indicating shape are conceived of as having a fundamental orientation toward substance in their lexical structure or at least in those lexical items for which the classifiers are applicable. Therefore the existence in a language of overt *forms* indicating shape (for example, the numeral classifiers) does not necessarily indicate special attentiveness to shape, as most earlier studies have argued, but rather may indicate a basic underlying orientation toward substance. Further, English and other languages with extensive obligatory pluralization are conceived of here as showing a relative emphasis on shape or form in much of their lexical structure dealing with objects. Thus English speakers can be expected to show exactly the relative preference for form-based classifications that Casagrande found long ago. Claims for a general English preference for form should perhaps be tempered, however, by the recognition that Maclay found that material was preferred over form as basis of classification for all three groups he studied: English, Navaho, and Pueblo.

Unfortunately, little information about English preference for shape or material as a basis for classification is available in the psychological literature. The problem is that the possibility that individuals might classify on the basis of material or substance has not traditionally been explored by psychologists, perhaps because it does not strike us – as speakers of English and other European languages – as a meaningful possibility. Not surprisingly, the few psychological studies which have considered this issue have been those concerned solely with the developmental acquisition of the count/mass distinction in English (for example, Gordon, 1985; Soja, Carey, and Spelke, 1985; Soja, 1987).

Although not part of the original design of the present study, certain ancillary data suggest that the differential sorting pattern reported here is a reliable phenomenon. In presenting these results to academic audiences, speakers of languages with numeral classifiers frequently mention that the substance-based alternatives seem more correct to them. Although some English speakers find the substance-based choices inconceivable, many can see and understand the alternative. But even so, they tend not to choose it. In a subsequent study (Lucy, 1990) where these triads were presented to a group of college-aged students in a classroom context, I found that 81% of monolingual English speakers preferred form choices ($n = 27$). Given other differences in the manner of administration, this is fairly close to the 92% rate reported in the present study. Only 40% of the bilingual students – mostly speakers of Asian languages – preferred form choices ($n = 10$). The sample was evenly divided between men and women so it was possible to establish that there were no sex differences in task performance for either group. After performing the task, these students were asked to indicate the basis for each of their selections; analysis of these responses showed that form and substance predominated as the basis for the selection, but that function/use, consistency/flexibility, size, and color were also invoked. Finally, pilot research with Yucatec- and English-speaking children (Lucy, 1989; Lucy and Gaskins, 1989) indicates that preschool-aged children from both groups prefer form as a basis of classification, but that around age eight Mayan children begin to show the characteristic adult preference for substance. By age eleven this preference is firmly in place. Importantly, this developmental study included female Yucatecan children, the older of whom showed a pattern of substance-based sorting identical with that found for adult Yucatecan men. In short, the behavioral patterns reported in the present study appear to be robust.

General discussion

It is important to emphasize some of the limits of the present findings and approach. First, both sets of tasks were exploratory – although in somewhat different respects – and this fact in itself dictates a certain amount of caution in interpretation. The picture task series was exploratory in the sense that it was carefully designed to examine a wide range of possible issues (only some of which have been reported here). Because a wide net was cast, it was still possible to get useful results even when certain aspects of the original design had to be abandoned *en route*. Nonetheless, these alterations in design may have had unintended effects and the findings need further verification. (It is clear now, with the advantage of hindsight, how more precise procedures could be designed.) The triads task was, by contrast, very loosely designed for a quite different reason: I initially found it difficult to believe that the Maya would actually sort on the basis of material even though this was clearly the implication of their number marking pattern. This response pattern deserves to be more systematically examined in further research.

Second, all experimental work is inherently problematic. One can never be sure to what extent the results stem from some unnoticed feature of the design itself rather than from some general disposition in the respondents. Even when task performance proves to be fairly reliable under many different conditions, its relation to everyday behavior remains problematic. A separate series of observational or ethnographic

F*

studies must be undertaken to establish the general validity and cultural significance of performance on these controlled tasks.

Finally, all the problems inherent in an experimental approach are compounded in the cross-cultural context. To take only the most obvious factor in the present case, most of the adaptations in procedures that were made with the picture tasks were made because of difficulties the original design produced for the Yucatecan men. These Mayan men clearly faced a much different assessment situation than did the US men. The Yucatec speakers were less thorough in the verbal description and recall tasks, were unable to rank order the full array of alternate pictures, were unable to work with the larger array of eleven alternates in the recognition tasks, did not spontaneously employ deductive strategies in the recognition tasks, and did not remember the pictures as accurately in the long term condition. Although the various modifications of the task procedures may have succeeded in allowing a fair contrast of the two groups with respect to the specific hypothesis at hand, from another point of view, the very need for the modifications is even more significant. The various Yucatec difficulties indicate another order of cognitive differences that must be better understood if the present results are to be properly interpreted.

Despite all of the above problems, however, the fact remains that the results of the cognitive assessment were consistently in line with expectations based on the general linguistic analysis. In general the two groups were in accord in their treatment of Animal and Substance referent types but differed in their responses to Implement referent types. Differences were observed both in the fundamental interpretation of the Implement referent types as shapes or materials, and in the salience of their number in various depicted contexts. These differences in the treatment of Implements showed up in tasks testing predictions derived from both overt and covert grammatical patterns, in tasks requiring diverse cognitive activities such as attention, classification, similarity judgment, and memory, in tasks involving both verbal and nonverbal response modes, and in tasks using both object and picture stimuli. Any alternative account of the results will have to account equally well for the overall pattern of results across a diversity of tasks and not just one result in an individual experiment. In short, it seems safe to conclude that there is good preliminary evidence that diverse language forms bear some relationship to characteristic cognitive responses in speakers.

4. Conclusions

Principal achievements

Language diversity and thought presented a critical analysis of previous empirical research on the linguistic relativity hypothesis and sketched the general theoretical and methodological parameters of an improved approach. The present volume operationalized this approach by developing a specific study comparing nominal number marking in Yucatec Maya and American English. Thus, the study can be evaluated both in terms of its success in meeting the theoretical and methodological goals, and in terms of the significance of the particular substantive findings.

Theoretical and methodological advances

The approach advocated here emphasizes that research on the hypothesis must be based on a comparative analysis of two or more languages, that differences between the languages should be used to generate hypotheses about possible nonlinguistic behavioral consequences, and that these hypotheses should be tested by careful comparative assessment of the individual behavior of speakers of the various languages. Further, it has been argued that such research will proceed most effectively at present if both the linguistic comparison and the language–cognition linkage are anchored in terms of linguistically defined referential categories.

Meeting the theoretical and methodological goals

The linguistic analysis in the present study focused on differences in pervasive morphosyntactic structuring of reference. Since the analysis looked widely within the grammar of each language, it was possible to see overall patterns and to discover relationships not anticipated at the outset (for example, the interaction of plural marking with unit marking). By selecting categories which had clear referential value, it was possible to anchor the linguistic comparisons in a meaningful way and to develop cognitive comparisons with respect to the same referential ground. By framing the analysis comparatively from the beginning, it was possible to contrast the two groups within a framework of broader cross-linguistic regularities and thereby formulate a neutral characterization of the differences in language pattern, that is, a characterization that did not privilege English language categories or conceptions of reality as more correct, accurate, developed, or complex.

Because the analysis began with a language difference and developed cognitive tasks on this basis, it was possible to formulate a linguistically relevant cognitive hypothesis from the outset (for example, treating number not as "counting" but as "one versus many," dividing referents into language-relevant categories, etc.). Further, the neutral linguistic characterization helped to assure a neutral cognitive prediction – a prediction of characteristic differences rather than a prediction of superior and inferior levels of performance. Neither group's cognitive *pattern* can in any meaningful sense be called "better" than the other. This is especially clear in the object-triads task. And any positive evaluation of the greater English accuracy with number would only reflect the English sense that accuracy in taking account of number in everyday behavior is important – more important, for example, than indicating the variability of the relevant units of countable referents. Any such evaluation would have to be balanced by a serious assessment of the cognitive implications of the relatively unelaborated system of English articles in comparison to the rich array of options available in Yucatec – an issue which has not been explored here.

The study also achieved the goal of demonstrating correlations between the characteristic structuring of reference in each language and the behavior of individual speakers on controlled tasks. In particular, it appears that the scope of pluralization and certain regularities in fundamental lexical structure predict the ways individual speakers will categorize and remember objects and their attributes. Because the assessment procedures employed familiar materials and relatively simple tasks, these controlled assessments of individual behavior should provide a reasonably valid index of habitual behavior in everyday contexts. Ideally, with time, it will be possible to supplement such controlled assessments with ethnographic evidence, and to link individual behavior with institutional structures and cultural beliefs. The use of familiar materials and simple tasks also made the cross-cultural comparison itself more meaningful since the modes of cognition that were assessed were minimally dependent on specialized cultural routines. Finally, although the experiments were designed primarily to provide controlled contrasts on crucial points of linguistic contrast, they were also structured so as to provide internal checks on the reliability of the comparison (for example, by including items where identical performance was expected) and to highlight qualitative differences (for example, by focusing on patterns of response rather than on absolute levels of response).

Much remains to be done in developing cognitive assessment procedures which not only adequately represent everyday situations, but also inspire confidence as to their suitability for widely different sample populations. However, to be fruitful, future work will, I believe, have to be formulated within a general methodological framework similar to the one developed here. That is, the larger claim being made is that the general structure of the approach advocated and illustrated here provides an effective one for investigating the significance of linguistic diversity for individual functioning – quite aside from the success or failure of any particular substantive analysis, hypothesis, or procedure. And crucial elements of the approach, such as formulating the research question comparatively from the outset, deserve to be employed generally in cross-cultural investigations of psychological functioning.

Contrast with earlier approaches

The current study draws heavily, if selectively, on earlier empirical work on the hypothesis. Despite this debt, however, the general structure of the empirical study contrasts markedly with that of previous research. The distinctive aspects of the present approach can be foregrounded by contrasting it with that of the color research tradition which has dominated earlier work.

This study begins with a comparison of the morphosyntactic structuring of reference rather than with a characterization of the referential range of a few lexical items in a single language. Where the color tradition initially attempted to build from the analysis of one language (the "intralinguistic" design), the present study begins comparatively. No matter how deeply one examines a single language, one cannot hope thereby to discover radically different structurings of reference. Where the color tradition dealt with lexical items severed from their grammatical roots (it doesn't matter, for example, whether the terms are verbs or adjectives or both), the present approach regards the "content" of lexical items as derived in part from the overall structure of reference in a language. (The requirement that color terms be "monolexemic" appears to be a move in this direction, but one which has never been justified theoretically or empirically. What is the relation between what gets lexicalized in a language and its overall structure of reference?) Where the color tradition took reality as a nonlinguistic given and asked how a language reflected this reality (or, at best, how diverse languages partition the "given" differently), the present study treats the characterization of reality itself as problematic and tries to build an informed calibration or characterization of reality on the basis of observed cross-linguistic regularities in the structures of reference. The proper characterization of the domain of study is itself at stake from the outset, rather than presupposed. From the point of view taken here, development of a grounded metalanguage for adequately characterizing the cross-linguistic fact constitutes the central research problem. When concern with grammatical structure is joined with concern for common referential function, the approach effectively begins to deal with structural–functional regularities – not with structural parallels alone (for example, similarities in formal marking) or functional parallels alone (for example, similarities in referential values). The heart of the relativity hypothesis lies precisely in this patterned interplay of structure and function.

This study also aims at identifying patterns of habitual individual conceptual thought. To this end, the emphasis is on contrasting qualitative cognitive patterns, rather than absolute accuracy of "encoding." Where the color tradition dealt with simple, artificial arrays of stimuli, the present study uses complex, naturalistically interpretable stimuli calibrated or characterized by reference to comparatively generated categories. Where most of the research in the color tradition focused on a single assessment task, the present study shows that a general cognitive disposition emerges across tasks and materials. Where the color tradition simply assessed perceptual confusions and linked them to language differences, the present study also attempts to explain such confusions in terms of fundamental differences in the conceptual interpretation of the very nature of objects.

Broader implications and significance

That the present study meets its own goals should be no surprise. It is important therefore to stress again exactly why those goals have been set up and, therefore, what the broader significance of meeting them is. The idea of a linguistic relativity is extremely controversial. For some it represents a threat to the very possibility of reasoned inquiry, whereas for others it represents a defense against the self-evident power of certain unpleasant ideas. It is widely debated and even more widely alluded to throughout the scholarly literature in the human disciplines. And even a cursory survey of this literature would reveal how much of the contemporary thinking hinges on its acceptance or rejection. Yet, insofar as one even imagines that such an important phenomenon might actually exist, there is a striking lack of research on it. The detailed analysis in *Language diversity and thought* should not obscure the fact that the number of studies reviewed is very small and that only a handful of these even come close to addressing the issue empirically. One can assert the truth or falsity of the relativity hypothesis pretty much at will without having to deal with any body of evidence – one way or the other.

The first and most essential aim here, therefore, has been to make the hypothesis investigable. So doing requires that both the hypothesis and the nature of good evidence be made precise. In achieving this precision, the hypothesis has been confined to rather narrow quarters and this will undoubtedly disappoint many. But the spirit of the effort here is similar to Geertz's (1973, p. 4) efforts to cut the culture concept down to size so as to insure its continued theoretical importance. The narrowing of focus, the insistence on precision, the requirement that certain formal conditions of evidence be met – all have been undertaken to give the hypothesis body and life.

Some advocates have produced sweeping and provocative formulations where relativity is assigned great significance and almost mystical qualities. In themselves, most of these claims cannot now, or perhaps ever, be proved or disproved. Indeed, the linkages of language and thought are often thought to be so pervasive and complex that no proof is possible. Yet it would help if, somewhere in the scores of articles which discuss the hypothesis, and the literally hundreds of articles which invoke it in passing, one could find references to cases where the proposal that language diversity was influencing – even determining – thought was successfully tested. (This immediately rules out all those individual case studies where the investigator sees some global "fit" between a given language pattern and some cultural or cognitive theme.) Whatever the more powerful global speculations might be – whether they concern vocabulary or grammar, reference or poetics, habit or ideology, structure or function – they all depend in the end on the ability to demonstrate *some* microlevel connections. This has been one aim of the present study, realized most clearly in the cognitive assessment which demonstrates narrow connections, but nonetheless very real ones, between language patterns and cognition.

Some opponents have produced extreme, and at times absurd, formulations where relativity is seen as an inherently unprovable thesis. In one sense, those holding this position are more justified in not conducting research since they feel it is pointless. Yet such critiques cut two ways: just to the extent the hypothesis cannot be proven when formulated in this way, it also cannot be disproven. This should be a cause of deep concern to these scholars rather than a cause for satisfaction. Not to confront the implications of the issue for their own work amounts to accepting a counsel of ignorance. It would be preferable for such skeptics, even while continuing to disbelieve, to make some serious attempt to explore what truth there might be in the relativity claim – or what limits there might be to their own. Grappling with the question of what can be known, that is, in a sense, grappling with both the reality and the limits of a relativism, has been another aim of the present study, realized most clearly in the linguistic analysis which demonstrated both commonality and differences in the linguistic construal of reality.

As outlined in the introduction to this work, the study here encompasses a very small piece of the territory which will ultimately prove relevant to tracing the relations of language and thought. Even within the framework of the possible influences of language diversity on thought, the study circumscribes a very small region. But the significance of the present study is that it provides a theoretical and methodological framework for exploring this area with some rigor. If microlevel connections of the sort proposed here can be firmly established, then researchers will be more justified in postulating the same sort of linkage in those domains and levels where, by the nature of the case, rigorous demonstrations will never be possible.

Substantive achievements

In addition to the above methodological achievements, the present study also produced a number of substantive achievements concerning the impact of patterns of number marking on thought.

Linguistic analysis

The goal of the linguistic analysis was to provide a comparative characterization of the two languages within a neutral cross-linguistic framework. The aim was to find an area in which the two languages differently structured a common domain of reference. It was crucial that the domain itself was first defined and articulated with reference to the contrastive analysis and not imposed on it a priori. That is, a global pattern of grammatical similarity both in terms of formal marking and semantic values was first identified before attempting to interpret it in terms of specific features of reference. The work began with an analysis of the two languages identifying points of structural–functional commonality, and only then moved to a systematic contrast in terms of a unified semantico-referential interpretation. This assured that the analysis preserved the integrity of both languages' categories.

The analysis showed that the number marking systems of English and Yucatec exhibit both similarities and differences. In both languages, Plural and Singular meanings are marked using roughly similar morpho-syntactic devices. Both languages mark singularity ('one') using various modifier forms – numeral classifer constructions in Yucatec and indefinite article and/or quantitative modifiers in English – and both languages mark plurality ('more than one') with nominal and verbal inflections. It is this broad similarity which makes it possible to state that we are dealing with "number marking" in both languages.

But the languages differ in their overall number marking configurations. They differ both in terms of the range of nouns for which number marks typically apply, and in terms of whether or not that marking is obligatory. English speakers obligatorily signal both singular and plural for a large group of lexical nouns, whereas Yucatec speakers optionally signal plural for a comparatively small group of lexical nouns. Whereas Yucatec speakers must use a numeral classifier to indicate an appropriate unit before applying singular marking to a noun, English speakers only need to indicate a unit for a small range of nouns. Thus, the specific patterns of marking in the two languages are quite distinct.

When these patterns of differences are interpreted in substantive terms, it becomes clear the Yucatec and English structure a similar semantico-referential domain quite differently. Yucatec speakers are treating all nouns in much the same way English speakers treat nouns semantically marked as [−animate, −discrete] – the so-called "mass" nouns of traditional grammatical analyses. Interpretively, in Yucatec all nouns are like our "mass" nouns in that they are semantically neutral with respect to logical unit or shape. This interpretation of Yucatec lexical structure is consistent with the obligatory specification of a unit to indicate Singular (and specific quantitative multiples) and with the optionality and restricted range of Plural marking. By contrast, English divides its lexical nouns into two groups, those with a presupposable unit as part of lexical structure and which may take Plural and Singular marking with indefinite article, and those lexical nouns which function like the Yucatec lexical nouns in requiring unitizers and lacking the plural.

Significantly, the complementary relationship between obligatory unitization and obligatory pluralization found in these two languages apparently holds for other languages. The regularity operates at two levels. First, typological characterizations of whole languages reveal a general asymmetry between the tendency to have obligatory pluralization and the tendency to have obligatory numeral classification.

Secondly, within languages which have both plural marking and numeral classifiers, the two patterns of marking tend to be in complementary relation. That is, the same factors differentiating languages can also be used to differentiate lexical nouns within languages. (Clearly, this approach will also help in identifying whatever cognitive universals might contribute to language structure.) The demonstration of this complementarity for plural marking in terms of referential features seems fairly solid; however, there is as yet no independently established set of features governing the scope of unitization. Overall the two patterns suggest a semiotic/linguistic restructuring of experience for the purposes of verbal communication. The question then becomes whether these restructurings matter for cognition and in what ways.

Cognitive findings

The general goal of the cognitive portion of the study was to test whether the specific linguistic patterns of Yucatec and English corresponded with observable patterns of individual cognitive performance. The specific goals were to form plausible hypotheses, test them with a variety of tasks and materials, and find distinctive patterns, that is, where the two languages show similar patterns, cognitive patterns should agree; where they differ, cognitive patterns should differ in the appropriate ways. Although the studies reported here are rough and preliminary because of their exploratory nature, they nonetheless suggest that language patterns do affect cognitive performance.

The central expectation was that language-specific patterns of grammatical number marking (for example, scope of pluralization and unitization) would correspond to more general cognitive dispositions towards referents among speakers of the languages. On the basis of the linguistic analysis and the semantico-referential interpretation of it, two general hypotheses were formed. First, English speakers should habitually attend to the number of various objects of reference more than should Yucatec speakers. In particular, they should habitually attend to number for the wider array of referent types for which they obligatorily mark number. Second, English speakers should attend relatively more to the shape of objects and Yucatec speakers should attend relatively more to the material composition of objects.

The results of the cognitive assessment were consistently in line with these expectations. The overall configuration of results across the tasks indicates a basic and reliable difference between the two groups. In the picture description and recall tasks, English speakers were more likely to mention number (in one way or another) than were Yucatec speakers and the pattern of mention for each group followed the general pattern of frequency for plural marking in the languages. English speakers mentioned number more often for Animal and Implement referents than for Substance referents; Yucatec speakers mentioned number more often for Animal referents than for Implement or Substance referents. In the nonverbal picture tasks involving similarity judgment and recognition memory, English speakers showed a greater sensitivity to changes in the number of an Animal or Implement than to changes in the number of a Substance, whereas Yucatec speakers showed a greater sensitivity to changes in the number of an Animal than to changes in the number of an Implement or a Substance. These patterns suggest strongly that the frequency of pluralization in each language influences both the verbal and nonverbal interpretation of pictures.

The results of the object triad sorting tasks also followed expectations. Yucatec speakers showed a strong tendency to group objects on the basis of common material composition and English speakers showed a strong tendency to group objects on the basis of common shape. These patterns suggest that the underlying lexical structures associated with the number marking in the two languages have an influence on the nonverbal interpretation of objects. These results are especially important. It has been emphasized in this study that in the analysis of number marking no firm line can be drawn between lexical and syntactic facts. The results of this classification task imply that the grammatical contribution to lexical reference can affect the interpretation of the referents of those lexical items. And the task indicates that a covert lexical structure – which, from one point of view, underlies and accounts for the overt differences in number marking patterns – can have direct effects on cognition. Although this triads task and the picture task series look quite different both in procedures and in content, they deal in fact with two aspects of a single, integrated morphosyntactic configuration in each language. Since each experiment can only isolate a single element of the configuration for examination, multiple studies are necessary to assess the full impact of the linguistic differences.

Overall, the two groups responded similarly both grammatically and cognitively to Animal and Substance referent types, but differed in their responses to Implement referent types. Differences were observed both in the fundamental interpretation of the Implement referent types as shapes or materials and in the salience of their number in various depicted contexts. Significantly, these differences in the treatment of Implements emerged in tasks testing predictions derived from both overt and covert grammatical patterns, in tasks requiring diverse cognitive activities such as attention, classification, similarity judgment, and memory, in tasks involving both verbal and nonverbal response modes, and in tasks using both object and picture stimuli. Any alternative account of the results will have to address this overall pattern of results across a diversity of tasks, and not just one result in an individual experiment. In short, there is good preliminary evidence that diverse language forms bear a relationship to characteristic cognitive responses in speakers.

Directions for future research

Future research will need to engage a number of important problems left unaddressed in the present work.

Refinements

The present work needs to be refined in a number of ways. First, there is a need to establish the *reliability* of the present results for English and Yucatec speakers. There were enough ambiguities in the present study to warrant caution in extrapolating from them too quickly. In future work it should be possible to construct more focused and precise versions of the existing tasks and stimuli, as well as to devise new ones. It is especially important to find new nonverbal tasks. Finally, it would be desirable to extend the triads approach to see whether there are differences in the interpretation of Animal and Substance type objects, in understanding of part–whole relations, and so forth.

Second, there is a need to establish the *validity* of the experimental findings as indices of everyday behavior. This will involve ethnographic analysis to explore whether everyday behavior reflects the conceptual orientations detected in controlled settings. Further evidence can be sought in the array of institutional structures and systems of beliefs characteristic of the societies. Here we move beyond the assessment of individual characteristics to a consideration of cultural forms. With regard to English speakers, it will be of interest to explore the possible relation (in both directions) between microlevel attentiveness to number and form, and macrolevel cultural valuation of quantification and formal analyses. With regard to Yucatec speakers, the connections between microlevel attention to substance, and the orientation to substance in certain origin myths, warrant particular attention. The crucial problem in such analyses is providing some rigor to the extensions and comparisons. The methodology for such analyses connecting language and culture in this way remains poorly developed at present.

Generalizations and extensions

The present work also needs to be generalized and extended in certain ways. There is a need to show the *generality* of the substantive findings for other languages and cultures. Two kinds of language data will be important. First, there is a need to explore additional systems of number marking that fit within the existing framework so as to confirm or qualify the observed correlations of linguistic pattern with cognitive performance. This would involve among other things exploring languages at other points on the continuum defined here (for example, Chinese, Tarascan, Hopi) so as to check the generality of the language-based predictions. Second, there is a need to explore additional linguistic types (for example, languages without obligatory plurals or classifiers) and incorporate them into the analysis if possible.

With the addition of further languages to the present sample, one could begin to explore the issue of *causality* more directly: is it language structure *per se* that is producing the observed differences? As has been noted throughout, it is not possible to establish definitive causal linkages with correlational data alone. Four sorts of data can, however, provide some information on this issue. First, synchronic comparison with sufficiently precise predictions can be used to systematically rule out some alternative hypotheses by reference to crucial cases. So, for example, if one believed that the English pattern was due to extensive formal education and not to language structure, then one would want to study cases where a Yucatec type language was associated with a system of formal education or where an English type language was associated with the absence of formal education. Given the specificity of the hypotheses developed here, such comparisons should be diagnostic. Second, such synchronic comparisons can occasionally be supplemented by cases of historical transformation. Here the introduction or disappearance of a cultural or linguistic configuration can be examined with respect to the cognitive consequences. To continue the example just given, the introduction of schooling into a society without a concomitant change in official language can provide the sort of natural case study that can test for schooling as a potent alternative hypothesis for certain cognitive effects.

Third, comparison at the level of individuals can provide important evidence in some cases. Within a society there may be sufficient differentiation by age, gender, social group, etc. to warrant a language-internal comparison. To continue the education example, there may be both schooled and unschooled populations in a given society, and comparing the performance of these populations might be sufficient to rule out education or language as the operative variable. Other individual characteristics such as bilingualism may also be relevant to judging some hypotheses, although the complexities of interpreting bilingual data are considerable.

Fourth, some competing hypotheses can be ruled out by reference to characteristic cognitive patterns emerging during child development. In general, children should look relatively alike in their cognitive performance early on in the language learning process and should diverge later. Depending on the synchronization of such development with other cultural and linguistic experiences, it may be possible to eliminate some competing alternatives. To continue the example presented above, if characteristic English cognitive patterns emerge before school age, this would weaken the possibility that schooling is the primary antecedent, although it would not necessarily be definitive since a "schooled society" will presumably exhibit a different preschool socialization pattern. (The preliminary evidence mentioned in chapter 3 suggests that the critical shift does in fact occur during the school years.)

Extending the method to new linguistic categories is also important. A large number of known typological variations among languages can readily be utilized in studies of the type developed here. The key in each case is identifying patterns where there is a framework of referential commonality in conjunction with substantial structural–functional variation (for example, in categories such as voice, aspect, etc.). These categories will provide the crucial opportunities to evaluate the linguistic relativity issue in a rigorous way. Of course not all language categories will fit neatly into typological frameworks. Some very important categories may not be widespread or readily subsumable under an analysis of their denotational values. In such cases, it will be more difficult to evaluate whether there are real cognitive effects. The warrant for regarding observed correlations as significant in such cases will have to come from having established the general pattern of language–thought relations in the more rigorously investigable cases of the type discussed here.

The functional dimension

Finally, the present work needs to be complemented and completed by a focus on the differing *functions of language* with regard to thought. This variable has essentially been bracketed here, except for the conscious attempt to measure habitual thought by minimizing the need for specialized skills in the tasks and to focus on obligatory grammatical categories which are frequently used. The positive results of the present study along with other evidence (cf. Lucy, 1981b) suggest that cultural differences in modes of thinking and the uses of language were not a decisive factor in this case.

However, certain sorts of specialized modes of thought (for example, science, philosophy, etc.) may be more or less language-dependent when compared to habitual everyday thought, and certain sorts of specialized uses of language (for example, literacy, poetic traditions, etc.) may have more or less influence on thought than does everyday usage. For example, to take the education example one step further, formal schooling produces a special kind of language use specifically designed to enhance thinking abilities. Such specialized uses may shape, amplify, or minimize structural effects, but are analytically distinguishable from them. The breadth and significance of any structural effects must ultimately be mediated by such patterns of language use. In some cases, a whole culture may use language for thought in a highly characteristic manner. Thus, from a culture–comparative point of view, even the notions of "ordinary language use" and "habitual thought" will themselves have to be subjected to critical examination and then either refined or discarded. Ultimately, one wants an account of language and thought interactions in terms of the interplay of linguistic structure with the various psychological, cultural, and semiotic functions of language (Lucy, 1991). By identifying one of the ways that distinctive lexico-grammatical categories may have effects on thought, the present study provides the foundation upon which one can ask how specialized uses of such language categories can shape, amplify, or suppress such effects.

Appendix A. Construction of picture stimuli

Basis of the decision to use line drawings

Stimuli used in the picture task series consisted of line drawings of typical Mayan village scenes and included specific numbers and types of objects relevant to the hypothesis in question. Constructed stimuli were used rather than actual village settings because it is very difficult to control the occurrence of objects (especially animate ones) in natural settings and because it is difficult to replicate the same setting across subjects and cultures. Artificial arrangements of objects were not used because it was difficult to include complex contextual features (for example, forest, house interiors), because it was difficult to include effectively many types of objects (for example, smoke, clouds), because pretesting revealed that small replicas of objects evoked unusual responses among the Yucatec subjects (for example, replicas of animals elicited great amusement), and because the practical difficulty of rapidly manipulating arrangements of objects made them difficult to use in some of the nonverbal tasks (for example, recognition memory).

Photographs of artificial arrays of objects would have solved this last problem, but not the others. Photographs of natural settings were rejected in part because they presented some of the same difficulties as the natural settings, especially the difficulty of setting up the situations to photograph so as to include the appropriate objects of interest and to exclude unwanted elements. More importantly, however, in pretesting photographs inevitably evoked too great an interest on the part of the Maya as to the *particulars* of who was involved, what they were doing, where the photograph was taken, etc. It can be argued that this was a desirable aspect of photographs, better reflecting speakers' actual responses to situations. Nonetheless, such responses could not be controlled across individuals within the Mayan group (for example, it could not be assured that every person had relatives, dogs, houses, etc. known to him represented in equal proportions in the stimulus set) nor could the responses of the US subjects be in any sense equivalent with respect to such details. Finally, film and video tape were rejected for many of the reasons associated with photographs. In addition they are extraordinarily novel media for the Maya, they require a reliable source of electricity which was unavailable, local repair was difficult to obtain in Mexico, and there were complex legal restrictions on the transport and use of such equipment in Mexico.

Drawings thus represented a compromise approach which allowed the introduction of many natural elements, but in their general (or indefinite) form and with precise control. Line drawings were chosen when pretesting revealed that colored drawings did not improve picture interpretation enough to offset the practical problems of reproduction. Further, line drawings are a familiar medium to Mayan men as features of Mayan village life are routinely depicted by such drawings in school materials, government pamphlets and posters, packagings, etc. Pretesting of stimuli showed that most drawings were readily interpretable, especially if *familiar objects* were presented in their *appropriate settings*. US subjects, or course, are highly skilled in the interpretation of line drawings even when the latter two conditions are not met.

Development of original pictures

This section explains some of the background details involved in the construction of the picture sets described in the main text. The picture sets themselves are reproduced further below in this appendix.

Selection of standard objects

Each picture contained certain *standard objects* which were introduced into the pictures by design so as to be able to sample speakers' responses to different types of objects. The full list of standard objects is represented in table 37. The first double column of this table indicates the general object type and its several subdivisions. These correspond in most cases to known linguistic category boundaries, although not necessarily those of Yucatec or English. The second column lists the items actually depicted. The third set of columns indicates the number of times each object was pictured in each picture set so that its weight in the final results will be clear.

Each set of three pictures contained 36 standard objects. In each set of pictures, nine were Animals, nine were Container Objects, nine were Implements or Tool-like Objects, and nine were Substances. Whenever

Table 37. *List of standard objects*

Category		Object	Number of times used		
			Set 1	Set 2	Set 3
Animal	human	human	3	3	3
	domestic	dog	1	1	1
		horse	1	1	1
		pig	1	1	1
		turkey	1	1	1
		chicken	1	1	1
	forest	bird	1	1	1
Container	rigid I	bucket	1	1	1
		barrel	1	1	1
		bottle	1	1	1
		tinaja	1		
		paila		1	
		pileta			1
	rigid II	water gourd	1	1	1
		calabash	1	1	1
		gourd	1	1	1
	flexible	mesh bag	1	1	1
		sack	1	1	1
Tool	hand tool	machete	1	1	1
		broom	1	1	1
		pulley	1	1	1
		ax			1
		shovel		1	
		sickle			1
		ladder	1		
		hose		1	
		scale			1
		knife		1	
	household	candle	1		1
		griddle	1	1	1
		stool	1	1	1
	clothing	hat	1	1	1
Substance	edible	corn dough	1	1	
		bean			1
		corn			1
		meat, fat	1	1	1
	rigid	rock	1	1	1
		firewood	1	1	1
	loose	dirt, trash	1	1	
		corn gruel	1		

Table 37. (*cont.*)

| Category | Object | Number of times used | | |
		Set 1	Set 2	Set 3
	puddle		1	1
	moving water	1	1	1
	cloud	1	1	1
	smoke	1	1	1

Human includes examples of men, women and children. *Tinaja, paila,* and *pileta* are Spanish terms for various large vessels usually used for holding water or for food preparation.

possible, the same standard objects were used across the three sets. Thus, instead of 108 different objects (i.e., 36 + 36 + 36) there were only 46; absolute minimum would, of course, have been 36. It was not possible to achieve this minimum since the goal of constructing scenes with thematic unity precluded portraying all objects equally often. Notice that the Human category is given a count of 3 since it is used three *separate* times as standard object as explained below.

Counterbalancing of standard objects

In principle, each individual picture was to contain 12 standard objects (i.e., one-third of the set of 36) and considerable effort was expended to achieve this. However, once more, since not all objects were compatible with all scenes, this was not completely achieved. Thus, the 36 standard objects for the first set were divided up 14, 11, and 11; those for the second set were divided up 12, 11, and 13; and those for the third set were divided up 13, 12, and 11. The distribution of standard objects by picture is given in table 38 which is an expanded version of table 19 presented in the main text. Interestingly, from an interpretive point of view, it was easy to include Animals and Containers in every picture. Tools (and other Implements) posed more difficulty since they interacted more with the thematic content of defining a scene. By contrast, Substances were easy to include from a thematic point of view but were very difficult from a representational point of view since so few could be adequately depicted by line drawings.

Table 38. *Inventory of standard objects and target objects by picture and type*

Picture set	Standard and target objects			
	Animate	*Container*	*Tool*	*Substance*
1.1	DOG 2 −	TINAJA 1 +	CANDLE 2 −	CORN DOUGH 1 +
	chicken 1	gourd 1	pulley 1	smoke 2
	human 3	bucket 2	stool 2	fat/meat 1
			griddle 1	moving water 1
1.2	HUMAN 1 +	SACK 2 −	AX 1 +	FIREWOOD 6 −
	horse 1	calabash 6	hat 1	rock 8
	bird 2	mesh bag 1		corn gruel 6
1.3	PIG 1 +	GOURD 1 +	MACHETE 2 −	CLOUD 2 −
	human 3	barrel 2	broom 1	trash 1 (many)
	turkey 2	bottle 1	ladder 1	
2.1	HUMAN 1 +	BUCKET 2 −	SHOVEL 1 +	SMOKE 2 −
	bird 2	calabash 1	broom 1	dirt mound 1
	dog 1	barrel 2	hose 2	moving water 1
2.2	HORSE 2 −	MESH BAG 1 +	PULLEY 2 −	PUDDLE 1 +
	pig 1	water gourd 1	machete 1	cloud 3
	human 2	sack 1	hat 1	
2.3	TURKEY 3 −	GOURD 2 −	STOOL 1 +	FAT/MEAT 1 +
	human 6	bottle 1	knife 1	rock 3 (+many)
	chicken 1	*paila* 1	griddle 1	corn dough 1
				firewood 3
3.1	CHICKEN 1 +	CALABASH 2 −	GRIDDLE 2 −	FAT/MEAT 1 +
	human 1	sack 1	candle 1	bean 1 (many)
	dog 2	mesh bag 1	stool 1	smoke 4
			scale 1	
3.2	HUMAN 2 −	BOTTLE 2 −	BROOM 1 +	CORN 1 (many) +
	pig 3	gourd 1	pulley 1	cloud 1
	turkey 1	bucket 1		puddle 1
				firewood 2
3.3	BIRD 2 −	BARREL 1 +	HAT 1 +	ROCK 3 −
	human 2	water gourd 1	sickle 1	moving water 1
	horse 1	*pileta* 2	machete 2	

Objects listed are the standard objects for each picture set. Numbers after the objects indicate the quantity in each original picture. Items in capitals were changed in one of the alternate pictures. '+' and '−' signs indicate whether the change was an increase or decrease. *Tinaja*, *paila*, and *pileta* are Spanish terms for various large vessels usually used for holding water or for food preparation. "Hat" indicates a hat not being worn.

Full content inventory

A definitive inventory of the content of the pictures is not possible since, on the one hand, the elements in a picture can be endlessly divided up into more and more minute elements, or, on the other hand, they can be interpretively grouped into various configurations. Nonetheless, an attempt was made to inventory the principal bounded entities in each picture and to balance them to some degree. For example, while the feature [± human] is not of specific concern in these experiments, it has been controlled for in the pictures. Every picture contains at least one human among its animates, and they are counterbalanced across pictures just as with all the other stimuli. Thus, these stimuli (or ones modeled on them) could be used to compare either English or Yucatec with a language where the expressions of quantity split on this feature. Inspection of the picture stimuli themselves will reveal other possible dimensions of contrast.

Development of alternate pictures

For each original picture, a set of five alternate pictures was developed for use in the nonverbal tasks. In each such picture the number of a *target object* was changed.

Selection of target objects

Target objects were selected from among the standard objects so as to maximize the sampling of different specific objects. The target objects are listed in table 19 and also indicated by capital letters in table 38. In each alternate picture, the number of one target object was changed by adding to its number (marked by '+' in table 38) so that it went from singular (one) to plural (more than one) or deleting from its number (marked by '−' in table 38) so that it went from plural (more than one) to singular (one).

For the purposes of these picture stimuli, it was not obvious whether a given object should be characterized on the basis of how it would be referred to in particular (i.e., the linguistic status of a typical lexical label) or on the basis of how most objects of its type would be referred to. For example, should target Substances be those things which are referred to by particular linguistic expressions that are formally [− animate, − discrete] or should they be those things which have the physical properties typical of most [− animate, − discrete] expressions. Under the first interpretation, *fog* and *cloud* would be classed differently, under the second they would be classed together (both in the *fog* category). In the present study the second approach was used because it was the most conservative with respect to the hypothesis. This led to the inclusion of *cloud*, *rock*, and *puddle* in the Substance category even though English speakers might regard them as [− animate, + discrete] or even, in the case of *cloud*, [+ animate, + discrete].

Selection of the number of alternates

Originally, each set contained eleven alternates, the five simple alternates discussed in the main text and six more complex alternates consisting of combinations of the four simple kinds of changes: alternates 2 and 3, 2 and 4, 2 and 5, 3 and 4, 3 and 5, 4 and 5. These additional changes were introduced originally to complicate the recognition memory experiments and thereby reduce the likelihood of answers based solely on deduction. The number of alternates was reduced when pilot work showed that Yucatec subjects would not be able to work effectively with the larger number of alternates. So only the smaller number of alternates containing these minimal changes was actually used with the sample. No attempt was made to work with the English subjects with this larger set, but, as mentioned in the main text, the English procedure was modified to reduce the possibility of deduction.

Counterbalancing changes in the alternates

As can be seen by inspecting table 38, the changes represented by the alternates were counterbalanced in various ways. First, increases and decreases of number were balanced so as to control for any difficulty which might be associated with the two types of change. For example, it might be that it is more difficult to recognize that something is missing from a picture than that something has been added. Thus, for each picture *set*, the twelve changes in number (i.e., pictures **2**, **3**, **4**, and **5**) were arranged so that six were increased and six were decreased.

Further, for each of the four types of object, the increases and decreases were balanced as closely as possible both within sets and across sets. Since each picture set altered only three examples of each type of object, the best possible balance was either two increases and one decrease or one increase and two decreases in number. Across all sets there were nine possibilities and the best possible balance was either five increases and four decreases or four increases and five decreases in number. Since alternates **3** and **4** were from the same general category (i.e., [− animate, + discrete]) it was possible to balance this category evenly across the entire set of eighteen items with nine increases and nine decreases.

Additional factors not related to the hypothesis but which might nonetheless be of interest (for example, relative size, location, and thematic salience of the target objects in the pictures) were also checked to assure that no object type was favored within each set.

Picture stimulus materials

Figures 7 to 15 show reproductions of the nine original pictures and their five alternates. The stimuli have been reduced here from their actual size which was five by eight inches. In each case, the original is in the upper left of the figure. Alternate **2** showing a change in an Animal is to the immediate right of the original. The second row contains alternates **3** and **4** with changes in the number of an Object–Container on the left and Tool on the right. The third row contains alternates **5** and **6** with changes in the number of a Substance – discrete change on the left and size change on the right. Specific items changed can be identified by reference to table 19 or table 38.

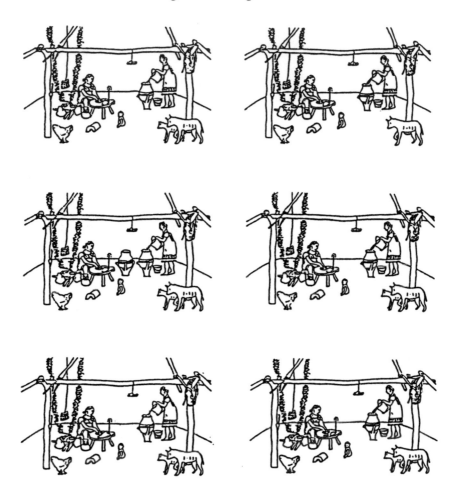

Figure 7   Picture set 1.1

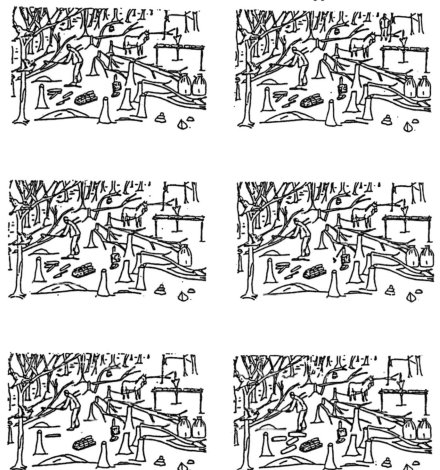

Figure 8　Picture set 1.2

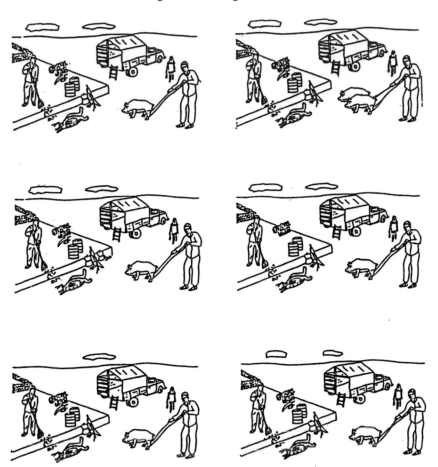

Figure 9   Picture set 1.3

Figure 10   Picture set 2.1

Figure 11   Picture set 2.2

Figure 12 Picture set 2.3

Figure 13   Picture set 3.1

Figure 14   Picture set 3.2

Figure 15   Picture set 3.3

Appendix B. Administration of task series

Subject characteristics and task sequence

A general description of subjects engaging in the tasks and the sequence of tasks was given in chapters 1 and 3. Tables 39 and 40 present additional specific details on these topics. Only tasks 6–12 in these tables have been reported here. The series 1 experiments concerned other issues and only served in the present context to familiarize the men with the task procedures. Unnumbered items represent supplementary procedures used with the preceding numbered task.

Counterbalancing of stimulus presentation

The picture stimuli were not easy to construct. Thus, it was desirable to use each picture in more than one task and to have every subject deal with each picture at some point, but not necessarily always in the same tasks.

Given five tasks (I–V), three sets of pictures (labeled 1, 2, and 3), and the requirement that a common picture set be used in Tasks I and V, and in Tasks II and III, six possible presentation orders (i–vi) are possible as indicated in table 41. On the basis of this, it made sense for subjects to be sought in groups of six since all possible orders could be equally represented.

Finally, since each picture set contained three originals (for example, 1.1, 1.2, 1.3), it was possible to order the presentation *within each set* in six possible ways as well. As there were not enough subjects to completely counterbalance this factor, the six possible combinations were assigned randomly (without replacement) to the six occurrences of each set associated with each six subjects.

Table 39. *Maya task and subject data*

									Subject identification number										
	1	2	3	4	5	6	7	8	9	10	11	12	13	14	15	16	17	18	19
									Personal information[a]											
Estimated Age	34	39	46	21	23	19	41	31	22	24	31	18	29	27	55	49	59	32	20
Schooling	1	0	0	1	1	1	1	0	1	1	1	1	1	1	0	0	0	1	0
Literacy	1	0	0	1	1	1	1	0	1	1	1	1	1	1	0	0	0	1	0
									Series 1 experiments[b]											
1. Descript.	x	x	x	x	x	x	x	x	x	x	x	x	0	0	0	0	0	0	0
2. Recall	1x	1x	1x	1x	2x	2x	2x	2x	2x	2x	2x	2x	0	0	0	0	0	0	0
3. Recogn. I	1x	1x	1x	1x	2x	2x	2x	2x	2x	2x	2x	2x	0	0	0	0	0	0	0
4. Recogn. II	1x	1x	0	1x	2x	2x	2x	2x	2x	2x	2x	2x	0	0	0	0	0	0	0
5. Naming	x	x	x	x	x	x	x	x	x	x	x	x	0	0	0	0	0	0	0
									Series 2 experiments[b]											
6. Descript.	0	x	x	x	x	x	x	x	x	x	x	x	x	0	0	0	0	0	0
7. Recall	0	1x	1x	1x	2x	2x	2x	2x	2x	2x	2x	2x	2x	0	0	0	0	0	0
PreDescr.	0	x	x	x	0	0	0	0	0	0	0	0	x	0	0	0	0	0	0
PostDescr.	0	0	0	0	x	x	x	x	x	x	x	x	0	0	0	0	0	0	0
Probes	0	0	x	x	x	x	x	x	0	0	0	0	0	0	0	0	0	0	0
8. Classific.	0	x	x	x	x	x	x	x	0	x	x	x	x	0	0	0	0	0	0
9. ST Recogn.	0	1x	1x	1x	2x	2x	2x	2x	0	2x	2x	2x	2x	0	0	0	0	0	0
10. LT Recogn.	0	3x	3x	3x	3x	3x	3x	3x	0	3x	3x	3x	3x	0	0	0	0	0	0

11. Triads I	x	0	0	x	0	0	0	0	0	0	x	0	0	x	x	x	x	x	x
12. Triads II	x	0	0	x	0	0	0	0	0	0	x	0	0	x	x	x	x	x	x
Probes	0	0	0	0	0	0	0	0	0	0	0	0	0	0	0	0	0	0	0
13. Triads III	0	0	0	0	0	0	0	0	0	0	0	0	0	x	x	x	x	x	x

[a] 1 = yes, 0 = no, other numbers = ages
[b] 0 = task not administered
x = task administered
1x = administered, memory assessed after 30 second delay
2x = administered, memory assessed after 60 second delay
3x = administered, memory assessed after 60 minute delay

G

Table 40. *English task and subject data*

	Subject identification number												
	21	22	23	24	25	26	27	28	29	30	31	32	33
Personal information[a]													
Estimated Age	21	21	21	19	21	21	22	19	20	24	20	19	27
Schooling	16	14	15	14	16	15	15	14	14	15	15	14	14
Literacy	1	1	1	1	1	1	1	1	1	1	1	1	1
Series 1 experiments[b]													
1. Descrip.	x	x	x	x	x	x	x	x	x	x	0	x	0
2. Recall	2x	2x	2x	2x	2x	2x	2x	2x	2x	2x	0	2x	0
3. Recogn. I	2x	2x	2x	2x	2x	2x	2x	2x	2x	2x	0	2x	0
4. Recogn. II	2x	2x	2x	1x	2x	2x	2x	2x	2x	2x	0	2x	0
5. Naming	x	x	x	x	x	x	x	x	x	x	0	x	0
Series 2 experiments[b]													
6. Descript.	0	x	x	x	x	x	x	x	x	x	x	x	x
7. Recall	0	2x	2x	2x	2x	2x	2x	2x	2x	2x	2x	2x	2x
PreDescr.	0	0	0	0	0	0	0	0	0	0	0	0	0
PostDescr.	4x	0	4x	0	4x	4x	0	0	4x	4x	0	0	0
Probes	0	0	0	0	0	0	0	0	0	0	0	0	0
8. Classific	x	x	x	x	x	x	x	x	x	x	x	x	x
9. ST Recogn.	2x	2x	5x	5x	5x	5x	5x	5x	5x	5x	5x	5x	5x
10. LT Recogn.	3x	3x	3x	3x	3x	3x	3x	3x	3x	3x	3x	3x	3x

Series 3 experiments[b]

11. Triads I	x	x	x	x	x	x	x	x	x	x	x	x
12. Triads II	x	x	x	x	x	x	x	x	x	x	x	x
Probes	0	0	0	0	0	0	0	0	0	0	0	0
13. Triads III	0	0	0	0	0	0	0	0	0	0	0	0

[a] 1 = yes, 0 = no, other numbers = ages or years of schooling
[b] 0 = task not administered
x = task administered
2x = administered, memory assessed after 60 second delay
3x = administered, memory assessed after 60 minute delay
4x = administered at the end of the series
5x = administered, 60 second delay, one-by-one administration

Table 41. *Order of presentation of picture sets by task*

Task	Presentation Order					
	i	*ii*	*iii*	*iv*	*v*	*vi*
I	1	1	2	2	3	3
II	2	3	1	3	1	2
III	2	3	1	3	1	2
IV	3	2	3	1	2	1
V	1	1	2	2	3	3

Numbers in the columns (i.e., 1, 2, and 3) represent the ID numbers of the three picture sets.

Appendix C. Scoring conventions and summary data for verbal tasks

The production of quantitative measures for the verbal picture description and verbal picture recall tasks was relatively complicated. This appendix provides information on the coding and scoring procedures used for these two verbal tasks.

Sample transcripts

Description

The following is one verbal description of the stimulus shown in figure 2.

I see a man that's giving uh food to a group of three sows. In the background is a- a some kind of a hut with a thatched roof and behind that are what seem to be palm trees and in the very far distance there is a stone wall. Over that there is a cloud. To the right of that- of the scene is a well that has a bucket on the edge of it and in the front foreground of the photog- of the picture there seems to be a pile of rocks. Uhm, at the left (of) the picture there are two uh bundles of sticks in the foreground. On the left there's a hen or a rooster – I'm not sure which. Uh, leaning against the hut there is a broom and uh two bottles. One looks like it's empty, the other is upright. And a young man is walking toward the older man that's feeding the sows. And there is a cloud over the stone wall.

(Picture 3.2.1, Subject 25)

Recall

The following is one verbal recall response to the stimulus shown in figure 2.

OK. It- There's a hut in the background, or a house with- it's made out of some kind of bamboo or sticks that are upright, and there aren't any windows, but there is a door and it's closed, and there's a thatch roof. And there's a broom leaning against it and a bottle on the ground. And there is a turkey in the yard –

it's a pretty big turkey. And there is a well with water on the outside, similar to the well in the other picture, with a pulley and a rope and a bag and supported by sticks over the well part. And there are a couple of big trees, and then there are some tropical trees. It looks like there's bananas on one of them. And there is a man who's throwing food to three pigs out of some kind of like bowl. And there's a little boy running towards the man in shorts, and it looks like he's yelling something at him. And, uh, there's a large pile of something that the man's standing near – I can't tell if it's rocks or what – and that's about it.

(Picture 3.2.1, Subject 26)

Coding Procedures

The following codes were used to indicate the type of mention of each target in the verbal description task and, for those mentions which involved nominal lexemes, the overt syntactic signs of number which accompanied the mention.

- − = no mention of the item. Misidentification of an item which nonetheless produced a clear, direct description of the item using a noun was coded as a mention by one of the P, S, or U codes described below.
- ~ = no explicit nominal form but weakly implied mention either because a commonly or closely related item was described by another noun or because an action typically associated with the object was described by one of the verbs. Indication of the specific nature of these implications is given in the notes to the tables and each indication is cross referenced to the table by data-point coordinates: type of target (A = Animal, C = Container, T = Tool, S = Substance), picture set (1, 2, 3), individual picture number (1, 2, 3), subject identification number (1 through 31).
- + = no explicit nominal form but strongly implied mention. Same general criteria and data-point coordinate system are used as in the previous code (i.e., ~).
- U = unmarked nominal form (i.e., no overt mark of [± discrete] status). Included here are nouns whose singular status can 'only' be deduced by knowledge of the covert [± discrete] status of the noun.

U. = unmarked form where one might deduce singularity on the basis of nonlinguistic, cultural norms. The only repeated case (five instances) of this possibility occurred in Yucatec because villagers tend to own only one each of certain domestic animals (for example, horses) and certain material possessions (for example, axes, hats). Thus, a singular may be reasonably deduced when a noun referring to such items is accompanied by a third-person possessive pronoun cross-referencing to a singular [+ animate] noun. Hence, the use of *'u-p'óok* 'his hat' when only one man has been mentioned implies that there is only one hat in the picture. Scoring the U.'s as S's does not change the pattern or significance of the major finding.

U_i = odd unmarked forms requiring special note where $i = 1, 2, 3$, etc.

P = plural number indicated 1) by overt inflectional marks *-s*, *-ó'ob'*, or irregular form, 2) by plural verb concord, 3) by specification of a number greater than one such as *two, three, ká'a-* or *ó'oš-* plus numeral classifier (for example, *-túul, -p'éel*, etc.), or 4) by other explicit enumeration (for example, *another*) in combination with an appropriate noun.

P_e = plural number, but an error because target actually consisted of a single object of the given kind.

P_+ = plural number by summation of two singulars, of a singular with an unmarked form, or of two unmarked forms; evidence of clear separation must be present, for example, "*a man* [+ some description] . . . *a man* [+ some other description]."

P_i = odd indications of plural number requiring special note where $i = 1, 2, 3$, etc.

S = singular number indicated 1) by *one*, 2) by *a* or *an*, of 3) by *'un-* plus numeral classifier (*-túul, -p'éel*, etc.) in combination with an appropriate noun.

S_e = singular number, but an error because target actually consisted of multiple objects of the given kind.

S_a = singular number in English, indicated only by free anaphoric pronoun: for example, "the pig is . . . one of the men is holding him" where the use of the animate pronoun form *him* overtly marks the discrete status of the lexeme *pig*. (This does not work as a deductive rule in Yucatec.)

S_i = odd indications of singular number requiring special note where $i = 1, 2, 3$, etc.

$?_i$ = uncodable items where $i = 1, 2, 3$, etc.

Scoring the results

Basic scores for mention of target and mention of number were derived for each of the twenty-four subjects on each of the four types of targets: Animal, Container, Tool, and Substance. Mention of target was assessed primarily by summing cases of explicit nominal reference (Us, Ps, and Ss). Mention of number was calculated only for the cases where the target was overtly mentioned (i.e., where there was some nominal form to which to attach a nominal number indication) and was assessed by summing the Ps and Ss. The most important measure is the ratio of the score for mention of number to the score of nominal mention of target: $(P + S) / (U + P + S)$. This is labeled as the Index value in the following tables. Secondary measures of implied mention can be calculated by including in the basic score for mention the items coded as + (strongly implied mention) and $\sim$ (weakly implied mention).

Tables of results

Tables 42, 43, 44, and 45 list the results for the verbal picture description and verbal picture recall tasks. In the tables, the responses of each subject to each individual picture on each type of target is given. Scores are arrayed so as to facilitate the comparison by type of target. Below each target type are the Index values for each subject. Following each table are notes explaining problematic individual scoring decisions. Notes marked + or $\sim$ are cross-referenced to the table by target (A = animate, C = container, T = tool, and S = substance), picture number (1.1, 1.2, etc.), and subject identification number (22, 23, etc.).

Table 42. *English scores on the verbal description task*

Subject		24	27	30	33	22	26	28	31	23	25	29	32
Picture Set		1	1	1	1	2	2	2	2	3	3	3	3
						Animate targets							
Picture	1	P	P	P	P	S	S	S	U	~	S	S	~
	2	S	S	S	S	P_+	P_+	P	P_+	P	P	P	P_1
	3	S	S	S	S	P	P	P	P	–	U	P	P
Index		$\frac{3}{3}$	$\frac{3}{3}$	$\frac{3}{3}$	$\frac{3}{3}$	$\frac{3}{3}$	$\frac{3}{3}$	$\frac{3}{3}$	$\frac{2}{3}$	$\frac{1}{1}$	$\frac{2}{3}$	$\frac{3}{3}$	$\frac{2}{2}$
						Implement (container) targets							
Picture	1	S_1	–	S	S	P	P	–	P	–	S	~	–
	2	P	P	P	P	S_2	S_3	P_2	P_3	P	P	P	–
	3	S_4	S_5	S_6	–	S_e	P	P	S_e	–	S	–	–
Index		$\frac{3}{3}$	$\frac{2}{2}$	$\frac{3}{3}$	$\frac{2}{2}$	$\frac{3}{3}$	$\frac{3}{3}$	$\frac{2}{2}$	$\frac{3}{3}$	$\frac{1}{1}$	$\frac{3}{3}$	$\frac{1}{1}$	$\frac{0}{0}$
						Implement (tool) targets							
Picture	1	P_+	P_+	+	P	~	S	–	+	–	–	–	–
	2	+	+	S	+	S_e	S_e	~	P_4	–	S	–	–
	3	P_5	P_+	P_6	S_e	S_7	–	–	S_8	U	S	U	S
Index		$\frac{2}{2}$	$\frac{2}{2}$	$\frac{2}{2}$	$\frac{2}{2}$	$\frac{2}{2}$	$\frac{2}{2}$	$\frac{0}{0}$	$\frac{2}{2}$	$\frac{0}{1}$	$\frac{2}{2}$	$\frac{0}{1}$	$\frac{1}{1}$
						Substance targets							
Picture	1	U_1	U_2	U_3	~	+	+	–	+	U	S_9	~	+
	2	P	~	U_4	U_5	U	U	U	S	+	U	+	U_6
	3	P	P	–	P	U	+	U_7	–	–	–	–	P_7
Index		$\frac{2}{3}$	$\frac{1}{2}$	$\frac{0}{2}$	$\frac{1}{2}$	$\frac{0}{2}$	$\frac{0}{1}$	$\frac{0}{2}$	$\frac{1}{1}$	$\frac{0}{1}$	$\frac{1}{2}$	$\frac{0}{0}$	$\frac{1}{2}$

S_1 = "the big vat" is coded as singular since the noun is modified by *big* which implies [+ discrete] yet does not carry a plural mark (-s).

S_2 = "a fish net" is accepted as reference to the mesh bag.

S_3 = "a bundle of sticks" is accepted as a reference to the mesh bag.

S_4 = "another thing" is accepted as a reference to the gourd.

S_5 = "a working object ... some other object" is accepted as a reference to a gourd.

S_6 = "one [item] shaped like a gourd" is accepted as a reference to the gourd.

S_7 = "a piece of a log" is accepted as a reference to a log stool.

S_8 = "a curved object" is accepted as a reference to a log stool.

S_9 = "a big bag" is accepted as a reference to meat.

P_1 = "they are" is accepted as plural reference to the two human targets even without explicit mention of human.

P_2 = "carrying goods it appears – flour or potatoes or something like that" is accepted as a reference to the mesh bag. Could also be scored as U or +.

P_3 = "some things which I can't identify" is accepted as a reference to the mesh bag. Could also be scored as U or +.

Table 42 (*cont.*)

P_4 = "hanging from the crossbar over the well there are several objects" is accepted as a reference to the two pulleys.

P_5 = "possibly, it reminds me of bow and arrow ... the thing to hold the arrows ... And something else that might be an animal ... a grasshopper standing up or something" is accepted as referring to the two machetes.

P_6 = "a ... tusk shaped item ... In fact, there are two tusk shaped items" is accepted as a reference to the two machetes.

P_7 = "Oh it could be in snow – there's footsteps in the bottom, looks like snow footsteps" is accepted as a reference to three rocks.

U_1 = "some sort of food with a batter" is accepted as a reference to corn dough.

U_2 = "kneads something" is accepted as a reference to corn dough.

U_3 = "some kind of a uh uh bread dough" is accepted as a reference to corn dough. The item is not coded as a singular both because of the explicit reference to *kind* rather than quantity and because of the hesitation between the article and the noun which appears to retract the *a* in this case.

U_4 = "he has bundled up some lumber" is given and the "lumber" is taken to include the loose pieces of wood.

U_5 = "chopping wood ... a bundle of sticks" is given and the "wood" is taken to include the loose pieces of wood.

U_6 = "feeding them ... (sow feed [? not clearly audible])" is accepted as a reference to corn.

U_7 = "food" is accepted as a reference to meat.

+ = "candle-lit" implies candle (T-1-1-30);
   "chopping" implies ax (T-1-2-24, -27, -33);
   "shoveling" implies shovel (T-2-1-31);
   "fire" and "burning" imply smoke (S-2-1-22, -26, -31);
   "butchering" implies meat (S-2-3-26);
   "feeding [pigs]" implies corn (S-3-2-23, -29).

~ = "various animals" and "animals are" may imply chicken; (A-3-1-23, -32);
   "pouring" may imply calabash (C-3-1-29);
   "digging" may imply shovel (T-2-1-22);
   "a water hole ... well" may imply pulley (T-2-2-28);
   "meal ... a meal" may imply corn dough (S-1-1-33);
   "bundle of firewood" may imply loose pieces of wood (S-1-2-27);
   "stuff" may imply meat (S-3-1-29).

Table 43. *Yucatec scores on the verbal description task*

Subject		1	4	7	10	2	5	8	11	3	6	9	12
Picture set		1	1	1	1	2	2	2	2	3	3	3	3
					Animate targets								
Picture	1	P	U	P	P	U	–	U	S	S	S	U	U
	2	S	U	S	U_1	S_e	P_+	U	P_+	P_+	P_+	P_1	U_2
	3	+	U_3	P_e	S	P	P	U	U	–	P	U	S_e
Index		$\frac{2}{2}$	$\frac{0}{3}$	$\frac{3}{3}$	$\frac{2}{3}$	$\frac{2}{3}$	$\frac{2}{2}$	$\frac{0}{3}$	$\frac{2}{3}$	$\frac{2}{2}$	$\frac{3}{3}$	$\frac{1}{3}$	$\frac{1}{3}$
					Implement (container) targets								
Picture	1	U	U	U	U	S	P	–	U	–	P_+	–	S_e
	2	P	–	~	U_4	~	–	–	–	–	–	U	S_e
	3	–	–	–	U	U_5	–	–	–	+	~	–	+
Index		$\frac{1}{2}$	$\frac{0}{1}$	$\frac{0}{1}$	$\frac{0}{3}$	$\frac{1}{2}$	$\frac{1}{1}$	$\frac{0}{0}$	$\frac{0}{1}$	$\frac{0}{0}$	$\frac{1}{1}$	$\frac{0}{1}$	$\frac{2}{2}$
					Implement (tool) targets								
Picture	1	U	–	S	U	U	–	–	–	–	+	–	~
	2	~	+	+	U	U	P	–	U	–	–	U	S
	3	U	–	U	U	U	–	–	–	U	S	U	S
Index		$\frac{0}{2}$	$\frac{0}{0}$	$\frac{1}{2}$	$\frac{0}{3}$	$\frac{0}{3}$	$\frac{1}{1}$	$\frac{0}{0}$	$\frac{0}{1}$	$\frac{0}{1}$	$\frac{2}{2}$	$\frac{0}{2}$	$\frac{2}{2}$
					Substance targets								
Picture	1	U	+	U	U_6	U	–	–	–	–	–	–	–
	2	P	U	U	+	–	U	–	–	U	+	+	U
	3	–	–	–	U	P_2	P_3	U	+	–	P	–	U
Index		$\frac{1}{2}$	$\frac{0}{1}$	$\frac{0}{2}$	$\frac{0}{2}$	$\frac{1}{2}$	$\frac{1}{2}$	$\frac{0}{1}$	$\frac{0}{0}$	$\frac{0}{1}$	$\frac{1}{1}$	$\frac{0}{0}$	$\frac{0}{2}$

P_1 = pronominal references in the description to drawing water and to feeding pigs would seem necessarily to refer to someone other than the "*champal* ('baby [small child]')" mentioned.

P_2 = "*ku-láal-ik le-koch-koh-a*' ('they pour [. . .?]')" and "*ku-láal-ik ha' yok'-ol tu-men k'éek-en-ó'ob*' ('they pour [hot] water over [it-zero anaphora] because [they are] pigs')" were given by the subject. However, the subject was prompted on this item by the experimenter: "*míin ku-šóot-ik k'éek-en wal-e*' ('perhaps he is cutting pig')" because he was completely unable to interpret this part of the picture, but he introduced the plural on his own (cf. P_3). Could perhaps be scored U or –.

P_3 = "*tun hó'och k'éek-en-ó'ob*' ('they are cleaning [scraping the skin of] pigs')" is taken to refer to the preparation of pig meat although the picture gives no evidence of multiple pigs.

U_1 = "*tun-si'(yée)t-eh b'àat* ('he is firewood-cutting with [an] ax')" is the only reference to the man in the picture.

Table 43 (*cont.*)

U_2 = "*páal* ('child')" is/has been used to refer to both of the humans in the picture (one who is feeding pigs and one who is nearby and has closed the door to the house) but not in a way which makes clear that more than one exists. "*wíin-ik* ('human person')" is also used but without implying plural number.

U_3 = "*k'éek'-en-a'* ('this pig')" was heard as "*k'éek'-en'-ó'ob'* ('pigs')" by an informant checking the transcription, but this seems to be incorrect to me. The picture contained only one pig.

U_4 = "*tinaja* (Spanish loan word for a 'large ceramic storage container for water')" was used with question intonation to describe two large sacks.

U_5 = "'*u-hòom-ah-il 'u-wah-il-ó'ob'* ('gourd for storing tortillas')" pluralizes the tortillas (*wah*) but not the storage gourd (*homah*).

U_6 = "'*u-táam 'um-p'éeh kib'* ('its drippings [or, residue] one [+ discrete] candle')" is given for the corn dough.

+ = "*le-man-k'éek'-en-a'* ('this pig buyer')" implies pig (A-1-3-1); "*tun-láal-ik le-ha'-o' ti'-kàab'-o'* ('he is pouring the water to the bees')" implies barrel (C-3-3-3, -12); "*wàah* ('tortillas/food')" and "*tun-pak-ach* ('she is tortilla-making')" imply corn dough (S-1-1-4); "*yá'ab' si' má'a-lob'* 'lots of good firewood'" in the context of a discussion of fallen, dried out trees and a bundle of firewood implies unbundled pieces of firewood (S-1-2-10); "*kòon-b'ak'* ('meat-seller')" implies meat (S-2-3-11); "*k-u-ţéen-t-ik 'u-k'éek'-en* ('he feeds his pigs')" and "*le-la' k'éek'-en tun-ţéen-tah* ('these pigs they are being fed')" imply corn (S-3-1-6, -9).

~ = "*b'á'aš* ('what?')" may imply sack (C-1-2-7); "'*u-kúuch* ('his load')" may imply mesh bag (C-2-2-2); "*tun-láal-ik b'á'ah* ('he is pouring something')" may imply barrel (C-3-3-6); "*tun-si'* ('he is firewood-collecting')," "*le-chan-máak-a' k'aš-ik si'* . . . šóot'-ik 'u-si'* ('this man finds firewood . . . cuts his firewood')," and "*tun-šot' si'* ('he is cutting [into pieces] firewood')" may imply ax (T-1-2-1, -4, -7); "*k'á'ak'* ('fire')" may imply griddle (T-3-1-12).

Table 44. *English scores on the verbal recall task*

Subject		22	23	28	29	25	27	32	33	24	26	30	31
Picture Set		1	1	1	1	2	2	2	2	3	3	3	3
						Animate	targets						
Picture	1	P	P	P	P	S	S_a	S	S	S	S	S	S
	2	S	P_e	S	S	P	P	P_a	P_a	P	P	P	P_a
	3	S	U_1	S	S_a	P	P	P	P	~	P	P	P
Index		$\frac{3}{3}$	$\frac{2}{3}$	$\frac{3}{3}$	$\frac{3}{3}$	$\frac{3}{3}$	$\frac{3}{3}$	$\frac{3}{3}$	$\frac{3}{3}$	$\frac{2}{2}$	$\frac{3}{3}$	$\frac{3}{3}$	$\frac{3}{3}$
						Implement	(container)	targets					
Picture	1	S	S	$?_1$	–	P	P	–	P	P_a	–	–	P_1
	2	–	–	S_1	S_1	S_2	S_3	–	–	P	S_e	–	P
	3	S	–	–	–	–	S	–	S	~	~	S	S
Index		$\frac{2}{2}$	$\frac{1}{1}$	$\frac{1}{1}$	$\frac{1}{1}$	$\frac{2}{2}$	$\frac{3}{3}$	$\frac{0}{0}$	$\frac{2}{2}$	$\frac{2}{2}$	$\frac{1}{1}$	$\frac{1}{1}$	$\frac{3}{3}$
						Implement	(tool)	targets					
Picture	1	S	–	S	–	S	+	U_2	S	S_e	S_e	S_e	P_a
	2	+	~	~	S	~	P	~	P	S	S	–	S
	3	P	–	–	–	S	S_4	–	–	S	S	S_a	S
Index		$\frac{2}{2}$	$\frac{0}{0}$	$\frac{1}{1}$	$\frac{1}{1}$	$\frac{2}{2}$	$\frac{2}{2}$	$\frac{0}{1}$	$\frac{2}{2}$	$\frac{3}{3}$	$\frac{3}{3}$	$\frac{2}{2}$	$\frac{3}{3}$
						Substance	targets						
Picture	1	+	~	$?_1$	U	+	–	–	–	S	P	U_3	U_4
	2	~	~	~	~	–	U	–	U_5	U	U	U	+
	3	P	–	–	–	–	U	+	$?_2$	–	–	P	P
Index		$\frac{1}{1}$	$\frac{0}{0}$	$\frac{0}{0}$	$\frac{0}{1}$	$\frac{0}{0}$	$\frac{0}{2}$	$\frac{0}{0}$	$\frac{0}{1}$	$\frac{1}{2}$	$\frac{1}{2}$	$\frac{1}{3}$	$\frac{1}{2}$

S_1 = references to "a large bag of grain" and to "food along the ground or a sack of some food" – not clear if these are a reference to the mesh bag or if it is to one of the two bags of grain (the target) to the lower right of the picture.

S_2 = "walking toward the well carrying two bundles uh it might be a sack to take the water home in" can refer to the single mesh bag only indirectly by pairing it with the sack in the other hand as one of "two bundles" or by mistaking it for a sack with which to carry water; scored as singular since number is clearly being applied to a container-like object. The alternative coding of P_e would not change the Index value. Coding as – [no mention] would change the mention score, but not the Index ratio.

S_3 = reference to a "bag" does not necessarily refer to the mesh bag (the target) rather than the sack also carried by the woman.

S_4 = "there's . . . that convex objects which . . ." mismatches nonplural demonstrative with plural noun. [Note: The *is* in *there's* does not reliably indicate a singular in English.]

P_1 = Target was two bowls, one in a man's hand and one on a table. Subject said "There were other bowls on the table," but did not mention bowl in the man's hand.

Table 44 (*cont.*)

U_1 = "pig on a leash" might be taken by some to imply singular pig.

U_2 = "I really don't know what type of tool he was using" might be taken by some to imply that a single type, hence a single tool, is involved here.

U_3 = "meat ... on hooks" might be taken by some to imply multiple pieces of meat.

U_4 = "meat hooks ... on which objects or meat of some sort looks appear to be a caldron on the first one and meat on the fourth one" might be taken by some to specify a single chunk of meat or to imply multiple chunks.

U_5 = "there was a large hog ... wallowing in some mud" might be taken by some as a positive specification a [−discrete] noun *mud* on the strength of the [unstressed] *some*, but this requires knowledge of the lexical status of *mud* as nonplural and hence [−discrete]. This construction is discussed in chapter 3.

$?_1$ = tape defect

$?_2$ = "They appear to be making some type of uh what looked to be a- a toy or something." So there is no toy there in the speaker's view, only the materials to make one, but these materials are not explicitly mentioned, so can only be coded as +. If coded this way, the Index value remains the same. If the guess of "a toy or something" which describes what will be the end product of the activity is coded as S, it would alter the Index value.

+ = "chopping" implies ax (T-1-2-22);
"digging" implies shovel (T-2-1-27);
"making a tortilla" implies corn dough (S-1-1-22);
"fire" implies smoke (S-2-1-25);
"feeding (pigs)" implies corn (S-3-2-31);
"a butcher shop" implies meat (S-2-3-32).

~ = "pouring" may imply barrel (C-3-3-24, -26);
"cutting" and "clearing" may imply ax (T-1-2-23, -28);
"well" may imply pulley (T-1-2-25, -32);
"mixing something" may imply corn dough (S-1-1-23);
"bundles of wood pieces," "bundles of sticks," "bundle of wood," and "some little pieces of wood in a bundle" may imply some unbundled pieces of firewood (S-1-2-22, -23, -28, -29).

Table 45. *Yucatec scores on the verbal recall task*

Subject		2	3	11	12	1	6	7	9	4	5	8	10
Picture Set		1	1	1	1	2	2	2	2	3	3	3	3
						Animate targets							
Picture	1	P	P	P	P	S_1	S	S	S	U_1	−	S	U_2
	2	S	U_3	S	S	U	P	P_+	P	P_+	P_+	P_+	P_1
	3	U_4	S	P_e	U	P	U	P_2	U	−	−	−	P
Index		$\frac{2}{3}$	$\frac{2}{3}$	$\frac{3}{3}$	$\frac{2}{3}$	$\frac{2}{3}$	$\frac{2}{3}$	$\frac{3}{3}$	$\frac{2}{3}$	$\frac{1}{2}$	$\frac{1}{1}$	$\frac{2}{2}$	$\frac{2}{3}$
						Implement (container) targets							
Picture	1	~	U	U	~	P	P_3	−	−	−	−	−	~
	2	−	−	−	−	−	−	S	U	−	−	−	−
	3	−	U	−	−	−	−	−	−	+	+	~	U
Index		$\frac{0}{0}$	$\frac{0}{2}$	$\frac{0}{1}$	$\frac{0}{0}$	$\frac{1}{1}$	$\frac{1}{1}$	$\frac{1}{1}$	$\frac{0}{1}$	$\frac{0}{0}$	$\frac{0}{0}$	$\frac{0}{0}$	$\frac{0}{1}$
						Implement (tool) targets							
Picture	1	−	−	−	−	+	−	U	−	~	~	−	~
	2	U	+	+	~	~	~	~	−	−	−	−	S_2
	3	−	S_3	−	U	−	−	S	−	S	S	−	U
Index		$\frac{0}{1}$	$\frac{1}{1}$	$\frac{0}{0}$	$\frac{0}{1}$	$\frac{0}{0}$	$\frac{0}{0}$	$\frac{1}{2}$	$\frac{0}{0}$	$\frac{1}{1}$	$\frac{1}{1}$	$\frac{0}{0}$	$\frac{1}{2}$
						Substance targets							
Picture	1	~	+	+	+	+	−	−	S	U	U	S	−
	2	+	U_5	~	−	~	~	U	+	U	U	+	U
	3	−	−	−	−	U	−	U	−	−	−	−	U
Index		$\frac{0}{0}$	$\frac{0}{1}$	$\frac{0}{0}$	$\frac{0}{0}$	$\frac{0}{1}$	$\frac{0}{0}$	$\frac{0}{2}$	$\frac{1}{1}$	$\frac{0}{2}$	$\frac{0}{2}$	$\frac{1}{1}$	$\frac{0}{2}$

S_1 = "'*un-túul* ('one [+ animate]')" given without any preceding noun phrase.

S_2 = "'*un-túul chan míis* ('one [+ animate] [diminutive] broom')" given where the expected response is "'*um-p'éeh míis* ('one [+ discrete] broom')." The response may be due to a speech error based on the similarity of *míis* to *mìis* ('cat') which would normally take the [+ animate] classifier.

S_3 = "'*um-p'éeh há'as* ('one [+ discrete] banana')" where the expected response was "'*um-p'éeh maskab'* ('one [+ discrete] machete')"; this appears to be a simple misidentification based on similarity of shape.

P_1 = Subject mentions that there are pigs and then says "*tun-láal-ik 'iš-ʼim ti'* ('he pours corn to them')." The only possible antecedent to the pronominal subject is "'*un-túul cham-pal* ('one [animate] baby [or small child]')." The presence of an older individual to which this pronoun refers is implied both by the presence of the child who would be tended and by the unlikelihood of a baby or small child feeding the pigs. Thus both the child and the adult are indicated, and a plural is implied by summation. If such reasoning is not invoked, the item would be scored S_e and the Index value would remain unchanged.

Table 45 (*cont.*)

P_2 = "*ká'a-túul 'úulum* ('two [+ animate] turkey[s]')" when there were actually three turkeys in the picture.

P_3 = "*cubos* (Spanish form for 'buckets')" is technically a plural and is so coded here, but since Spanish plurals when used by Yucatec speakers may take further plural specification with Yucatec morphology (for example, *cubos-ó'ob*') the actual number status of these forms is ambiguous. They may be regarded as unmarked or neutral with respect to number, since singular forms would be expected when referring denotatively to singular targets. Such forms appear to have a sense more like our generic plural (for example, dogs [as a species] vs cats [as a species]) in that they refer to the type of object.

U_1 = "'*u-noh-kaš* ('his large [full-grown] chicken' – *kaš* has its origin in the Spanish word *Castellano*)" is given. When only one man is mentioned as possessor in a context of contrastive reference (for example, his large chicken as opposed to his other chickens), a specific chicken and hence singularity might be implied, but no such contrast is operating in the present context.

U_2 = "'*u-chan-kaš* ('his small chicken')" presents a problem similar to that noted in U_1 but is even weaker because *chan* is such a general diminutive. It can be used to indicate not only small, not full-grown, or not full-size, but also to indicate speaker uncertainty – in which form it often merely indexes speaker unease and may indicate nothing about the modified noun itself.

U_3 = "*le-máak-k-u-ch'ak-che'-o*' ('the man who is chopping wood')" is given. In some contexts (as with U_1 and U_2) this form could be given a contrastive status which might imply singular, but it is clearly unmarked and, in the present case, the contrastive situation does not obtain.

U_4 = Transcribed as "*yéet-eh k'éek'en* ('and pig', i.e., unmarked for number)" but the recording is not clear and "'*un-túuh k'éek'en* ('one [+ animate] pig)" is also possible. The evidence for the current transcription is (1) there are three pigs close together so the explicit statement that there is one would be quite odd, (2) this subject used *yéet-eh* 'and/with' very frequently in similar ways, and (3) *yéet-eh* in its various abbreviated forms is consistently hard to hear on the tapes whereas '*un-túuh* was usually not problematic.

U_5 = "*ȼ'-u-láah-šóot-ik* ... *le-che'-[?]* ... *ȼ'-u-láah-wal-á'an-t-ik* ('finished he all-cut it ... the wood ... finished he all-cut-up-into-pieces it' [or, more idiomatically, 'he's finished cutting all of the wood, he's finished cutting it all up into pieces'])" is given. Six pieces of wood constitute the target. *che'* may indicate nearby trees which are being felled, the felled logs which are being cut up, or all the wood involved in the process. As the latter seems most likely, the item is scored here as a mention. Number is scored as U because it is not overtly signalled. The form *wal-á'an* refers to the activity of cutting, but by simultaneously indicating the manner and hence product of the cutting (cf. English *slice, shred*), it may thereby suggest plurality since the typical product would be multiple pieces.

+ = "*tun-láal-kab*' ('he is honey-pouring')" and "*tun-láal-ik ha*' ('he is
    pouring [it] water')" imply barrel (C-3-3-4, -5);

"*palear* (Spanish for 'to shovel')" implies shovel (T-2-1-1);

"*chak-che*' ('wood chop')" implies ax (T-1-2-3, -11, -12);

"*pak-ach (wah)* ('make tortillas')" implies corn dough (S-1-1-3, -11,
-12);

"*tun-si*' ('he cuts/collects-firewood')" implies there are some
unbundled pieces of firewood (S-1-2-2);

"*k-u-tóok-ik* ('he burns it')" implies smoke (S-2-1-1);

"*k-u-y-ich-kil* ('he [= pig] is bathing [himself]')" implies mud puddle
(S-2-2-1, -6);

"*k-u-¢en-t-a'al-(ó'ob')* ('pigs are fed')" implies corn (S-3-2-5, -8).

~ = "*k-u-chup-ik 'u-ha*' ('she is filling up her water [i.e., her supply of
    water]')" and "*tun-po*' ('she is washing [laundering]')" may imply
    tinaja (C-1-2, -12);

"*tun-lóop-ik* ('he is scooping it')" may imply calabash (C-3-1-10);

"*k'á'ak*' ('fire')" may imply griddle (T-3-3-4, -5, -10);

"*ch'é'en* ('well')" may imply pulley (T-2-2-1, -6, -7);

"*hàan-al* ('food')" may imply corn dough (S-1-1-2);

"'*un-kúuch si*' ('one-load firewood')" may imply some unbundled
pieces of firewood (S-1-2-11).

Notes

1 Background of the comparative research in Yucatan, Mexico

1 Wolf (1959) gives a good outline of the history of the entire Mesoamerican region. Coe (1980) and Morley, Brainerd, and Sharer (1983) provide an overview of Mayan history to the conquest. Farriss (1984) describes the colonial period in Yucatan.
2 For a general description of the Yucatan region, see Redfield (1941) and Moseley and Terry (1980).
3 An extensive description of traditional material culture is available in Redfield and Villa Rojas (1934).
4 Historically, communal labor had a religious character although after the Mexican revolution it became largely secularized. *Ejido* institutions in general and communal labor in particular have fallen into disuse in many other parts of the peninsula; see Redfield (1941, pp. 176–86) and Press (1975, p. 155).
5 See Redfield and Villa Rojas (1934) for details on kinship and family life.
6 Good descriptions of traditional agriculture are available in Redfield and Villa Rojas (1934) and Steggerda (1941).
7 Contemporary Mayan religious life is described in the general sources cited in the previous footnotes but no truly comprehensive treatment focusing on religion is currently available.
8 Steggerda (1941) made a general assessment of Yucatec Maya intellectual abilities. However, most of his measures and procedures would not be considered acceptable by present standards. See also the discussion of Galda's work in *Language diversity and thought*, chapter 6.
9 Many of these men also had some prior experience with experiments having participated in a separate series of experiments on color naming and color memory some 18 months earlier (see Lucy, 1981b). Six of the men did experiments 6 and 7 on a separate occasion but still in correct sequence.

2 Comparison of grammatical categories: nominal number in English and Yucatec

1 Much of the terminology in this section is drawn from Quirk, Greenbaum, Leech, and Svartvik (1972).

2   Utterances regarded as ungrammatical are preceded by an asterisk (*).

3   Only under unusual circumstances can this overt mention of kinds be omitted. Nonetheless, even in these cases, use of the Neutral frame still forces an interpretation of the referent in terms of kinds (for example, one cannibal to another: *would you like to eat boy for dinner or girl?*). A similar reference to kinds can be conveyed by the use of such nouns in certain generic or nomic constructions with Singular or Plural noun phrases (for example, *a man is bigger than a boy, boys always eat more than girls, boys will be boys*).

4   If this overt mention of unit is omitted, the resulting "elliptical" expression may still take an interpretation in terms of units if the context is supportive. In the absence of such contextual cues, an interpretation in terms 'kinds' is probably most common. Cf. Lyons (1977, p. 463).

5   Other pre-determiners such as quantitative multiples (for example, *three times a day*) and subjective estimators (for example, *nearly a dozen*) which do not have the same phrasal form will not be discussed here.

6   A rigorous set of terms for describing Yucatec argument structure has yet to be devised. I will use the terms *transitive* and *intransitive* here with approximately the same sense they have when applied to English.

7   Recall that gender is not marked in Yucatec pronominal forms. When the possessor would typically be a person, I have glossed the form with 'his'.

8   It is worth noting explicitly that Yucatec does not have a special "pluralization" classifier as is reported, for example, in Chinese.

9   The exception to the rule that classifiers are followed by a lexical noun or equivalent involves those classifier uses referring to iterations, especially temporal ones. As indicated above, these typically modify a verbal predicate and thus are adverbial in nature, although there are some borderline cases:

'óoš-wáac'	'three round-trips'
'óoš-wáac' t-in-mèen-t-ah	'I made three round-trips'
'óoš-wáac' ha'	'three loads (i.e., three round-trips-to-the-well's-worth = six buckets) of water'.

10 The general approach to the contrastive analysis in this section owes much to the methods and findings of Silverstein's (1976, 1981) work on case marking and noun phrase reference.

11 More precision could be indicated by giving specific probabilities rather than global "yes/no" judgments. Developing such quantitative values depends on employing a systematic procedure. Specific values developed from one such procedure are reported in chapter 3.

12 *Segmenting* is used in this work to refer to segmentation of a referent from its surround, that is, to the process of distinguishing a figure from a background.

13 See Silverstein (1981, pp. 236–38, fn. 12) for discussion of the limits of notional characterizations of formal linguistic facts and the necessity of recognizing in languages a *sui generis* formal organization.

14 This is the crucial shift in perspective that distinguishes the present approach from past ones. In essence we are following the agenda set earlier in *Language diversity and thought* (chapter 7), namely, to outline the pro-

cedures necessary to generalize Whorf's approach (chapter 2) so as to avoid the reductionism of Lenneberg's approach (chapter 5) or the detachment (approaching idealism) of Bloom's approach (chapter 6) by utilizing the linguistic advances of Silverstein's approach (chapter 4).

15   At first glance, it might seem that the color tradition moved in the direction of developing a neutral metalanguage for linguistic description in the work of Berlin and Kay. However, their metalanguage was hardly neutral in that it followed the English focus on "color" terms, ignoring characteristic non-colorimetric significations co-occurring in such terms in other languages. Secondly, the approach was hardly linguistic in a serious sense since it was irrelevant whether "color" terms were adjectives or verbs or a mixture of the two, whether they were primes or morphologically complex, etc. and since non-monolexemic forms were simply eliminated from consideration without reference to the characteristic structures of a language.

16   As mentioned in the previous subsection, the cross-linguistic justification for these features will be discussed below.

17   From the point of view of number marking alone, certain self-segmenting inanimate entities are so regularly grouped with the animates that the feature [± self-segmenting] (or [± self-individuating]) would be superior in terms of capturing cross-language number marking regularities. However, from the point of view of other grammatical categories, the feature label [± animate] apparently has substantial value (see Silverstein, 1976, 1981, 1986, 1987) and is therefore used here. It is possible that two separate features may need to be defined.

18   The feature [± discrete] corresponds to the feature [± count] provisionally used in some of my previous unpublished manuscripts (esp. Lucy, 1981a). I change the notation here because [± count] was ambiguous between a referential feature and a purely formal, distributional class of English which cannot, in itself, provide a basis for comparison with other languages. The change also brings the feature label into conformity with Silverstein's (1981, 1987) feature terminology.

19   Imprecision on this point in Lucy (1981a) apparently led Bowerman (1985, p. 1299) to draw the conclusion that there must be a fourth type of lexical noun phrase marked [+ animate, − count] giving as examples in English *poultry* and *livestock*. To the extent that [± animate] can be motivated as a referential feature of English, her lexical examples are better construed [− animate] – that is, as *unmarked for animacy from a morphosyntactic point of view*. (Speakers can apparently respond to this mismatch between their language categories and other cognitive bases of classification as evidenced in the unusual distributional potential of some such noun phrases – especially those denoting human referents [see the last two examples in table 5].)

20   The term "stable" is meant to encompass conventional (culturally specific) regularities of object form insofar as the conventional form is relevant to predication. Some linguists would include only "natural kinds." (Cf. Silverstein, 1987; Lyons, 1977, p. 465.)

21   In conformity with Silverstein's (1976) conventions, capital letters are used for noun phrase types and lower case letters for referential features (introduced below). However, the specific letter assignments used here do not correspond to his.

22 Comrie (1981, pp. 102–3) has made brief, somewhat similar suggestions about plural patterns being governed by an "animacy hierarchy."

23 This feature was used in his table 2. In his table 3 he used [± addressee].

24 I use the expression *cross-linguistic notional core* to capture the sense that similar positive values are being selected for signaling in many languages. We might also characterize such a regularity as a *salient contrast* to capture the sense that certain distinctions among referents are significant enough to elicit signaling in many languages.

25 This is a claim about the formal status of the feature hierarchy. The discovery procedure may, of course, involve noticing which referential features are directly relevant to case-marking.

26 The term "noun phrase" is preferred here to "lexical noun phrase" so as to encompass pronouns and other indexical forms which serve as complete noun phrases without a lexical noun head.

27 This is an instance where case marking is affected by number. The inclusion of these specific features in the same linear order with the others may be considered an artifact of the two-dimensional representation since they are apparently only relevant to indexicals of the speech event. They thus constitute an example of a "locally-nested sub-space ... not applicable outside that particular region of the higher-order space" (Silverstein, 1987, p. 19). With a more sophisticated representational device, these three features could be displayed on an orthogonal dimension.

28 Smith-Stark made a similar argument for number marking *features* proposing that "the organizing principle of the [feature] hierarchy ... can ... be described as encoding *likelihood of participation in the speech event*" (1974, p. 664).

29 Preliminary suggestions in somewhat different terms were made in Silverstein (1973, p. 20).

30 These phrasal modifiers were discussed above. Quantitative estimators operate somewhat differently (see Lyons, 1977, pp. 333–35).

31 Unlike the English case, however, Yucatec nouns are not grammatically unmarked since there is no contrasting set of nouns inherently marked for unit, that is, which can be enumerated without using a classifier construction.

32 Where appropriate, the chain of connection among referents covered by a single lexical item apparently referring to some common substance can extend quite far. For example, the lexeme *hú'un* can be used to refer to a type of tree, to the bark of the tree which traditionally was used to make a type of paper, to paper as a material, to any given piece of paper, and to items made of paper such as books.

33 The sortal–mensural division closely parallels the distinction in English between count and mass nouns. This suggests that at a deeper level there may be something akin to a count/mass distinction (or a referential feature [± discrete]) operating in some classifier languages. It is also possible, of course, that the distinction has been foisted on the data by linguists for whom the count/mass distinction is salient.

34 In the service of accounting for cross-linguistic patterns in the marking of (in)definiteness, Gil (1987) formulates a language typology which distinguishes, among other things, Type A languages which have obligatory

marking of nominal plurality from Type B languages which have obligatory marking of numeral classification. Gil (1987, pp. 255, 258) sees these two grammatical patterns as a "product" (or "corollary") of a "count–mass parameter" which he explains by reference to whether or not the *noun* is count or mass, that is, does or does not have a "natural" unit for enumeration. The circularity of accounting for the patterns in this way has been pointed out already. The other five correlates of Gil's typological division stem from a "configurationality" parameter which has to do with whether a noun phrase (or other syntactic unit) has internal (or hierarchical) constraints on the combination and permutation of its elements. The theoretical analysis is again underdeveloped and circular, but there seems to be little doubt that these additional phenomena identified by Gil do interrelate not only with each other but also, significantly, with those described in the present work. If a sound linkage can be established, then the overall configuration of meanings involved becomes much larger. Gil himself sees the implications of such a broad division of languages "for one version of Whorf's hypothesis of linguistic relativity" (1987, p. 268).

35   "Obligatory" marking patterns are compared here to simplify the analysis. As mentioned earlier, degrees of likelihood can also be used.

36   The English terms 'alive' and 'dead' in this gloss might not appear to refer to a type of unit. It is possible, however, to see the logical continuity of this distinction with those characteristic of other classifiers by thinking of animate entities as those which by their own properties separate and bound themselves off from a background, that is, self-unitize.

37   Herein lies the origin of a great deal of speculation about whether people speaking in this way actually regard a variety of non-animate objects in the world (for example, clouds) as animate.

38   To say that the lexical noun does not include [+ animate] as part of its meaning would not mean that the status of the lexical noun *phrase* in ongoing discourse would likewise be ambiguous. The animacy of the referent of a Yucatec noun phrase could be established overtly at some point if it was not clear on pragmatic grounds.

39   Only with the latter expression would we clearly exclude the possibility of a live pig.

40   And what has been said here for *-túul* can be said for other classifiers as well. For example, Friedrich's (1970) characterization of Tarascan shape-oriented classifiers in terms of reference to salient 'one-,' 'two-,' and 'three- (or unmarked) dimensionality' clearly suggests that the classifier applied in a situation has much to do with the point of view taken by the observer, since every object can always be construed as 'three-dimensional' (or unmarked). By contrast, the traditional characterizations of the meanings of these forms by such terms as 'long,' 'flat,' and 'round' suggest something inherent to the referents themselves and obscure the pragmatic dimension of classifier use.

3 Cognitive assessment

1   As indicated in *Language diversity and thought*, chapter 7, the focus on denotational reference should not be taken to imply this is the only

important function of language categories either in communication or in thought. In fact, the contrary is quite likely the case, at least for thought.

2   The tasks described were also exploratory in that issues other than those directly relevant to the current project were being investigated. These other issues will not be taken up here.

3   Three ambiguous items were included in the Substance category: cloud, rock, and puddle. Rationale for their inclusion is given in appendix A. Their presence should weaken the expected effects.

4   Error patterns involving introductions and rearrangements can sometimes be informative even under these conditions, but were not in the present case.

5   Initially, each picture set had been designed with eleven alternate pictures rather than five. In these additional alternates, the number of *two* of the target objects was changed simultaneously. The problem with using only five alternates is that it is possible to deduce by close examination which picture is the original since it is distinctive within the set – it is always the picture which is different from each of the others in *only one element* and *never the same element*. By contrast, the alternates each show one (common) element of difference from all other pictures (original and alternates) and a second (variable) element of difference from each of the other alternates. Deducibility of the identity of the original can not only confound the attempt to assess accuracy of recognition memory, but it can also raise the success rate of respondents up to a point where there would be no errors to analyze – and it is principally in the pattern of errors that information will be sought in this task. Deduction remained possible with the larger set of eleven alternates, but became much more difficult both to notice and to calculate. Yucatec pilot subjects found the full set of eleven alternates too difficult to consider and would not even attempt the task with this number. Therefore, only the smaller set of five alternates was used. No obvious cases of deduction were noted with the Yucatec sample. With the English sample, however, the deducibility of the identity of the original picture emerged as an immediate problem. To minimize this problem, the procedure used with the English sample was altered as described in the main text.

References

Allan, K. (1977). Classifiers. *Language*, *53*, 283–309.

Blair, R. W. (1965). Yucatec Maya noun and verb morpho-syntax (Doctoral dissertation, Indiana University, 1964). *Dissertation Abstracts*, *25*, 6606.

Blair, R. W. and Vermont-Salas, R. (1965). *Spoken (Yucatec) Maya*. Chicago: Department of Anthropology, University of Chicago.

Bowerman, M. (1985). What shapes children's grammars? In D. I. Slobin (ed.), *The crosslinguistic study of language acquisition*, Vol. 2: *Theoretical issues* (pp. 1257–319). Hillsdale, NJ: Lawrence Erlbaum Associates.

Bricker, V. R. (1974). The ethnographic context of some traditional Mayan speech genres. In R. Bauman and J. Sherzer (eds.), *Explorations in the ethnography of speaking* (pp. 368–88). Cambridge: Cambridge University Press.

(1979). WH-questions, relativization, and clefting in Yucatec Maya. In L. Martin (ed.), *Papers in Mayan linguistics* (Studies in Mayan Linguistics, Vol. 1) (pp. 109–38). Columbia, MO: Lucas Brothers.

(1981a). Grammatical introduction. In E. Po'ot Yah, *Yucatec Maya verbs (Hocaba dialect)* (pp. v–xlviii). New Orleans, LA: Center for Latin American Studies, Tulane University.

(1981b). The source of the ergative split in Yucatec Maya. *Journal of Mayan Linguistics*, *2*, 83–127.

Burns, A. F. (1983). *An epoch of miracles: oral literature of the Yucatec Maya*. Austin, TX: University of Texas Press.

Chao, Y. R. (1968). *A grammar of spoken Chinese*. Berkeley, CA: University of California Press.

Coe, M. D. (1980). *The Maya* (rev. edn.). London: Thames and Hudson.

Comrie, B. (1981). *Language universals and linguistic typology: syntax and morphology*. Chicago: University of Chicago Press.

Denny, J. P. (1976). What are noun classifiers good for? In S. S. Mufwene, C. A. Walker, and S. B. Steever (eds.), *Papers from the twelfth regional meeting, Chicago Linguistic Society* (pp. 122–32). Chicago: Chicago Linguistic Society.

(1979). The 'extendedness' variable in classifier semantics: universal features and cultural variation. In M. Mathiot (ed.), *Ethnolinguistics: Boas, Sapir, and Whorf revisited* (pp. 97–119). The Hague: Mouton.

Dirección General de Estadística. (1973). *IX Censo general de población, 1970*

[9th General population census, 1970]. Mexico, DF: Dirección General de Estadística, Estados Unidos Mexicanos, Secretaría de Industria y Comercio.

Durbin, M. and Ojeda, F. (1978). Basic word-order in Yucatec Maya. In N. C. England (ed.), *Papers in Mayan linguistics* (Studies in Mayan Linguistics, no. 2) (pp. 69–77). Columbia, MO: University of Missouri, Miscellaneous Publications in Anthropology, no. 6.

Farriss, N. M. (1984). *Maya society under colonial rule: the collective enterprise of survival*. Princeton, NJ: Princeton University.

Friedrich, P. (1970). Shape in grammar. *Language, 46*, 379–407.

Geertz, C. (1973). *The interpretation of cultures*. New York: Basic Books.

Gil, D. (1987). Definiteness, noun phrase configurationality, and the count–mass distinction. In E. J. Reuland and A. G. B. ter Meulen (eds.), *The representation of (in)definiteness*. Cambridge, MA: The Massachusetts Institute of Technology Press.

Gordon, P. (1985). Evaluating the semantic categories hypothesis: the case of the count/mass distinction. *Cognition, 20*, 209–42.

Greenberg, J. H. (1966). Language universals. In T. A. Sebeok (ed.), *Current trends in linguistics*, Vol. 3: *Theoretical foundations* (pp. 61–112). The Hague: Mouton.

(1972). Numeral classifiers and substantival number: problems in the genesis of a linguistic type. *Working papers in language universals, Stanford University, 9*, 1–39.

(1978). Generalizations about numeral systems. In J. H. Greenberg (ed.), *Universals of human language*, Vol. 3: *Word structure* (pp. 249–95). Stanford, CA: Stanford University Press.

Hanks, W. F. (1986). Authenticity and ambivalence in the text: a colonial Maya case. *American Ethnologist, 13*, 721–44.

Kalectaca, M. (1978). *Lessons in Hopi*. Tucson, AZ: University of Arizona Press.

Kautman, T. (1974). Meso-American Indian languages. In *The new encyclopædia Britannica: macropædia* (vol. 11, pp. 956–63). Chicago: Encyclopædia Britannica.

Killingley, S. (1981). The semantic grouping of mensural classifiers in Cantonese. *Anthropological Linguistics, 23*, 383–435.

Li, C. H. and Thompson, S. A. (1981). *Mandarin Chinese: a functional reference grammar*. Berkeley, CA: University of California Press.

Lucy, J. A. (1981a, November). *An empirical approach to the Whorfian question*. Paper presented to the Psycholinguistics Colloquium, Northwestern University, Evanston, IL.

(1981b, December). *Cultural factors in memory for color: The problem of language usage*. Paper presented to Annual Meetings of the American Anthropological Association, Los Angeles, CA.

(1989, April). *Vygotsky and the culture of language*. Paper read at the Biennial Meeting of the Society for Research in Child Development, Kansas City, MO.

(1990). (Bases of triads sorting in American English subjects). Unpublished data.

(1991, May). *Empirical research and linguistic relativity*. Paper presented at a conference on Rethinking Linguistic Relativity sponsored by the Wenner-Gren Foundation for Anthropological Research, Ocho Ríos, Jamaica.

(1992). Metapragmatic presentationals: Reporting speech with quotatives in Yucatec Maya. In J. A. Lucy (ed.), *Reflexive language: Reported speech and metapragmatics*. Cambridge: Cambridge University Press.

Lucy, J. A. and Gaskins, S. (1989, November). *Language diversity and the development of thought*. Paper presented at the Annual Meetings of the American Anthropological Association, Washington, D.C.

Lyons, J. (1968). *Introduction to theoretical linguistics*. Cambridge: Cambridge University Press.

(1977). *Semantics* (2 vols.). Cambridge: Cambridge University Press.

McClaran Stefflre, M. (1972). *Lexical and syntactic structures in Yucatec Maya*. Unpublished doctoral dissertation, Harvard University, Cambridge, MA. (No abstract published. Indexed as Stefflre, 1973.)

McQuown, N. A. (1956). The classification of the Mayan languages. *International Journal of American Linguistics*, 22, 191–95.

(1967). Classical Yucatec (Maya). In R. Wauchope and N. A. McQuown (eds.), *Handbook of Middle American Indians*, Vol. 5: *Linguistics* (pp. 201–47). Austin, TX: University of Texas Press.

(1970). El acento del Maya-Yucateco. *Actas de 39 Congreso Internacional de Americanistas (Lima)*, 5, 59–71.

Miram, H.-M. (1983). *Numeral classifiers im yukatekschen Maya*. Hannover: Verlag für Ethnologie.

Morley, S., Brainerd, G. and Sharer, R. (1983). *The ancient Maya*. Stanford: Stanford University.

Moseley, E. and Terry, E. (1980). *Yucatan: a world apart*. University, Alabama: University of Alabama.

Owen, M. G., III. (1969). The semantic structures of Yucatec verb roots. (Doctoral dissertation, Yale University, 1968). *Dissertation Abstracts International*, 30, 476B.

Press, I. (1975). *Tradition and adaptation: life in a modern Yucatan Maya village*. Westport, CT: Greenwood.

Quirk, R., Greenbaum, S., Leech, G. and Svartvik, J. (1972). *A grammar of contemporary English*. New York: Seminar Press.

Redfield, R. (1941). *The folk culture of Yucatan*. Chicago: University of Chicago Press.

Redfield, R. and Villa Rojas, A. (1934). *Chan Kom: a Maya village* (Carnegie Institution of Washington Publication No. 448). Washington, DC: Carnegie Institution of Washington. (Reprinted in 1962 by the University of Chicago Press.)

Sanches, M. and Slobin, L. (1973). Numeral classifiers and plural marking: an implicational universal. *Working Papers in Language Universals, Stanford University*, 11, 1–22.

Silverstein, M. (1973, January). *Hierarchy of features and ergativity*. Paper presented to the Chicago Linguistics Society, Chicago, IL.

(1976). Hierarchy of features and ergativity. In R. M. W. Dixon (ed.), *Grammatical categories in Australian languages* (Australian Institute of Aboriginal Studies, Linguistic Series, No. 22.) (pp. 112–71). Canberra: Australian Institute of Aboriginal Studies.

(1981). Case-marking and the nature of language. *Australian Journal of Linguistics, 1*, 227–44.

(1986). *Noun phrase categorial markedness and syntactic parametricization.* Paper presented at Eastern States Conference on Linguistics, State University of New York, Buffalo, NY.

(1987). Cognitive implications of a referential hierarchy. In M. Hickmann (ed.), *Social and functional approaches to language and thought* (pp. 125–64). Cambridge: Cambridge University Press.

Smith-Stark, T. (1974). The plurality split. In M. W. LaGaly, R. A. Fox and A. Bruck (eds.), *Papers from the tenth regional meeting, Chicago Linguistic Society* (pp. 657–71). Chicago: Chicago Linguistic Society.

Soja, N. N. (1987). *Ontological constraints on 2-year-olds' induction of word meanings.* Unpublished doctoral dissertation, Massachussetts Institute of Technology, Cambridge, MA. (No abstract published.)

Soja, N., Carey, S. and Spelke, E. (1985). *Constraints on the meanings of words.* Poster presented at the meeting of the Society for Research in Child Development, Toronto.

Steggerda, M. (1941). *Maya Indians of Yucatan* (Carnegie Institution of Washington Publication No. 531). Washington, DC: Carnegie Institution of Washington.

Straight, H. S. (1972). *Yucatec Maya pedelectology: segmental phonology.* Unpublished doctoral dissertation, University of Chicago, Chicago, IL. (No abstract published.)

Voegelin, D. F. and Voegelin, F. M. (1957). Hopi domains: a lexical approach to the problem of selection. *International Journal of American Linguistics, 23*(2, Pt 2, Memoir 14).

Wolf, E. R. (1959). *Sons of the shaking earth.* Chicago: University of Chicago Press.

Whorf, B. L. (1946). The Hopi language, Toreva dialect. In H. Hoijer (ed.), *Linguistic structures of native America* (pp. 158–83). New York: Viking Fund. (Written in 1939.)

(1956). *Language, thought, and reality: selected writings of Benjamin Lee Whorf* (J. B. Carroll, ed.). Cambridge, MA: The MIT Press. (Original works written 1927–1941.)

Index

Printed in the United States
87526LV00005B/256-303/A